THE BEGINNING AND THE END

NIKOLAI BERDYAEV

The Beginning and the End

⊕

Translated by
R. M. French

Foreword by
Boris Jakim

SEMANTRON PRESS

Philmont NY

First Edition, Harper & Brothers, New York, 1952
Second, enlarged edition © Semantron Press 2009
Semantron is an imprint of Sophia Perennis LLC
Foreword and Biography © Sophia Perennis 2009
Translation by R.M. French

For information, address:
Sophia Perennis, P.O. Box 931
Philmont NY 12565

Library of Congress Cataloging-in-Publication Data

Berdyaev, Nikolai, 1874–1948
[Opyt eskhatologicheskoi metafiziki. English]
The beginning and the end / Nikolai Berdyaev;
2nd, enl. ed.

p. cm.
ISBN 978 1 59731 264 6 (pbk)
ISBN 978 1 59731 199 1 (hbk)

1. Metaphysics. 2. Eschatology. I. Title.
B4338.B43O6913 2009
263—dc22   2009022948

Cover design: Michael Schrauzer

CONTENTS

PART FOUR
THE PROBLEM OF HISTORY AND ESCHATOLOGY

CHAPTER VIII

CHAPTER IX

FOREWORD

Written at the beginning of the world apocalypse which was World War II, *The Beginning and the End* (Russian title: *An Essay on Eschatological Metaphysics: Creativeness and Objectification*) is Nikolai[1] Berdyaev's main book on eschatology. He describes his book as an "essay in the epistemological and metaphysical interpretation of the end of the world, of the end of history" (p. vi, present volume); hence he calls it an "eschatological metaphysics." Let it be noted, though, that for Berdyaev the eschatological outlook is not limited to the prospect of the end of the world; it embraces every instant of life. Every instant of our lives, we are required to put an end to the old world and to begin a new world.

What does Berdyaev mean by "the metaphysical and epistemological meaning of the end of the world and of history"? What it denotes for him is "the end of objective being and the overcoming of objectification" (p. 231, present volume). But what is "objectification"? We are cast into a world of objects, into an objective world, which has a metaphysical meaning for us; or rather this objectified world is a construction of our own minds. This objectification is the fall of the world: the loss of the world's freedom, the alienation of its parts. The world of appearances (of objects) acquires a grandiose empirical reality which exercises compulsion upon us. These objectified constructions begin to live an independent life and give rise to pseudo-realities. Even though it is our own construction, we cannot escape this objectified world; we too can become objectified—parts of this objectified world, slaves to it. But our

---

1. "Nikolai" is the more correct form of Berdyaev's first name. The original translations of Berdyaev's works into English used "Nicolas"; in order to avoid confusion this spelling is retained on the cover and title page.

inner spiritual experience cannot become an object; spirit cannot be objectified. This is how Berdyaev puts it: "Objectification is the ejection of man into the external; it is an exteriorization of him; it is the subjecting of him to the conditions of space, time, causality, and rationalization. But in his existential depth man is in communion with the spiritual world and with the whole cosmos" (p. 60, present volume). In his existential depth, man cannot be objectified. "The true, deep-down existence of man, his noumenal self, does not belong to the world of objects. The end of the world will be an end of that world of objects" (p. 233, present volume).

Berdyaev explores the relation between God and this objectified world. He asserts that God does not act everywhere in this objectified world; God was not the Creator of this fallen world; He does not act and is not present in plague and cholera, in hatred, in murder, war, and violence, in the suppression of freedom. Rather, God is present and acts only in freedom; He is present in Truth, Beauty, Goodness, and Love, but not in the world order. "God shows himself in the world in truth and right, but he does not dominate over it in virtue of his power. God is Spirit and he can operate only in Spirit and through Spirit" (p. 152, present volume). The objectified, fallen world seems dominant now; God, however, will have the last word, but this can be conceived only in terms of eschatology. In the eschatological perspective, freedom is opposed to objectified being and creativeness to the objective order. The world of freedom invades the objectified world and acts creatively within it. Man, as a creatively active and free being, as a spiritual being, is transforming the fallen world into a spiritual world. That is true eschatology.

Berdyaev points out that creative activity has an eschatological nature; it is upward flight toward a different world. However, even the results of creative activity can be objectified: The possibility of creation presupposes an infusion of the Spirit into man (what is called inspiration); and this elevates the action of creative power above the world. But the world demands that the creating mind should conform to it: the world seeks to make its own use of creative acts, to defuse the eschatological character of these acts. The creating mind must give bodily form to its images (e.g., in works of art) of the other world, to its ecstasy; and it is obliged to do this in accordance with the laws of this world. Creative power is noumenal in its origin but it is in the phenomenal world that it reveals itself. "The world does not come to an end. It is held back from doing so. But it ought to come to an end. The creative act of man is an answer to the call of God; it ought to prepare the end of this world and the beginning of another" (p. 185, present volume). But, as yet, it does not. For Berdyaev, there has been one historical creative failure more terrible than all the others: the failure of Christianity, the failure of the work of Christ in the world. "There is nothing more horrifying and more gloomy than the objectification in history of that fire which Christ brought down from heaven" (p. 187, present volume).

This leads Berdyaev to ask the following question: Is it possible to achieve the conquest of this objective world? Is it possible to achieve, not the annihilation of what is "earthly," but its liberation and transformation, its transition to a different scheme of things? He answers this question by saying that the kingdom of God is not merely a matter of expectation, but is being founded: its creation is beginning already here and now on earth. And for this creation it is required that we should interpret eschatology in an active and creative way. A key element of this creation of the kingdom of God is a personalist spiritual revolution, a revolution which would mean the end of the objectified everyday world and a transition to the kingdom of freedom, which is the new era of the Spirit.

For Berdyaev the end of the world is a divine-human enterprise: man not only endures the end, but he also prepares the way for it. Man's creative activity is needed for the coming of the kingdom of God: God is in need of this activity and awaits it. "What one needs to do at every moment of one's life is to put an end to the old world and to begin a new world" (p. 254, present volume).

BORIS JAKIM
2008

PREFACE

I have for a long while wanted to write a book in which I should describe my metaphysical position as a whole. I use the word 'metaphysics', but my readers must not give it here its traditional and academic meaning. I am concerned rather with the kind of metaphysics which is disclosed in the spirit of, for instance, Dostoyevsky, Kierkegaard, Nietzsche, Pascal, Boehme, St Augustine and similar writers, that is to say, as they put it nowadays, with existential metaphysics. But I prefer another word, and that is eschatological metaphysics. I want to survey all problems in the light of eschatology, in the light which streams from the End. And I speak of my metaphysical position as a whole in spite of the fact that my way of thinking is fragmentary and aphoristic and moves by fits and starts. But inwardly there is an integral character which belongs to my thought, and that integral character is present in every part of it. My thought moves largely round one centre, I have always been badly understood, and many misunderstandings have constantly arisen, not only among people who were hostile to me, but even among those who were sympathetically disposed. It is of course I myself who am to blame for this. I have done but little to make my general outlook understood. I have announced it, but I have not developed it systematically.

My philosophical thinking does not take a scientific form: it is not ratiocinative, it belongs intuitively to life. Spiritual experience lies at the very foundation of it, and its driving power is a passion for freedom. I do not think discursively. It is not so much that I arrive at truth as that I take my start from it. Among the philosophers whose thought does take a scientific form, I owe most to Kant, and it is with Kant that I begin in this book. But it is not altogether in the usual way that I expound Kant's metaphysics. As I deal with the problems of metaphysics I find myself in many respects indebted to Boehme amd Dostoyevsky. Of all the writers of the ancient world it is Heraclitus with whom I have the greatest affinity. I should describe my book as an essay in the epistemological and metaphysical interpretation of the end of the world, of the end of history, that is to say it is a book on eschatological epistemology and metaphysics. So far as I am aware no interpretation of that kind has been made hitherto. Eschatology has been left as a part of dogmatic theology, and not the most important part at that. It is not, however, by any means to be inferred from this that I am committed to a proclamation of the end of the world in the near future.

I might call my book 'an untimely meditation'. It is very closely associated with the spiritual experience which has been evoked by the catastrophic events of our time. But the ideas expressed in it are opposed to the prevailing ideas of our day, and turn rather towards other centuries. I have very little sympathy with an age which is characterized by the prevailing influence of masses, quantities, and technological science, and by the dominance of politics over the life of the spirit. I have written the book at a terrible time. It is shorter than I could have wished. There is a great deal in it which is not adequately developed and clearly set forth. I was afraid that catastrophic events might prevent my finishing it. I have not addressed myself to the average normal, socially organized and organizing mind. From my point of view that would have been objectification. I recognize the fact that as a thinker I belong to the aristocratically radical type. The description which has been given of Nietzsche, as an 'aristocratic radical' might be applied to me. It has been my wish to think, to apprehend and to form my judgments of value simply and naturally, taking things in their essential nature, and without having to square accounts with anything, and without accommodating my opinions to anything. But to the pride and isolation of the cultural élite I have always felt a negative reaction. It has not come within my purview to indicate ways of organizing the human masses. There are many who are eager to do this without my adding to the number. There are fewer by far who are eager to grasp the meaning of what is happening to the world and to man. I should like to belong to their number. My thought is not by any means abstract, it is concerned above all with a revolution in the mind, in other words, with the liberation of the mind from the power of objectification. Nothing but a radical change in the set up of the mind can lead to vital changes; a wrong attitude of the conscious mind is the source of the slavery of man.

At the root of the metaphysical considerations of this book there lies an acute sense of the evil which reigns in this world, and of the bitter lot of man as he lives in it. My thought reflects a revolt of human personality against an illusory and crushing objective 'world harmony', and the objective social order, against any form of investing the objective world order with a sacrosanct character. It is the fight of the spirit against necessity. But it would be a mistake to number me among the pessimists and those who do nothing but deny. I belong to the believing philosophers but my faith is of my own sort. For the rest, I hold that the most complex and the most problematic must at the deepest level coincide with what is simplest and clearest.

Paris - Clamart,
    December, 1941.

PART ONE

The Problem of Knowledge and Objectification

CHAPTER I

*1. A metaphysical interpretation and critique of Kant. Two
Worlds: appearance, and things-in-themselves, nature and
freedom. Kant, Plato, German mysticism, German idealist
metaphysics after Kant. 2. The dialectic of German idealism
from Kant through Hegel to Nietzsche. 3. The problem of freedom in French philosophy of the nineteenth century. Themes
of Russian philosophical and religious thought. 4. The emotionally passionate character of cognition. Existential metaphysics as the symbolism of spiritual experience. 5. Truth
which is beneficial, truth which is ruinous, and saving truth.
Truths and the truth. The criterion of truth*

I

Man finds himself in the world, or has been thrown into
it, and as he stands facing the world he is confronted
by it as by a problem which demands to be solved.
His continued existence depends upon the world, and he perishes
in the world and by the action of the world. The world nourishes
man, and it destroys him. The world environment into which he
is cast in mysterious fashion from some source or other, everlast-
ingly threatens man and arouses him to conflict. And man devotes
himself to the extraordinarily venturesome task of getting to know
the world and that which may to some extent be discovered
behind it. Man is small in comparison with that which he wants to
get to know, he is small compared with the world. He is terribly
small if he is looked upon as one of a number of objects.

Nor is there anything more astonishing, more touching and
more disturbing, than these efforts of the human spirit to break
through darkness towards the light, through what is meaningless,
towards a meaning, to break its way through the servitude which
necessity imposes, towards freedom. Man measures his powers

with the universe, and in the act of knowing seeks to rise above the limiting conditions and the solid massiveness of the world. He can recognize light, meaning, and freedom for the sole reason that light, meaning and freedom are there within his very self. And even when man regards himself as merely a creation of the world environment and as wholly dependent upon it, even then he rises above it and reveals in himself a higher principle than the data which the world provides, and unveils the presence within him of a stranger from another world, from a different idea of the world.

The knowledge would not be possible if man belonged solely to nature, if he were not spirit also. The acquisition of knowledge is a struggle, it is not a passive reflection. Philosophy, which has aimed at integrated knowledge, has sought not only to know the world, but also to change it. It is futile for Marx to appropriate this idea to himself, it forms a part of all true philosophy. Philosophy not only wants to perceive meaning, it desires that meaning shall be triumphant. Philosophy will not come to terms with a meaningless world datum, it seeks either to break through to another world, a world which has meaning, or to discover the wisdom which brings light into the world, and changes human existence in it for the better. Thus the most profound and most distinctive philosophy has, behind the phenomenon, the appearance, discovered the noumenon, the thing-in-itself; behind the necessity of nature it has revealed freedom, and behind the material world, spirit. And even when philosophy denies the 'other', the noumenal, world, it still projects upon the future a better world, a higher condition of the world in time to come, and this is, after all, in some sense noumenal.

From the time of Greek philosophy men have given the name being (*ousia, essentia*) to the subject matter of profound knowledge. We shall see all the difficulties which are connected with ontology. Ontologism does not appear to me to be the highest philosophical truth. But accepting the conventional terminology it may be said that in seeking knowledge, the philosopher has

4

sought to solve the riddle of being. And there are two paths, or two starting-points, in seeking a solution to the mystery of being. Either being is known and unriddled from the side of the object, taking the world as the starting-point, or it is known and un-riddled from the side of the ego, that is from man. This ought to form the basis of distinction between different tendencies in philosophy. But in the history of philosophical thought this distinction is complicated and involved.

In reality the philosophy of the ego, as distinct from the philosophy of the world begins with the revolution brought about by Kant,[1] although he had his predecessors, such as for instance St Augustine and Descartes, and in some material respects, Socrates and Plato. A fundamental discovery in philosophy was made by Plato and Kant who must be regarded as the greatest and most original philosopher in the history of human thought.

After Plato and Kant the philosophers who followed them in part developed their ideas and in part distorted them, and it is of great importance that this fact should· be grasped. But Plato's philosophy, as indeed Greek philosophy as a whole, was not yet a philosophy of the ego, it was not the apprehension of being from the point of view of the subject, and arising out of the depth of human existence. Greek thought was directed to the object and it is German thought alone which has turned towards the subject. But it did in fact succeed in discovering in the object the world of ideas, through the subject, through the participation of man in that higher world.

A naïve realism is the general outlook of the greater part of mankind. It would not be true to say that it is the general view of the world taken by mankind in its primitive state. That view was extraordinarily complex, it was a myth-creating process, animism,

[1] See R. Kroner: *Von Kant bis Hegel.* 2 Vols. This is the best history of German idealism. I am much indebted to it in the understanding and interpretation of Kant and the great idealists of the beginning of the nineteenth century.

totemism and belief in magic. But the power of workaday prosaic experience over man inculcates a naïvely realistic acceptance of the world. This visible world, this world of the senses, this world of phenomena, as philosophers were in due course to call it, exercises too much compulsion upon man, it subjugates him too much to itself, for it to be easily possible for him either to harbour any doubts of its true reality, or to rise above it. Yet all profound philosophy begins from such a doubt, and takes its rise from an act of spirit which lifts itself above the data which the world provides.

Is the true, the most real thing that which most insists upon one's acknowledgment of it? Philosophical knowledge is an act of self-liberation on the part of the spirit from the exclusive claims of the world of phenomena to be reality. And this is the amazing fact: the world as a whole, as the cosmos, is never a datum in our experience of the phenomenal world of the senses. The phenomenon is always partial. The cosmic whole is an image which is grasped by the intellect. The power of the world over man as he seeks to know it is not the power of the cosmic whole, it is the power of phenomena, which are shackled to necessity and the ordered rhythm of nature.

A naïvely realistic distortion of the world is always based upon confusion, the constructions of the mind enter into it. This compulsorily perceptible world which is the only real world for prosaic workaday experience, and the only 'objective' world, is a creation of man, it expresses the direction in which his mind tends to move. When the ordinary everyday person naïvely says: 'I regard as real only what I can perceive with the senses' he is, by so saying, and without being aware of the fact, regarding the reality of the world as dependent upon himself. And that is why philosophical empiricism was a form of idealism. Naïve realism is subjectivism at its worst.

The only real world of appearances is this human world of yours, and it depends upon your limitedness, upon the self-alienation of the spirit within you. Man exteriorizes his own enslave-

6

ment, he projects it upon the external, and he pictures it to himself as constraint exercised by an exterior reality. Purely intellectual criteria of reality are impossible, reality depends upon the dialectic of human existence, upon a dialectic which is existential, not intellectual. Being is anxiety, as Heidegger says, because I am in a state of anxiety and I project it upon the structure of being. When I say that the world is matter, and spirit an epiphenomenon of matter, I am saying that I am overwhelmed and enslaved by the materiality of the world. The phenomenal world, so staggeringly real, is dependent not only upon our reason but to a still greater extent upon our passions and emotions, our fear, our anxiety, our interests and our sinful slavery. Transcendental passions and feelings exist, and it is they above all that create our world, our reality.

At a certain stage in human self-consciousness, philosophy emerges out of dualistic thought, out of the distinction between the world of sense and the world of ideas, of phenomena and noumena, of appearances and things-in-themselves. Such an emergence was achieved by Plato and Kant, and this is the reason for their surpassing importance and depth of thought. The philosopher discovered that the world of the senses, the phenomenal world, is not the true world, nor is it the only world. But Plato and Kant deduce from this different and flatly contradictory conclusions about the act of knowing. In Plato's view true knowledge (*epistema*) was possible of the world of ideas only, of the noumenal world. Knowledge of the world of sense is not true knowledge. Kant's opinion, on the other hand, was that real knowledge, scientific knowledge, is a possibility only in regard to the phenomenal world. So far as the noumenal world is concerned knowledge is an impossibility; it is only moral postulates that are possible. Here the scientific spirit of the modern writer made itself heard. But we have already seen that Kant's philosophy was two-sided and inconsistent and thus lent itself to different interpretations. Kant has been regarded sometimes as an idealist and sometimes

7

as a realist. At times he has been accounted a metaphysician and at other times an anti-metaphysician.

I am convinced that Kant has not been accurately understood. He was a metaphysician and he ought to be interpreted from a metaphysical point of view. He was a metaphysician of freedom, even, it may be, the only metaphysician of freedom, and in this respect my attempt to set forth my own metaphysics of freedom will be derived from Kant. When Kant appeared the tragic side of the act of knowing came to light. It was an important event in the history of European thought. It is essential to grasp his vital and existential meaning. Epistemological optimism was a property of Greek philosophy, as it was also of mediaeval scholasticism as well as of the rationalist philosophy of modern times. The perceptional activity of the reason was taken in no naïve way, it was accepted dogmatically. Even earlier philosophy had turned its attention to the reason and investigated it. Greek philosophers had even discovered reason, but they had a dogmatic belief in the capacity of reason to apprehend being, in the correspondence between the concepts devised by reason and the object which is perceived. They saw reason in being itself, and it was that which made rational knowledge possible. According to Plato the noumenal world or the world of ideas is an intellectual and rational world. In St Thomas Aquinas it is only the intellect which comes into touch with being and apprehends it, since being itself is permeated by intellectuality. Spinoza and Leibniz believe in being in the same way. Universal reason apprehends things with the help of general concepts.

In this there was a naïve self-confidence on the part of the reason which lasted until the time of Kant. But the doubt arises whether the reason did not communicate its own properties to the object of its perception. And may it not be that its perceptional ontologism is based upon this transference to being of that which is a matter of its own devising and owes its origin to concepts? Is not the activity of the reason which has not been subjected to criticism a source of its impotence?

8

Kant, with his extraordinary critical acuteness was the first to note the confusions which might be engendered by the reason and to reveal its contradictions. The doctrine of transcendental illusion which owes its origin to reason is perhaps the aspect of his teaching in which his genius is most conspicuously displayed. Kant's doctrine of antinomies ranks among the greatest discoveries in the history of philosophical thought and merely requires amplification and development. With clear insight Kant perceives the confusion between the process of thinking and being, and the way in which thinking accepts as objective being that which it itself produces. He overcomes the power of the object over the subject by bringing to light the fact that the object is the offspring of the subject. Kant's great discovery which makes a sharp cut in the whole history of human thought and divides it into two parts, consists in this, that what refers merely to appearances and phenomena must not be transferred to what is noumenal, to things-in-themselves.

Kant's dualism was not a defect; it is quite the greatest merit of his philosophy. What was to be a defect in his followers was their monism. It is not true to say that Kant makes an end of all metaphysics; he merely makes an end of metaphysics of the naturalistic rationalist type, metaphysics which are derived from the object, from the world, and he reveals the possibility of metaphysics based on the subject, of a metaphysics of freedom. There is eternal truth in the distinction which Kant draws between the order of nature and the order of freedom. It is precisely Kant who makes existential metaphysics a possibility, the order of freedom is indeed *Existenz*.

It is generally supposed that Kant seeks only to give a secure basis to science and morals, but it is not only that, he has also a metaphysical interest and he wishes to make a stand in defence of freedom, he would see in it the essential nature of the world. The thing-in-itself is unknowable from the side of the object; from the side of the subject it is freedom. It would seem that those who regard Kant as the foe of all metaphysics, allow the possibility of naturalistic objective metaphysics only. But another path for metaphysics opens out. Man is aware of himself not only as a phenomenon. The establishment of the frontiers of reason at once reveals also the ground of a different sort of knowledge. The old uncritical metaphysics was based upon a confusion of subject and object, of thought and thing, and for that very reason it was permeated with a false objectivity. It is an absolute mistake to interpret Kant's philosophy as 'subjectivism' and psychologism or to confuse his theory of knowledge with the physiology of the organs of sense.

People see in Kant a false 'subjectivism' precisely for the reason that they are under the sway of a false 'objectivism', and within the objectified world which arises from the subject. Critical philosophy is, of course, philosophy of the subject not of the object, and just for that reason it is not 'subjective' in the bad sense of the word and is 'objective' in the good sense. It is bound to arrive at setting spirit in opposition to being in its 'thingness', and creative dynamic in opposition to congealed being.

The subjective necessity of scientific knowledge and the moral law is, according to Kant, linked with the fact that the subject in his view is transcendental mind, spirit, that is to say, true 'objective' being. The relations between the 'subjective' and 'objective' are entirely paradoxical and throw the ordinary terminology out of gear. But here Kant is not completely consistent or thoroughgoing and the concept of the object is with him especially weak and unstable.

Kant's criticism of the ontological proof of the existence of God is of great importance. It is directed against false ontologism in general. Ontological proof is based upon a confusion of the logical predicate with reality, of the idea of being with being. Kant strikes a blow at the old metaphysics which were based upon a confusion between the product of thought and reality. It is interesting to note that in Kant the limitations and metaphysical weakness of reason are associated with its cognitive activity. Reason is not active in cognition only. It is active also in the formation of the object-world itself, of the world of phenomena.

Pre-Kantian philosophy had an inadequate view of this activity of reason and, therefore, accepted its metaphysical claims to reflect real entities. Kant's criticism denied the applicability of concepts to things-in-themselves. They can be applied only to appearances. Transcendental ideas have only a regulative, not a constitutive application. But there is in idealism a danger of regarding reason as concerned only with itself and thought as having immediate apprehension only of thought.

Such is one side of Kantian criticism; but there is also another. Kant is the central event in the history of European philosophy. But the spirit of the philosophy of modern times as a whole is different from the philosophy of the Middle Ages and of antiquity. With Nicholas of Cusa, with Descartes and in part with Spinoza, with Leibniz, Locke, Berkeley and Hume, a new orientation of philosophical thought begins. The relation between the philosophies of modern and mediaeval times must be understood in a different way from that which is commonly accepted. The view usually adopted is that mediaeval philosophy was Christian, whereas the philosophy of modern times is non-Christian or even anti-Christian. But in actual fact it is rather the reverse of this which is true. Mediaeval scholastic philosophy was fundamentally Greek; it did not pass beyond the bounds of ancient thought; it was a philosophy of the object, that is to say it was cosmocentric. Modern philosophy, on the other hand, has become a philosophy of the subject; it is anthropocentric and its centre of gravity is transferred to man. But this means that Christian emancipation from the power of the objectified world over man had not yet made its way into thought in the Middle Ages, whereas in modern times Christianity does enter into thought, it carries on its work unseen within it and leads to the autonomy of man and of his thought.

11

The philosophy of the ego, of the subject, in German philosophical thought has a Christian basis and its theme is Christian. A truly Christian philosophy cannot be one which expresses a servile dependence of man upon the object and upon the world. St Thomas Aquinas was, of course, much more of a Christian than Hegel was, but in its theme and in its line of direction his philosophy was less Christian than Hegel's, not to speak of Kant's. That philosophy did no more than add an upper storey of theology to a purely Greek philosophical foundation, and that theological storey was infected by Aristotelian categories of thought. The scholastic metaphysics was naturalistic.

It follows as a matter of course that a different spirit made its way into philosophical thought. It is to be found above all in St Augustine who was a predecessor of the philosophy of modern times. It was in St Gregory of Nyssa too, and among the great scholastics, to some extent in Duns Scotus. According to Duns Scotus man rises above nature, not through the intellect but by the will, the intellect is determined from without, whereas the will is self-determination.[1] And our attitude to the age of the Enlightenment also requires some re-valuation. It has been settled too much by the reaction of the Romantic epoch. The Enlightenment is an important moment in the history of the spirit, in the dialectic of reason, and it ought not to be identified with the superficial French Enlightenment of the eighteenth century. Enlightenment is not the same thing as rationalism, although rationalism played a great part in the age of the Enlightenment.

Kant gave us a profound definition of the Enlightenment. According to him it is man's way out from the impossibility of using his reason without the help of another. It means that man, having been set free from his swaddling clothes, begins to make use of his own reason.[2] Kant was of the opinion that we are still not living in an enlightened age but only in an age of enlightenment.

[1] See Landry: *Duns Scotus*, and Seeberg: *Die Theologie des Johannes Duns Scot.*
[2] See Kant: *Der Frage Beantwortung: 'Was ist Aufklärung?'*

But this is a contradictory dialectic process. In an age of enlightenment the reason is permeated by self-conceit which weakens it. It limits itself by the fact that it regards itself as having unlimited power.

Kant not only proclaimed the truth of enlightenment as against the enslaving power of authority, but he also marks out the limitations of the Enlightenment by weakening the principle of rationalism and setting free the sphere of faith. He admits the claims of reason only in the sphere of phenomena and not in the noumenal sphere. Man stands in his full stature only when he arrives at his years of enlightenment, that is to say when he begins to make independent use of his reason and ceases to rely only on the authority of others, in other words when he discovers freedom of spirit which is the value and dignity of the image of God in him. And let there be an end of saying that this means rationalism, for that is just boring and commonplace.

The philosophy which I wish to present in this book is certainly not rationalistic. It will probably be found to be even irrationalistic, but I cherish the hope that it is enlightened philosophy in the Kantian sense of the word. There is a further error which sets the spirit of *sobornost*[1] in opposition to freedom. Free spirit is a corporate spirit, not that of the isolated individual. *Sobornost* cannot but be free. We ought to appraise Kant afresh and get new understanding of him; but this presupposes a criticism of him also, albeit from a different point of view than has hitherto been the case.

Kant denied intuition in metaphysical apprehension. Contemplation presupposes the presence of an object, but the transcendent object, the thing-in-itself, is not present in contemplation. At the same time Kant recognizes intuition of the noumenal world as the world of freedom. He admits only pseudo-scientific metaphysical knowledge and submits it to doubt and exposes its illusions.

But why should another sort of knowledge be impossible, one which is not open to the Kantian criticism? Such a knowledge is

[1] See page 131 for the meaning of this word.

implied by Kant himself. He does not explain why knowledge of the world of appearances is true scientific knowledge while at the same time it has nothing to do with true reality. It is not only the transcendental dialectic of reason which gives rise to illusions. The scientifically knowable phenomenal world also is itself an illusory world as the philosophy of the Upanishad recognizes. The upshot is that the truly real world (things-in-themselves) is unknowable whereas the unreal world (appearances) can be known.

Kant recognized that there is a metaphysical need implanted in our nature; it is deeply inherent in reason. But he repudiates spiritual experience as a basis of a possible metaphysics. Or rather, to put it more accurately, he reduces spirituality to practical ethical postulates which open up another world to view. But Kant would not acknowledge outright that non-conceptual, spiritual, existential apprehension of a noumenon is a possibility. He was right only in the negative sense: the whole apparatus of our knowledge by concepts is applicable only to the world of appearances. It is a curious thing that in the denial of the possibility of intellectual contemplation without external sensations, in the recognition of such a possibility only for higher beings than man, Kant was akin to St Thomas Aquinas.

The criticism, however, of purely intellectual contemplation seems to me to be true. If intuitive knowledge is possible it cannot be purely intellectual, it can only be integral, concrete, that is to say it must also be emotional and volitional. Thinking and knowing are always emotional, and the emotional is the deciding element. Judgment presupposes freedom and a choice of the will. Judgments of value are emotional and volitional. It was a fundamental mistake in Kant that he recognized sensuous experience, in which appearances are the data, but he did not recognize spiritual experience, of which the data are noumenal. Man remains, as it were, corked up in the world of phenomena; he is unable to break out of it, or able to break out only by way of practical postulates. Kant regarded man as, from man's

14

point of view, an appearance; man was not revealed to himself as a noumenon.

But in what does the source of the impotence of reason lie? The reason is divided. It has metaphysical needs and metaphysical claims, and at the same time it is fitted to know only the world of appearances and these are its own creation. Kant revealed this dividedness of the reason and to him it was a tragic experience. But, while admitting metaphysical presuppositions for the practical reason, Kant by the very fact of so doing acknowledges that there may be knowledge which is not intellectual but volitional and emotional. He admits a very great deal; he creates real metaphysics. This metaphysical interest plays a part in him in no degree smaller than that of scientific interests or purely moral interests; it was even existentially fundamental for him. The noumenal world was revealed to him as the world of freedom. He knows what the thing-in-itself is and it is only in respect of method that he gives the impression of knowing absolutely nothing about it. Kant was not a phenomenalist, nor was he in the least degree a noumenalist. He set a very high value on the thing-in-itself and placed all his hopes in it. For that reason he could not be a thorough-going idealist and he repudiated the name 'idealist' as applied to himself.

Kant's critics have above all exposed the contradictions in the very concept of the thing-in-itself. One of the first to do this was Solomon Maiman. But in Fichte's rejection of the thing-in-itself the profound dialectic of German idealism came to light. In the Kantian recognition of things-in-themselves there was much difficulty and it gave rise to contradiction. But the subsequent development of German philosophy rejected things-in-themselves much too lightly, and this has had fateful results. Kantian dualism in which a great deal of truth was brought to light, was replaced by monism. Reason cannot by itself arrive at the thing-in-itself not even as at a concept which marks a boundary.

What is most contradictory and inadmissible was in Kant's view to regard the thing-in-itself as the cause of appearances since to him causality is the transcendental condition of knowledge of the world of appearances only. This has often been pointed out. It introduces complications into the Kantian distinction between form and content. Content is given by the thing-in-itself while form `is given by reason, by the transcendental mind. But if the thing-in-itself can be revealed, this can take place only from the side of a subject; from the side of an object it cannot be revealed. Behind appearances, behind objects there are no things-in-themselves at all; they are behind subjects only. Things-in-themselves are entities and their existence. The thing-in-itself is not the cause of an appearance; the thing-in-itself (if indeed we are to retain that not entirely satisfactory name) is freedom, not a cause; and as a result of a certain line of direction taken by freedom it gives rise to the world of appearances. This was how Fichte was thinking when he wrote of the primary act of the ego. We shall see the sort of consquences which followed from this.

The most thorough-going idealist was Hermann Cohen to whom thinking and its product are all that there is. The mistake of thorough-going idealism has lain in this, that to it the ego was not the individual entity, not personality. It was the error of impersonalism and that is what is basically wrong in German metaphysics. Given that as the case it was easy to deny the difference between appearance and the thing-in-itself, in the divine intellect which performs the act of knowing. Kant was not an impersonalist. On the contrary his metaphysics are personalist. But his mistake lay in the very admission of the existence of pure reason and pure thought. Pure thought does not exist; thought is saturated with acts of volition, with emotions and passions and these things play a part in the act of knowing which is not simply negative; they have a positive role to play.

But this is not the main point; the main point is that Kant uses the words 'object' and 'objectivity' inaccurately and inconsistently. In the end, objectivity is with him confused with reality and truth; he aims at getting to know things objectively and he seeks to find a basis for objective knowledge. To him the transcendent itself was not free from association with the name of object, but if there is such a thing as the transcendent there is nothing which is less an object than it. Kant, like the majority of philosophers, still fails to discover the truth, which is a paradox in form, that the 'objective' is precisely 'subjective' while the 'subjective' is 'objective'. For the subject is the creation of God while the object is the creation of the subject. The meaning which Kant puts into the words 'object' and 'objectivity' contradicts that philosophy of the subject, of the ego, which is fundamental to his thought. Objectivity was accepted as identical with general-validity.

But it is that general-validity above all which convinces me of the truth of my understanding of objectivization. And at the same time it is clear to me that general-validity is sociological in character. The transcendental mind cannot be regarded as immobile; it is moblie and depends upon the social conditions which obtain among human beings. But social relations among human beings do not belong only to the world of phenomena; they belong to the world of noumena, to primary life, to *Existenz*. The transcendental mind of Kant is very different from the transcendental mind of Attila, and they were faced by totally different worlds.

But the mobility of the transcendental mind does not mean a denial of the truth that the Logos shows through in it. The degree to which the Logos permeates the mind depends upon the spiritual state of human beings. The distinction between appearance and the thing-in-itself lies not in the relation between subject and object but in the actual things-in-themselves, in a qualitative condition of that which is called being. But in any case the object is always appearance.

2

German philosophy as a whole was inoculated with German

mysticism, and it is possible to show the underground activity of this mysticism in it. Kant shied at it, but Hegel recognized the fact and had a very high opinion of Boehme. German mysticism introduced the idea of newness into the history of spirit. Originally this had not found any philosophical expression. The effects made themselves felt in philosophical thought only at the end of the eighteenth century and at the beginning of the nineteenth. The speculative mysticism of Eckhardt and his followers was still in the line of descent from neoplatonism. But in Boehme a new feeling for the world becomes evident.

Boehme was not a neoplatonist in any forthright sense, and was a stranger to the tradition of both ancient and mediaeval Latin thought. He was inoculated with a strain derived from the Kabbala. What was new in him was the interpretation of cosmic life as a passionate struggle between diametrically opposed principles. In the depth of being, or rather before being, is the Ungrund, a dark, irrational bottomless depth—the primordial freedom. The eternal cosmic order envisaged by ancient and Latin thought is melted down in a stream of fire. The only writer of the ancient world who was a kindred spirit to Boehme was Heraclitus.

To Latin thought, reason, like the light of the sun, lay at the foundation of the objective world order, and that same reason was to be found in the apprehending subject. To Boehme, an irrational principle lies at the basis of being, primordial freedom precedes being itself. Thus a new theme is stated for German mysticism, a theme which went beyond the confines of Greek thought. The voluntarism of German metaphysics is associated with this. This voluntarism is to be seen already in Kant. Kant maintains that freedom is a primary principle. We see the same thing in Fichte also. The primordial act of the ego is connected with freedom, which precedes the world: it comes into actual effect out of the Ungrund. Hence Goethe's saying—'*Im Anfang war die Tat*'.

According to Hegel, in spite of his panlogism, the becoming of the world is impossible without non-being. Hegel, as Kroner put

18

it, irrationalized even the concept itself and introduced a passionate dialectical struggle into it. The link which existed between Baader, Schelling, Schopenhauer and the theme propounded by Boehme, is clearest of all. Being is irrational, but man is called upon to bring a rational principle into it. In Hegel's view, God arrives at self-consciousness in man, in the philosophy of Hegel himself. In E. Hartmann's opinion too, God, who in a senseless, unconscious, outburst created the pain of being, nevertheless arrives at self-consciousness in man.[1] German metaphysics rationalized the theme of Boehme's mystical gnosis, it was in that that its strength was to be found, but therein lay its weakness also. At the very outset German mysticism revealed the divine depth in the primary foundation of the soul and thereby transferred the centre of gravity to the subject (Eckhardt and Tauler).

Thus the spiritual ground for a philosophy of the subject, of the ego, was already created, and it became possible to supersede the ancient and mediaeval Greek and Latin philosophy which was directed towards the object. When the matter was stated in purely philsosophical terms, it was inevitable that thought should pass through a period of dualism, of which there was none in the neo-platonism of Eckhardt though there was in Boehme. It is to this moment that the philosophy of Kant corresponds. And in Greek thought the passage through dualism in Plato is analogous to it. And further, just as the philosophical thought which came after Plato sought to overcome dualism and pass over to monism, so in the same way the like process of overcoming dualism and establishing monistic systems, took place in the philosophical thought which followed Kant.

By the dualism of the world of the senses and the world of ideas in Plato, a question was posed which subsequent Greek philosophers endeavoured to decide. Aristotle already seeks to overcome dualism and later on Plotinus and neoplatonism do the same. The Platonic doctrine of two worlds was converted by Aristotle

[1] See E. Hartmann: *Die Religion des Geistes*.

into a monistic doctrine of one world within which there exists the distinction between form and content, between act and potentiality. Plotinus also is a monist; according to him, everything moves from above downwards by way of emanations.

In the monist system this world is an unfolding of the other world, the other world is immanent so far as this world is concerned. Plato regarded being as an attribute of perfection: being, in his view, is a derivative from the Good, from the Supreme Good. There is, therefore, a strong ethical element in his philosophy; it cannot be called ontological in the exact sense of the word. Dualism and an ethical line of approach are always associated with one another. Aristotle constructed a system of ethics which had its influence even upon Thomas Aquinas, but his philosophy did not have an ethical bearing as a whole. The wrongness in this world of the senses was a cause of suffering to Plato, but there is no such feeling in Aristotle. In Plotinus everything is reduced to mystical contemplation. In the neoplatonists Iamblichus, Proclus and others, there is an attempt at a mystical revival of paganism, Plato's ideas become gods. To Plato the life of a philosopher is the practice of death. Aristotle wishes to live in this world, and has the sanction of the higher world for life in this. Form and act are the higher elements operating in the lower, acting in matter, in potentiality. It might be said that Aristotle was the Hegel of Greek philosophy, while Plotinus was the Schelling. They both alike moved away from the Platonic dualism towards monism. It is impossible to deny the services which Aristotle rendered, and the importance of Plotinus, who was a very great mystical philosopher. But the development of Platonism towards monism was a mistaken solution of the question that had been raised. Unity was not attained.

Christianity also overcomes the dualism of Plato, but it acknowledges the fallen state of this world and, therefore, that to pass through dualism is unavoidable. A new eschatological element appears in Christian thought. This has not been sufficiently brought to light, but it makes all forms of monism impossible within the confines of this objectivized world. The philosophy of Plato was a philosophy of species. *Eidos* is species. The problem of the person and of individuality, therefore, did not arise within the limits of this philosophy. Plato was disquieted by the plurality and mobility of the world of sense. But what is still more disquieting is its fettered condition, its necessity and its impersonality. Monistic unity is unattainable from and through the object, it is only in the subject and through the subject that it can be reached. Kant starts, as Plato did, from the dualism of phenomenon and noumenon, of appearance and the thing-in-itself, and for the new age of thought from the dualism of nature and freedom. It was in this way that the theme which the Great German metaphysicians developed was stated. I repeat, that a process of thought took place which was analogous to what had happened in Greek thought—a development in the direction of a false monism. The thing-in-itself was set aside. The subject, the self, the universal ego became the architect of the world. It might be put in this way, that post-Kantian idealistic metaphysics regarded the transcendental subject as the thing-in-itself. A hypostatization of 'consciousness in general' took place. As Nicolas Hartmann puts it, consciousness is not confronted by the thing-in-itself, the thing-in-itself lies behind it. It is on this soil that the new metaphysics spring up.

German idealism, of Kant and the rest, differs from neoplatonic, it is transferred to the subject, to the inward. It is not the ideas, but the apprehension of them, which is the distinguishing mark of knowledge. In Plato the ideas are archetypes of the world of sense, in Kant the same relation holds good between the ego and the world of sense. Apprehension of the transcendental conditions of knowledge becomes for the German idealists the apprehension of metaphysical being. Kant did not aim at a total knowledge of nature, to him the world as a whole was not a datum in experience. Hegel and Schelling do have such an aim. There is a firm grip upon moral principle in Kant, and also in Fichte. The ethical knowledge of self lies at the basis of even the logic of Kant. It is moral responsibility which creates the ego. The unconditioned is in the sphere of obligation. Man is free not as belonging to nature but as being endowed with the power of practical reason. Morality does not depend upon the object. German idealist metaphysics are not concerned with the object, nor with the world, nor with being, but with the subject, with reason, thought, and with responsibility.

Fichte's monism is ethical pantheism, he wants to re-make the world. In Kant the metaphysics of freedom are dualist. In Fichte they become monist. In his system there are no longer two worlds, as there are in Indian thought, and in Plato and Kant. There is only one world, postulated by the universal ego. Freedom of thought exists only in rational beings. The act of the spirit, as recognized by us, is called freedom. The only source from which freedom flows is conscience. Fichte maintains the supremacy of conscience. It is simply thanks to the bidding of duty that the world exists. My will is the first thing, it must operate through itself.

But in contradiction to his monism of the ego, Fichte sees in the world the interplay of self-acting and independent wills. To German metaphysics as distinct from Latin, reason in itself is essentially irrational. In Fichte, the ego postulates for itself an antithetic non-ego, and by this means acquires its content. *Einbildungskraft* produces empirical objects. But nature is merely a hindrance to the ego. The relation between the individual empirical ego and the Absolute ego, is left unexplained. It was here that Fichte's monism broke down. Which ego performs the primary act? Fichte confuses the creation of the world by God and an act performed by man. Neither does he distinguish between evil and good infinity. An endless output of effort—that is Fichte's last word; Spirit exists to the extent in which it actualizes itself. Consciousness rests upon the intuition of the act.[1]

In Schelling thought and being are identified. In considering

[1] I am not speaking now of the Fichte of the period of *Anweisungen zum seeligen Leben*.

the dialectic of thought after Kant, the early writings of Schelling are of particular interest.[1] Knowledge cannot be based upon the object. The object exists only for the sake of the subject, for the sake of knowledge; object and subject exist for the sake of each other. The unconditioned cannot be a thing; it lies within the absolute. The ego is anterior to the antithesis of subject and object. Appearance is a conditioning of the ego by the non-ego. The Absolute is not appearance, nor is it the thing-in-itself. The essence of the ego is freedom, and freedom is the beginning and the end of all philosophy. The concept refers to objects only. The ego is not a datum in the form of a concept. Intellectual contemplation is not directed upon the object. The ego is one only, there is no other ego for it. The ego, the basic principle of philosophy, is God, the Absolute. Kant wrote the *Critique of Pure Reason*, but he did not reveal the way to another metaphysic of reason. In Fichte, Schelling and Hegel, reason becomes divine. It is only on that account that dualism passes into monism. But the Absolute ego is not transcendent. Egress from the ego would be transcendent. Dogmatic metaphysics had seen reality in the non-ego, not in the ego. After Kant it was possible to see metaphysical reality only in the ego. The thing-in-itself is not an object, it is a subject and, therefore, not a thing. According to Schelling the source of self-consciousness is in the will.

Without contemplation we should have no knowledge of movement. It is only by freedom that freedom is recognized. The 'I' can become 'I' only through the 'thou'. Schelling's philosophical thought is informed by aesthetic contemplation. He passes from a philosophy of the ego, to a nature-philosophy, combining a criticism of Kant's capacity for judgment with the scientific teaching of Fichte. Kroner says truly that in Schelling Spinoza has conquered Kant. The monist tendency leads towards Spinoza.

Hegel is the most consistent of idealists, and in him idealism passes into a special sort of realism. He seeks to return to reality

[1] Especially his *Vom 'Ich' als Prinzip der Philosophie.*

23

and the concrete by means of a dialectic of understanding. Hegel brings the dynamic of life into thought and conception. He gives new life to the law of identity. An antithesis which is thinkable is to him an antithesis which can be overcome (*Aufhebung*). Movement is itself existent contradiction. 'Only the absolute idea is being, unceasing life, which knows itself to be truth and the whole truth.[1]

Reason itself is truth revealing itself to itself. To Hegel, philosophical idealism means that the finite is not regarded as the truly existent. Freedom is true necessity. There is a changed attitude to reason in Hegel, it is no longer the reason of Kant. Thinking, ratiocination, becomes the dialectical life of the Deity, of the world Spirit. Logic is turned into ontology. According to Hegel's logic the concept submits to passions and is endowed with a mysterious life. Hegel is the first in the history of human thought to introduce the dynamic into logic; he breaks with the thousand years' reign of Aristotelian logic. There is absolutely no dualism in Hegel, but there is antithesis, as the law of thinking and being. Philosophical thought in the past had been aware of dialectic—it is to be found in Plato, in Nicholas of Cusa and in Kant. Heraclitus was already aware of the idea of antinomy. Antinomy and antithesis are by no means evidence of weakness of mind. On the contrary through its fixing of boundaries it represents a great achievement of reason. According to Nicholas of Cusa *docta ignorantia* is the highest form of knowledge. The dialectic of antithesis is to be found in Zeno, Heraclitus, Plato, Nicholas of Cusa, Boehme, Hamann and Kant. But as contrasted with Nicholas of Cusa and Kant, in Hegel the identity of opposites is attained by dialectical development. He introduces a new element.

Hegel's philosophy is a philosophy of the spirit. It maintains the supremacy of spirit over nature. The potency of spirit is in nature. Spirit is the unity of subject and object, of the self and nature, of the process of thinking and the outlook which results from it. It is the essence of Hegelian monism that spirit organizes itself as re-

[1] See Hegel: *The Science of Logic*. Part 2. Section 3. Chapter 3.

24

ligion, art, the State, the soul, and nature. For him, therefore, objective spirit exists, and that I regard as the principal error of Hegel
and of the monistic doctrine of the spirit. Kroner insists that Hegel
has irrationalized the concept and has, therefore, introduced the irrational into the history of philosophical thought. Dialectic is the
unrest and the life of the concept. But the unrest is brought to an
end, the contradiction is overcome, the dialectical process comes
to an end in a higher synthesis. It was here that Hegel broke down.

The self-directed movement of thought is revealed in dialectic,
but it is consummated within the confines of this objective world.
The contradiction disappears, it does not lead on to the end of this
world. But Kroner denies that Hegel was a panlogist. Everything
is spirit, the world is spiritualized. To Hegelian universalism the
whole is the truth, and separate propositions are true only as part
of the whole. Spirit sets itself in opposition to nature. The absolute
reason carries its antithesis within itself. The Absolute is the surmounting of the opposition between the inward and the outward.
The opposites are identical. The self-alienation of spirit takes place
in Hegel, and that perhaps is the most remarkable thing about him.
But the Hegelian universal monism failed for this reason, that the
Absolute is actualized in the form of absolute necessity. Because of
that, however much Hegel may have talked about freedom, he
does not know freedom. Hegel asserts the identity of spirit with
philosophy, his own, the Hegelian philosophy. This is the most
dreadful philosophical pride which the history of philosophy
knows. Kroner speaks of the eschatological and prophetic
character of German idealism. There is truth in this. There is the
idea of an end in German metaphysics, there is striving towards an
ultimate consummation.

But this final consummation is thought of in an immanentist
manner, within the confines of this world in which spirit is
decisively revealed by way of dialectical development. What
was fundamentally wrong about those idealist systems of metaphysics was their monism, which is an impossible thing within the

limits of a fallen world, their mistaken, anti-personalist conception of freedom. Kant was more in the right with his dualism, his metaphysics of freedom and his ethical personalism. In Hegel's view the idea stands high above everything. But the living creature ranks higher than the idea. To Hegel the most exalted thing of all was history in which the victorious march of the world-spirit is disclosed. He wrote about the cunning of reason in history. He does not understand the conflict between personality and history; history is not a tragic thing to him; he was an optimist.

Schopenhauer makes a different deduction from Kant. He preserves the Kantian thing-in-itself and in this he was right. He understands objectification in a different way, not upon optimistically evolutionary lines, and in this also there was much that is true. But he arrives at monism from the opposite end, at monism of the Indian type; and he certainly does not understand history, just as Indian thought does not understand it either. Indian philosophy is monistic in so far as it regards the plurality of this world as unreal and illusory.[1] This is of a different type from Hegel's. Hegel was a typical European and in him the German strain is combined with the Hellenic. If German idealism developed Kant's theme in the direction of monistic metaphysics and reveals creative philosophical genius, neo-Kantianism develops it in the direction of an entire repudiation of metaphysics: it is under the sway of an age of scientism, and reveals a decline in philosophical creativeness. But they all, in fact, distort Kant; no-one has been true to the Kantian metaphysics of freedom which presupposed dualism.

The most thorough-going and extreme neo-Kantian, Hermann Cohen, affirms pan-methodism. For him truth is method, and idea is obligation. Another neo-Kantian, Rickert, denies the two-fold nature of the world which both Plato and Kant acknowledge. But there is much truth in his position that the act of knowing is above

[1] I must defend myself by admitting that there have been pluralist systems in Indian philosophy, but it is monism that has been predominant. See R. Grousset *La philosophie indienne*.

all an act of valuing, and that it is only a judgment of value which can be either true or false. In his view *a priori* is a form of mind which has transcendental rather than psychological significance. This is neo- Kantianism.

But in the last resort the philosophy of values turns into a new scholasticism; and there is a deathly pallor about it. Phenomenology is in danger of turning into the same sort of thing. The opinion has been put forward that Kant was not a metaphysician, that he reduced philosophy simply to the theory of knowledge and to ethics. The value of this judgment needs drastic reconsideration. The controlling motive in Kant was metaphysical; it was the defence of the world of freedom from the power of phenomena.

Kant's dualism cannot be overcome by the monistic idea of a development of spirit in the world. Spirit (noumenon) is not revealed and does not develop in a continuous uninterrupted process in the world of history (phenomena). It only breaks through into the phenomenal 'objective' world, but it is then that freedom of the spirit overthrows the necessity of the world. Kant was inconsistent but essentially he was more in the right than Fichte, Schelling and Hegel. Evolutionism (albeit of the spiritual and not the naturalistic type) is just as mistaken as monism.

The optimism of this evolutionary monism is certainly not justified by the real and actual process of the world and of history. There is no such thing as objective spirit. There is merely the objectification of spirit, and that is a distortion; it is estrangement from itself and it is an adaptation to the world as we have it. Spirit, which is freedom, is objectified in the historical process, in culture, but it is not revealed, it does not come to light in its existentiality. The creative fire of the spirit cools down. Objectification is a process of cooling. We shall see that the dualism of Plato and still more of Kant raises the subject of eschatology: monism is possibly only in an eschatological setting.

There are three ways of overcoming dualism and attaining to

27

unity. Either you regard the world of sense and plurality, the mobile phenomenal world, as an unreal and illusory world. Real knowledge may be only knowledge of Brahman and this knowledge is possible because Atman, the subject in the act of knowing is identified with Brahman. Or you regard the spiritual noumenal world as unfolding itself and developing within this phenomenal world: nature and history are stages in the self-revelation of spirit. This is metaphysical evolutionism which may turn even into materialism. Or again there is a third possibility. You may see spirit and freedom merely breaking through in this phenomenal world, that is to say you refuse to see in this an uninterrupted process. You see a process which is liable to be broken off, and you connect the attainment of monistic unity with the coming of the end of this world of phenomena and with the Kingdom of God.

In that case the end and the coming of the Kingdom of God are not conceived as belonging only to the other world. We come into touch with the end in every creative act of spirit. The Kingdom of God comes not with observation. The noumen operates in phenomena, but this is not uninterrupted evolution and not the true rhythmic order of necessity. The two first types of surmounting dualism appear to me to be erroneous, and in my opinion only the third type is true. Monism is a metaphysical heresy. It is the denial of the existence of two natures, two principles, the denial of the operation of God and of response to God in the creative act of man.

Faith is possible only if it be granted that dualism exists both in the visible world, the world of compulsion, and in the invisible world, the world which is revealed in freedom. In Kant the foundation stone of true metaphysics was laid. In the affirmation of German idealism that God is obligation, and that in the process of the world and history there is a becoming of God, there is a measure of truth is spite of the religious and metaphysical error which this teaching contains. It is true that God is the supreme value, the supreme good, truth and beauty. God is not a reality in the same sense and of the same kind as the reality of the natural world. God is spirit, not being.

3

During the nineteenth century in Germany a dialectic of idealism was developed by one genius after another, from Kant, through Hegel and Feuerbach, to Max Stirner and Nietzsche. It was not only a logical dialectic, or simply an evolution of thought. It was the unfolding of a vital existential process across an abyss of contradiction. In Kant's philosophy a turn is definitely made towards a philosophy of the ego, of the subject, as against a philosophy of the world, of the object. This presupposes to begin with a dualism between appearance and the thing-in-itself, between the order of nature and the order of freedom. Fichte is absorbed in the subject and its creative act, the thing-in-itself is set aside, the ego presents itself as the Divine Ego, and through the subject monism is reached. In Kant a distinction is drawn between being and obligation. In Fichte obligation swallows up being. In Schelling and Hegel, on the other hand, it is obligation which is swallowed up.

Schelling (not, however, in his first period) turns again towards the object, and towards Spinoza. The dialectic of subject and object reaches its climax in Hegel who discovers becoming as the identity of non-being and being. The concept turns into being in its uniqueness, it experiences a vital unrest and dialectic passions. The world process is a dialectical development and through it the self-revelation of the Spirit takes place. Reality, therefore, is rational and only the rational is real. This is monism, and it cannot be called a philosophy of the ego, of the subject. The Universal Spirit completely engulfs personality and turns it into one of its instruments. The cunning of reason in history makes use of the human personality and of every individual way of deceit. Hegel strove after concreteness, and he arrived at the abstract at its very height, in which human existence vanishes. Great concreteness is to be found only in the *Phenomenology of the Spirit*.

29

Schopenhauer followed another route which led from Kant. At the outset he was true to Kant's dualism of appearance and the thing-in-itself. But through the subject he discovers a single metaphysical principle of the will, and also arrives at a monism in which man, personality and individuality vanish. Schopenhauer's philosophy is more concrete just because of its extreme inconsistency. It does not stand up to logical criticism just because of its great existentiality. But Schopenhauer stands apart, he is outside the unfolding destiny of German idealism.

There comes a glut of metaphysical systems, and a violent reaction of thought against metaphysics in general. There comes a turn towards reality, the concrete reality which had disappeared, material reality though it may have been. Hegelianism dialectically passes into its opposite and gives birth to dialectical materialism. A transition from Hegel to materialism was plainly possible, whereas such a transition from Kant would have been out of the question. Feuerbach made his appearance, and then Marx, both deriving from Hegel. The philosophy of the subject which maintains the primacy of thought over being leads to the assertion of the supremacy of being over thought and to extreme objectivism. Thus is the dialectic of the destiny of thought fulfilled. Feuerbach raised a lament over man who was disappearing. In his anthropological philosophy there was a presentiment of the possiblity of an existential philosophy.[1] Feuerbach's materialist deviation was not only not necessary to his anthropologism, but is clearly a contradiction of it and threatens a new disappearance of man. Man may vanish not only in idea, in concept, in abstract thought, he can disappear even more in matter, in society which is controlled by economics, in the life of the race. Feuerbach's religion of humanity is a religion of race, not of personality.

In Max Stirner the dialectic reaches the limit of individualism and anarchism. The philosophy of the ego is turned into the deification of the ego. Here, he says, is this unique, this given 'I'.

[1] See in particular his *Grundsätze der Philosophie der Zukunft*.

Stirner justly rebels against the idea of mankind, against the power of the breed over the individual. The whole world is the property of the single ego, nor is anything higher than it. The single ego refuses to be a part of the world or of society or of anything at all; everything is simply a part of it. And in all this there is a great measure of truth although it is set forth in a false and weak philosophy. In Stirner the tones of German mysticism can be heard and echoes of the Renaissance doctrine of man as a microcosm. Here the development of one side of German idealism to the extreme limit is to be seen.

Fichte had taught a doctrine of the primary sovereign ego which was not the individual but the universal ego. Stirner definitely identifies the individual ego with the universal and maintains its priority and supremacy. It declines to be made subordinate to anything or anybody whatever. The ego which does not seek to know another, whether the ego of God or the ego of other men, is bound to reach the position of Max Stirner. That is an inevitable dialectical movement. Thought had to pass through this experience; it is one of the boundaries of thought. If there is no God, then the self is God and in that case not the self in general and not mankind within my ego, as in Feuerbach, but my separate unique ego. And further, another question comes into view; on what are the claims of this ego based? It can hardly be merely a natural phenomenon dependent in all respects upon natural and social environment, and an insignificant little part of this world. Stirner's anarchism hangs in the air.

The dialectic development from Hegel and Feuerbach to Marx takes an entirely different direction, it moves not to the limit of individualism but to the limit of collectivism. The labouring society, the social collective, is regarded as the only thing, and everything as its property. In Max Stirner concrete human persons disappear in the universal claims of the Unique One; the limit of universalism swallows up the individual which has no support in anything. There is no difference between saying that there is no-one and nobody except myself and saying that there is no 'I'.

In Marx the concrete human person disappears in the universal claims of the social collective, of the perfect society which is to be achieved in the future. Both points of view are alike anti-personalist. The anti-personalist spirit of Hegel is hidden away in them, the anti-personalism of monism. Marx started from humanism and his original themes were humanist. In his early work he rebels in the name of the dignity of man, against the process of dehumanization which is due to the capitalist régime, but in the last stage Marx's humanism passes into anti-humanism.

The most extreme and the most audacious case was Nietzsche. His appearance was an important fact in the destiny of mankind in Europe, not only in the intellectual sphere but in the existential too. Nietzsche was a man whom the Christian message touched to the quick, but he broke with the ethics of the Gospel as he did also with humanistic ethics. He proclaimed a morality of the lord and master. Nietzsche revolts against logical universalism and general moral obligation, against the dictatorship of logic and ethics: he deifies the force of life and the will to power. He opens up a Dionysiac world, a world which is passionate and tragic, which has no desire to experience happiness, like the 'last people'. Nietzsche wanted to be a man exclusively of this world, to be true to this earth. But his theme is a religious one and his thought is controlled by a passion which is religious. The idea of superman is one which belongs to the religious order and in it both God and man disappear, while a third sort of being makes his appearance. Thus the dialectic of humanism is completed in the period in which he struggles against God. Dostoyevsky reveals this with all the force of his genius and he had already propounded Nietzsche's theme. Philosophically speaking the most important point was that in Nietzsche the attitude to truth is drastically altered. Truth is created by the will to power. This was a crisis in the very idea of truth, to which philosophers had remained faithful. Pragmatism has popularized Nietzsche's idea of truth and made it trivial, as something which can be created in a conflict for power, as a weapon at the disposal of the forces of life.

If we are to understand Nietzsche it is most important to grasp the fact that he had by no means any eager desire for the realization of a final victory of the will to power. The will to power does not build empires. What interested him was simply the experience of the uplifting impulse and ecstasy in the struggle for power. Afterwards ruin and disaster might follow. His pathos was linked with *amor fati*. But in the dialectic of German thought in the nineteenth century Fichte, Hegel, Feuerbach, Max Stirner, Karl Marx and Nietzsche were anti-personalist, albeit in different ways; it was not within their power to rescue the value of personality.

The genius and the existential significance of this thought are not to be denied. But in it the heresy of monophysitism came to light again, the acknowledgment of one nature only and of one principle. It was the engulfment of man, of the personal human features, by the world-ego, by the self- revealing world-spirit, by the human race, by the Unique One, by the social collective, or by the superman and his will to power. It was this system of thought which prepared the way for and made possible existential and personalist philosophy. But it could not itself effect a transition to it. It was in a different dialectical movement. The service it rendered was that it came near to the problem of the end and touched upon eschatology.

The return to Kant which came afterwards with the neo-Kantians was a transition to a central position. It was a fact of little significance and it reflected the dominance of scientism, whereas in Kant the possibility of existential and personalist philosophy had been disclosed and that is the only way out from the crisis in philosophical thought. Behind the crisis in philosophical thought is hidden a crisis in life. It will be clear that what I understand by existential philosophy is not the philosophy of Heidegger and

Jaspers. I attach value to these but I do not regard them as existential philosophers.

The French philosophers of the nineteenth century did not display the metaphysical depth or the creative philosophical imagination of the German. There was no such development of the genius for dialectic in French thought. It was more individual and that by fits and starts. French philosophical thought does not get into touch with ultimate problems, with those that lie on the frontiers; it is not eschatological. The vital destiny of man does not come into view in it.

But there is a greater psychological subtlety in the French thinkers. There are no such violent outbursts among them; and they are not under the sway of the seductive lure of monism. Personalist tendencies find greater expression among the French (compare Maine de Biran with Fichte, or in another field Proudhon with Max Stirner and Karl Marx). It was in fact French philosophy of the nineteenth century which raised the problem of freedom and interpreted freedom in a different way from that in which Hegel had understood it, for Hegel had regarded freedom as the child of necessity. It was an anthropological philosophy rather than cosmological. Maine de Biran, the Swiss Secretan, Renouvier, Lecky and Boutroux fought against determinism and defended the philosophy of freedom.

At times the problem of freedom is confused with the traditional problem of the schools about the freedom of the will, and this was due to an anthropological tendency in psychology. But the independence of man is defended in the teeth of cosmic necessity. To German metaphysicians life appeared as a cosmic mystery and in this same cosmic mystery the personal features of man are easily lost to sight. French philosophy has come nearer to Kant although it has frequently interpreted Kant's philosophy too much from the psychological point of view. Hegel's universal determinism in which freedom and necessity are identified was alien to this philosophy. Renouvier was particularly incisive in his

34

criticism of Hegelianism. In so far as French philosophy was rationalist, this rationalism was a limiting influence. There was no process of irrationalizing reason as in Hegel. French philosophical thought maintained its equilibrium in a central position. Neither Max Stirner nor Karl Marx nor Nietzsche could have appeared in France.

The French philosophers' critique of freedom is often just, but the realization of destiny does not make itself felt in it. In Heidegger there is a sense of something fateful, there is nothing fateful in Bergson. The English genius found its outstanding expression in literature and poetry, not in philosophy. The ultimate problems and final breaks come to light only in German and Russian thought. But the eschatology of Russian thought and its concern with ultimate problems were revealed in the great literary figures of Russia rather than in its professional philosophers. This concern with ultimate problems and eschatology is to be found in Dostoyevsky and in Tolstoy, in the outbreaks of Russian nihilism, in K. Leontiev, in Fyodorov and in Vladimir Soloviëv (in the last in a confused form) as well as in a number of thinkers at the beginning of the twentieth century.

Our creative philosophical thought has been tinged with a religious spirit, and a yearning for the Kingdom of God is disclosed in it, together with a sense of the impossibility of reconciling oneself to this world. Its fundamental problems were not questions about the theory of knowledge, about logic or abstract metaphysics. They were problems concerned with the philosophy of history, the philosophy of religion and ethics. Certain themes can be shown to be specifically Russian. Among such themes I place the subject of God-manhood and of eschatology and again the theme of the end of history.

A keen criticism of rationalism was associated with the interpretation of the act of knowing as an act of the integral mind, in which a combination of the spiritual powers of man plays its part. and not only of the individual man but also of man in his corporate

35

capacity. With the philosophy of history was connected the specifically Russian problem of the conflict of personality with world history and world harmony. This is a subject which finds expression in terms of the greatest genius in Dostoyevsky. The problem of theodicy is present in all Russian thought. It takes possession of the Russian soul and governs it. It is to be found in Russian anarchism and in Russian socialism.

The opposite pole was the suppression of personality in Russian political institutions and in the form taken by Russian Marxism. In Belinski there was a revolt of personality against the world-spirit, world-history and world-harmony, and the new enslavement of personality to society in the social harmony that was to come. The idea of God-manhood, the development of which was principally due to Vladimir Soloviëv, and the religious philosophy of the beginning of the twentieth century means the mutual penetration and the union of two natures, the Divine and the human, while the distinction between them and their independence is preserved.

The doctrine of God-manhood presupposes commensurability between God and man, the presence of the divine principle in man, and at the same time it does not admit monistic identity. The divine-human process not only occurred individually in the God-man, it ought also to take place in mankind, in human society. In Soloviëv the doctrine of God-manhood assumed too evolutionary and optimistic a character and was not sufficiently free from the influence of Hegel and Schelling, but this is not a fundamental aspect of it. The actual act of knowing may be conceived as a divine-human process in which the two principles operate.

This is distinct from the monistic interpretation of knowledge, in which it is either a divine process (Fichte, Schelling, Hegel) or one which is exclusively human (positivism). In Russian thought also the way was prepared for the possibility of existential philosophy, and in this respect the greatest significance attaches to Dostoyevsky's anthropology and the problems with which he dealt.

4

The discovery of reason by Greek philosophy was an important event in the history of knowledge. Man brought into the light forces which had hitherto been in a dreamlike state within him. He took possession of his reason and reason became independent. The emotional life of man had depended upon his impressions of the world of sense and his thought was entirely under the sway of mythological feelings about the world and of tradition. Reason, however, is both itself free and it is a liberating agent; it both enriches man and impoverishes him.

The philosopher believed that reason lifted him up to the world of ideas, to the noumenal world. This opinion Kant subjected to criticism. But almost throughout the history of philosophy the apprehending mind remained faithful to the conviction that cognition is a purely intellectual act, that there exists a universal reason and that reason is always one and the same and remains true to its nature. But in reality cognition is emotional and passionate in character. It is a spiritual struggle for meaning, and it is such not merely in this or that line of thought or school, but in every true philosopher even although he may not recognize the fact himself. Cognition is not a dispassionate understudy of reality. The significance of a philosophy is decided by the passionate intensity of the philosopher as a man, as one who is present behind his effort to know. It is decided by the intensity of the will to truth and meaning; it is the whole man who takes knowledge of a thing. Dilthey who was one of the forerunners of existential philosophy, says with truth that thinking is a function of life. The whole man, not reason, constructs metaphysics; it is not the autonomy of the intellect which needs to be asserted, but the autonomy of spirit, the autonomy of the knowing person as a complete being.

The process of thinking cannot be separated from the person who thinks and the person who thinks cannot be separated from the corporate experience of his brothers in spirit. The know-

37

ing person may, as an effect of his cognition, attain to an objective coolness of expression, but this is a secondary process of objectification. What is primary is the man's intuition as one who exists in the fullness of existence. Man apprehends emotionally to a greater extent than intellectually, and the view that emotional cognition is 'subjective' in the bad sense of the word while intellectual cognition is 'objective' in the good sense is entirely wrong, and in any case it is expressed in terms which are inaccurate. To quicken the subject matter of knowledge into life is in any case a process which is emotional rather than intellectual in character. The intuitivism of Bergson and Scheler as well as of Schelling, to say nothing of Nietzsche, is non-intellectualist.

Purely intellectual discursive knowledge constructs an objectified world out of touch with reality. What is decisively important in knowledge is not the logical process of thought, which ranks as an instrument, and which takes control only in the centre of the path, but the emotional and volitional tension is attributable to the spirit as a whole. Knowledge is a creative activity, not a passive reflection of things, and every act of creation includes knowledge. Intuition is not only the perception of something; it is also a creative penetration into meaning; and more than that, the very existence of meaning presupposes a creative condition of spirit.

Phenomenological philosophy requires passivity on the part of the subject. Existential philosophy, on the other hand, requires activity and passion in the subject. The world of ideas, the noumenal world, assumes this activity and passion of the spirit; it is not a congealed world which is devoid of the movement of life. An act of cognition is an act of transcendence; it is a way out from the closed circle and a way which opens out upwards. It is possible to conceive of the transcendent only because of the existence of such a transcending act. But the transcending act is an intense effort of the whole being. It is its uplifting power and its state of exaltation.

38

The pursuit of a metaphysics which is completely scientific in form, of metaphysics as a strict and objective science is the pursuit of a will o' the wisp. Metaphysics can only be the apprehension of spirit, in spirit, and through spirit. Metaphysics is in the subject, which creates spiritual values and makes a transcending act, not into the object but into its own self-revealing depth. Metaphysics is empirical in the sense that it is based upon spritiual experience. It is a symbolism of that experience. Philosophical knowledge is knowledge attained by means of images to a greater extent than knowledge reached through concepts. The concept is important only as playing a secondary part. In Hegel the concept does not possess its traditional logical significance; it acquires not only a metaphysical but even an almost mystical meaning.

The principal and decisive thing about the philosopher has not by any means been the assertions which he has contributed for objective use. The apprehending mind has never discovered truth by the assistance of the logical apparatus by which he endeavours to convince others. Philosophical knowledge is the knowledge of truth, of what is true and right, not of being, for the apprehension of truth is an uplifting movement of the spirit towards truth; it is a spiritual ascent, an entering into truth. There is, however, a social aspect of knowledge and too little attention has been paid to it. Knowledge is a form of communication and intercourse among human beings. At the same time knowledge is above all a gesture on the part of him who seeks it, which places him face to face not with some other, or others in general, but face to face with truth. It is to stand facing the primary reality which philosophers have been fond of calling 'being'. Human knowledge and philosophical knowledge in particular, depends upon the spiritual condition of men, upon the scope of their minds, and the forms of communion and community which exist among men have an enormous part to play in this.

Philosophical knowledge is personal in character and the more personal it is the more important it is. But the personal character of knowledge does not mean the isolation of personality. Personality gets to know things in communion and community with the world and with men; it enters into union with world experience and world thought. Knowledge is at the same time personal and social. The degrees of spiritual community which hold among men are here of very great importance.[1] All this leads to the fundamental truth, that knowledge is anthropological, but this will not by any means denote relativism.

There is one very important truth which must be recognized in the theory of knowledge, and that is that the person who knows is himself existent, that he himself is 'being', and that the recognition of the meaning of the world is possible only in the subject, not in the object, that is to say in human existence. It is indeed in this that the truth of existential philosophy is to be found. If it is not to be naïvely and unconsciously anthropocentric, philosophy must be consciously and critically anthropocentric. Philosophy is anthropocentric but the philosopher ought to be theocentric.

Comprehension of the mystery of the world in human existence is a possibility only because man is a microcosm and a microtheos. There is no cosmos in the object world of phenomena. There is no God in the objective world order, but there is a cosmos in man. God is in man, and through man there is a way out into another world. That protagonist of the humanist theory of knowledge, F. S. Schiller, says with truth that a depersonalization and dehumanization of knowledge has taken place and that the personalizing and humanizing of it is imperative.[2] Man is the measure of things, but there is a higher measure than man. St Augustine was perhaps the first to turn to the existential philosophy of the subject. He set forth the principle of interior experience and of the credibility of the mind to itself. He recognized doubt as a source of

[1] I have written a great deal on this subject. See in particular my *Solitude and Society*.
[2] See F. S. Schiller: *Étude sur l'humanisme*.

40

credibility and as a proof of one's own existence. To him the soul was the whole personality.

The theory of orderly and regular development in knowledge does not settle accounts with the invasion of individuality. It may be taken as beyond doubt that the act of appraisal which has such an immense part to play in cognition, is performed above all by feeling not by the intellect. Nietzsche, who did his philosophizing with a sledge hammer, said that the philosopher ought to be one who gives instructions and imposes commands. This means that in philosophical knowledge a rearrangement of values and the creation of values take place. Philosophy seeks to break out from the slavery of this world into another world, towards a perfect free life, and deliverance from the suffering and ugliness of the world as we have it. To strive after objective knowledge is an illusion and in any case it is a mistake in terminology. Dispassionate knowledge there cannot be and never has been among real philosophers; it can only exist in dissertations which are devoid of any creative gift. Even in Spinoza himself knowledge was nothing if not passionate. Intellectual passion may be a source of perceptual transcendence. Plato, the greatest of all philosophers, was an erotic philosopher. There was an erotic pull in the rationalist Spinoza, and in the panlogist Hegel, to say nothing of such philosophers as Kierkegaard and Nietzsche.

The philosopher has fallen in love with wisdom. In real true-born philosophy there is the eros of truth; there is the erotic attraction of the infinite and the absolute. Philosophical creativity is intoxicated with thought. Philosophical cognition can only be based upon experience, upon spiritual experience, and within that it is the spirit as one whole which accomplishes the act of cognition. There is bitterness in knowledge. But knowledge is by nature a liberating agent. Philosophical knowledge is called upon to set man free from the power of the objectified world and from his intolerable servitude to it. Not the will to power but the will to meaning and to freedom is the driving force of philosophical

41

knowledge. As a system of concepts metaphysics is an impossibility, it is possible only as the symbolism of spiritual experience.

The conflict between subject and object, between freedom and necessity, between meaning and the lack of it is, in the language of metaphysics, a symbolic conflict which in 'this' provides symbols of 'another'. Behind the finite the infinite is concealed, and it gives signs of its presence. The depth of my ego is steeped in infinity and eternity and it is only a superficial layer of my ego which is illuminated by the mind, rationalized, and recognized on the basis of the antithesis between subject and object. But out of the depth signs are given, whole worlds are there, and there is all our world and its destiny. Hartmann is right when he says that the problem of cognition is a metaphyscial problem, and Heidegger is right when he says that we understand the *Existenziele* as an interpretation of our own selves. But what is truth? That is the eternal question. The answer that the Gospels give to this question has its importance even in philosophy.

5

The aim of philosophical knowledge certainly does not consist in the knowledge of being, in a reflection of reality in the mind of the person who knows. Its aim is the knowledge of truth, the discovery of meaning, its purpose is to give an intelligible sense to reality. Philosophical knowledge, therefore, is not passive reflection, it is an active break-through, it is victory in the conflict with the meaninglessness of world reality. What I want to know is not reality but the truth about it, and I can recognize this truth only because there is in me myself, in the knowing subject, a source of truth, and union with truth is a possibility. The fact that there is in front of me a writing-table and I am writing with a pen on paper is not truth. It is something received by the senses and a statement of fact. The problem of truth is already posed in my writing. There is no truth of any sort in the object; truth is only in the subject.

Truth is related not to the phenomenal world but to the noumenal, to the world of ideas. Truth is a relation, but this relation is by no means the one between subject and object; it is not the repercussion of the object in the subject. Truth is not to be understood in the spirit of epistemological realism or at any rate if it is to be taken as realism, then it is realism of an entirely different kind. Truth has two meanings. There is truth in the sense of knowledge of reality and there is truth which is reality itself. Truth is not only an idea, and a value, it is also an entity, something which exists. 'I am the Truth'. Truth is not that which exists; it is the meaning of that which exists, the Logos of it; but this meaning is that which, or he who, exists.

According to Heidegger truth exists only to the extent that *Dasein* exists. Truth does not exist outside and above us; it is a possibility because we are within it. Heidegger is of the opinion that absolute truth is a remnant of Christain theology, but in point of fact it is precisely Christianity which must deny truth outside that which exists and outside him who exists. Truth is a creative act of spirit in which meaning is brought to birth. Truth stands higher than the reality which exercises compulsion upon us, higher than the 'real' world. But still higher than truth is God, or to put it more truly—God is Truth.

A thorough-going materialism has to reject the idea of truth as pragmatism has to reject it. Marx, still preserving some connection with German idealism, has a divided mind in this matter; Lenin is naïve; but their descendants refuse truth and so do Nietzsche's. Nietzsche was alone in boldly acknowledging the truth of illusions, the offspring of the will to power, but he still recognizes an aristocratic quality which those who have popularized him deny. There is in truth an aristocracy of ideas and meaning. But the idea and the meaning are not to be torn away from the existent and existence. Truth is the meaning of the existent, and meaning is the truth of the existent. This found its expression in the doctrine of the Logos which is not bound to be tied to the limits of Platonism

43

and to a static ontology. Truth is meaning born in God before all ages, in God the existent One. And this birth is repeated in all who exist, and because of it personality emerges into view.

Personality is not the offspring of a generic process; it is the child of meaning, of truth. There is a concrete universalism in truth which not only is not opposed to personality but presupposes its existence. Truth is not a reflection of the world as it is and as it appears, it is a conflict with the darkness and evil of the world. The apprehension of truth is a self-kindling of the light (the Logos) in existence (in being) and this process takes place in the depth of being; it is not in opposition to being. I use the word 'being' in the conventional sense before investigating the essence of the problem of 'being'.

Truth is certainly not knowledge of the object. Truth is a victory over objectification, in other words over the illusory and transparent nature of object being. Truth certainly reflects nothing, just as the reality of spirit reflects nothing. Truth is spiritual, it is in the spirit, it is the victory of spirit over the non-spiritual objectivity of the world, the world of things. Spirit is not an epiphenomenon of anything, everything is an epiphenomenon of spirit. Truth is the awakening of the spirit in man; it is communion with spirit.

It may be supposed that all that I have just said refers to Truth but not to truths, not to those partial and relative truths which science discovers in the natural phenomenal world. What is there of the noumenal in such truths as 'twice two are four' and 'all bodies expand when heated'? Is meaning revealed in such truths? There is Truth with a capital letter and there is truth with a small letter. This needs elucidation. All the little and partial truths receive their light from the whole major Truth. All rays of light come from the sun. Philosophers have in their different ways expressed this in the doctrine of the Logos, of universal reason, of the general validity of transcendental thought.

But transcendental thought is mobile and its structure depends upon the character and quality of the cognitive mind and upon the subject matter to which cognition is directed. The Logos is a sun which shines down upon a fallen objectified world, and the logical apparatus of cognition is worked out to correspond with the state of that world of objects. This is epistemological adjustment to the world for the sake of victory over the world. If science is under the sway of determinism, if it is looking for casual links and does not discover primary creative movements in the life of the world, the blame for this does not lie with science but with the state of the world. But the light which science sheds upon the world arises, albeit not in a direct line, from the primary source of the Sun of Truth, The lie begins with the affirmation of scientism, that is to say, with a false philosophy.

But can the acknowledgment of the one whole entire Truth of the universal Logos be combined with the existential type of philosophy? If philosophy has to be personal, if it is based upon personal experience if the subject puts his own experience with all its contradictions into the act of knowing, does not universal Truth disintegrate into partial truths and do we not fall into the power of relativism? The usual and generally accepted views on this point must be dismissed. They are due to the limitations of rationalism. The old antithesis between the individually personal and the individually common is false and has to be superseded. Truth lies outside that antithesis; the individually personal is the most existential of all things and perhaps the most universal too; it is the most spiritual, and it is that which is most closely linked with meaning. The ego is steeped in its own depth and there it comes into touch with the noumenal spiritual world. This has been better understood by mystics than by philosophers.

But the universality and entirety of self-revealing Truth is certainly not the same thing as general validity. General validity exists precisely for the objectified world, for the world of phenomena. It indicates forms of communication within this disconnected world. It is an adjustment to a fallen state. What is of general validity is due to discontinuity, it is communication within discontinuity. The whole logical apparatus of proof exists for the sake of those who are disconnected from me, and do not see the Truth which is perceptible to me; it exists for those with whom I am not united in the Truth. There is an analogy between general validity in the field of logic and general validity in the field of jurisprudence. Truths which are of general validity and are proved are, therefore, just those that are least universal; they are under the power of objectification. Universal Truth, on the other hand, lies outside the process of objectification. It is in the highest degree existential, and it is derived from spirit, not from the world. In spirit, that is in spirit which has not been objectified, the universal and the individually personal are united. Truth is not revealed through objectification nor through subordination to the world; it is revealed through the transcending act, through a way-out which lies beyond the confines of the antithesis between the subject and object. Truth is not objective, it is subjective, but subjective in the sense of spiritual depth, removed from that superficial subjectivity which stands in opposition to objectivity.

Where, however, is the criterion of truth to be sought? Too often this criterion is looked for in something which lies on a lower level than truth, it is sought in an objectified world with its general validity. People look for the criterion of the spirit in the material world, and thus they fall into a vicious circle. Discursive thought can provide no criteria at all for final truth; its place is wholly in the middle part of the road; it is unaware of that which belongs to the beginning as well as of that which belongs to the end. All proof rests upon the undemonstrable, upon what can be postulated, perceived and created. There is a chance but there is no guarantee. The very search for guarantees is a false line to take: it means the subordination of the higher to the lower. The freedom of the spirit knows nothing of guarantees.

The one and only standard of truth is Truth itself, it is the radiant light of its sunshine. All other criteria exist only for the

46

objective world of the commonplace and for the sake of social intercourse. I never demonstrate truth for my own sake. I have to demonstrate it only for the sake of others, In regard to knowledge I live in two worlds, on the one hand in a world which is primary, existential, and in which communion with Truth is possible, and on the other hand in a secondary world, an objectified world, in which Truth is communicated to others and is demonstrated, a world in which Truth is crumbled into a multitude of truths as a consequence of adjustment to the fallen state of the world. Florensky says that the credibility of truth is given potentially, not actually.[1] This means that the Truth is within me, in the depth of me, in the depth of the knowing subject, since I have my roots in the noumenal spiritual world. But it is within me in a drowsy state and awaking of it demands a creative act on my part. The awakening of the spirit within me is an awakening to truth. The criterion of truth is in the spirit, in spirituality, in the subject which has come to recognize itself through the spirit. It is not in the object. Truth is not received from without, it is received from within, The knowledge of truth makes me free. But the actual knowledge of truth cannot but be free itself. Every external criterion of truth which is derived from the lower world is opposed to freedom of the spirit in the apprehension of truth, and it does not liberate. Truth is not due to the object, not even to 'objective being'. It is due to the spirit. Spirit is in the subject, not in the object, in the noumenon, not in the phenomenon. And science which knows the world of phenomena, the object world, the world of necessities, moves out of the spirit and down from it, descending by degrees of objectification, by stages of dissociation and general validity.

Pragmatism was an attempt to provide a new answer to the question of the criterion of truth, by starting from the true proposition that knowledge is a function of life. Pragmatism is right in regard to the technical results of science, but truth is nevertheless in direct opposition to pragmatism. A vitally flourishing state of

[1] See his *Pillar and Ground of the Truth*.

affairs, success, profit, interest, all these things are marks rather of falsity than of truth. Truth is certainly not a useful and serviceable thing in this world; it renders no services, it may even be destructive and ruinous to the ordering of the things of this world; it demands sacrifices and has even led to martyrdom. Truth does not so much liberate and save within this world as liberate and save from this world. The thorough-going acceptance of the truth of the Gospel right through to the end, an agreement to bring it to effective realization, would lead to the destruction of States, civilzations, and societies which are organized according to the law of this world. It would lead to the perishing of this world which is in every respect opposed to the Truth of the Gospel.

And so people and nations have amended the Gospel. They have filled it up with 'truths' that belong to this world, 'truths' which were really pragmatic because they were a lie and an adjustment to a lie. The recognition and confession of Truth have no connection with use and profit; their connections are with hazard and danger, But pragmatism in all its forms has no knowledge of Truth, which stands above the world and judges it. It is only the tragic pragmatism of Nietzsche which is free from this adjusting optimism, if indeed it is in place to speak of his pragmatism. The pathos of Nietzsche is due to his *amor fati* and with him victory is associated with ruin. Bergson's philosophy of life and his biological metaphysics are likewise optimistic.

Existential philosophy must be distinguished both from the philosophy of life and from pragmatic philosophy. It is associated with the experience of tragic conflict. There is in it no cult of life as the highest criterion; it is not biological in character. Life has judgment passed upon it by Truth-and-Right. What is important is not the quantitative maximum of life, not its flourishing condition in the world, nor its power, but the quality of it, its intensity, its moving and pathetic character, which carries over and beyond the frontiers of life.

The recognition of Truth does not by any means indicate a

primatively joyful blooming of life and an increase of its strength. It may mean the exposure of the fallen state of the world, the testing experience of the pain which accompanies all life, the conflict between personal destiny and the destiny of the world, between existential experience and enslaving objectification, the struggle of freedom with the necessity which it encounters. Truth is saving, but it saves for another world, for the eternal world which begins in temporal life, but begins with suffering, with grief and frequently with what seems like hopelessness. The acceptance of Truth right through to the end, to the last of its vital deductions, is to give assent to the perishing of this world and to its coming to an end.

I am not speaking of truths which denote adjustment to the world of phenomena, to the inevitable process of objectification, but I am speaking about Truth, as the primary source of light, as what is true and right in its entirety. Knowledge within the objectified world does admittedly reveal truths. There is a reflected light in it which helps us to take our bearings in the darkness of this world, but it does not reveal primary and original Truth, which is the beginning and the end. It is science, not philosophy, which is the discoverer of principles and laws which give men their bearings within reality. But supreme Truth is eschatological and by this very fact exposes the conventional lie of pragmatism, the falsehood of an optimistic cult of life.

Truth is not of the world but of the spirit. It is known only in the transcendence of the object-world. Truth is the end of this object-world, and it demands assent to this end of it. Such is the Truth of Christianity when freed from social adjustments and distortions. But such also is in essence the Truth which was to some extent revealed to the messianic prophetic thought of ancient Israel, to the religious philosophy of India, to Persian dualist eschatology and to many thinkers, such as Plato, Plotinus, Eckhardt, Boehme, Pascal, Kant, Schopenhauer, Kierkegaard, Dostoyevsky and Tolstoy.

All philosophy, theory of knowledge, ethics, philosophy of history should be constructed with an eschatological outlook, but, as we shall see, by no means eschatological in the sense in which the word is usually understood. Knowledge seeks the Truth and truths; it ardently seeks to be purified from all that darkens and distorts the process of knowing, to achieve the self-purification of the subject. But he who knows may know the falsehood of the world, its defilement and pollution. Knowledge may be the discovery of the truth about a lie. In that case truth is a judgment upon the falsity of the world, it is light which exposes the darkness. And the proclamation of the Truth is the end of the world of falsehood. In every true act of knowing the end of the world comes, the end of enslaving objectivity.

There have always been different types of philosophers. They have been distinguished from one another by a varying structure of the mind behind which lay different directions in which the spirit moved. In Greece there were Parmenides and Heraclitus, Democritus and Plato; they endeavoured to establish types of philosophical world outlook.[1] The distinction among the types depended upon what principle was taken as the basis of classification. One and the same philosopher may fall into one class in one connection and in another connection into another class. Dilthey proposes to recognize three types of philosophical world-outlook: naturalism, objective idealism and idealism of freedom. In this conventional classification I should decidedly be placed in the class of idealism of freedom. On the same grounds this might be called realism of freedom so long as reality is not understood in a naturalistic way. I would suggest the following series of antitheses:—

1. Philosophy of the subject and philosophy of the object.
2. Philosophy of the spirit and naturalistic philosophy.
3. Philosophy of freedom and determinist philosophy.

[1] See, for example, Jaspers: *Psychologie der Weltanschauungen*, and also Dilthey's works.

4. Philosophy which is dualistically pluralist and monistic philosophy.
5. Philosophy which is creatively dynamic and statically ontological philosophy.
6. Personalist philosophy or the philosophy of personality and the philosophy of universal common sense.
7. Eschatological philosophy, the philosophy of discontinuity and evolutionary philosophy; the philosophy of continuity.

Within this list of antithesis I define my own philosophy as being of the subject, of spirit, of freedom; as being dualistically pluralist, creatively dynamic, personalist and eschatological. Up to the present time philosophy has to a very small extent been eschatological. Eschatology has been related to the sphere of religion only. But eschatology can have and ought to have its epistemological and transcendental metaphysical expression, and I shall aim at such an expression. It is imperative to build up a philosophy of the End. This has little in common with the various interpretations of the Book of the Revelation and it does not imply an expectation of the end in some definite year. Eschatological philosophy springs from a philosophical problem raised already by Plato.

Philosophical monism was an attempt to solve the eschatological problem within the confines of this world, to assert a unity without taking the end into its purview. In my opinion the central thought of eschatological philosophy is connected with the interpretation of the Fall as objectification, and of the end as the final and decisive victory over objectification. The choice of the type of philosophy is settled by the spirit of the philosopher as a whole, by decision and emotion rather than by the intellect. But the human intellect itself is also inseparable from the existence of the whole man, from choice of his will and from his emotional experience.

CHAPTER II

1. Subject and Object. The subject as that which exists. The mystery of objectification. Genesis of the world of appearances. 2. Existential experience. Primary intuition and the social character of knowledge. The concept, as a limitation and protection. Orientation in the environmental infinity. 3. Illusions of consciousness. Transcendental illusion (Schein) in Kant. Dualism and revolution of thought. Two worlds. 'The other world'

I

From the days of Kant German philosophy has always taken the relation between subject and object as its starting point. The problem has been stated as that of the relation in which reason, thinking, the mind stands to being. From this point of view the object has frequently been represented as being, while the subject has not been taken as being, but simply as standing face to face with being. The object, so to speak, stands over against me, it lies outside me. Objectivity has been almost identified with what is true, and what is true with general validity.

The paradoxical nature of the position lay in the fact that the guarantee of objectivity was not in the object but in the subject. It was in the subject that those transcendental *a priori's* lay which alone made knowledge even a possibility, and it was they which constructed the object. Subject and object are correlatives. According to Kant transcendental forms are applicable only to phenomena. But the pre-eminence of the subject over the object is evident. The object exists simply for the sake of the subject, but the subject possesses an inner existence of its own.

The terms 'object' and 'objectivity' have been left in a very shaky, precarious and uncertain state. Formerly, in Duns Scotus, for instance, that which refers to the concrete subject-matter of thought was called the subject, while that which referred to representations was given the name of object. Even in so critical a writer as Kant the use of the word 'object' is ambiguous. Hegel, in contradiction of his own point of view at the outset, recognizes the existence of objective spirit, whereas he should have recognized only the objectification of spirit. In any case the accepted use of the word 'object' is contrary to the redirection of philosophy from object to subject, from the world to the ego which was brought about by Kant and German idealism; and it is surely necessary to recognize that the object is not the thing-in-itself, the subject is the thing-in-itself. The object, on the other hand, is only a phenomenon and an appearance for the sake of the subject. To be the object means to be for the sake of the subject; the object is always that which makes its appearance for the sake of another. The world of appearances is the outcome of objectification. Objectificaton, however, is brought about by the subject and it indicates the trend and the condition of the subject.

There is no greater mistake than to confuse objectivity with reality, The 'objective' is that which is least real, least existential. The Thomists in particular are fond of setting their metaphysical realism in contrast to phenomenalism. But it would seem that they entirely fail to admit the existence of the realism which is based upon recognition of the metaphysical reality of the subject as noumenon, as spirit.[1] The transcendent cannot be in the object and cannot become the object. It is in the subject, it lies beyond the very antithesis of subject and object. It was an error in Kant to think that in the contemplation of ourselves we act upon ourselves in such a way that our subject apprehends merely an appearance.

Subject and object are correlatives only in an epistemological sense. There is no such correlativity in the metaphysical sense. The subject is also that which exists; it is not only the transcen-

[1] This is particularly striking in Gilson. See his Le Réalisme Méthodique.

dental *a priori* as a condition of sense experience and of the possibility of knowledge of appearances. Truth is hidden in that which exists, and therefore, truth is subjective, not objective. The truth is the ego and not the non-ego. One must definitely refuse to apply the adjective 'objective 'to truth. What is called objective truth is that which is furthest removed from the Truth. The ego, man, can be a source of truth, when he is steeped in his own depth, he can be in the truth, whereas the object, on the other hand, cannot be in it. Hence we shall see that the knowledge of truth is dependent upon the social relations which obtain among men.

In the phenomenology of Husserl the intentional act liberates from the individual and becomes the basis of objectivism.[1] But in this way Husserl denies the human character of knowledge, and this is one of the results of Platonic universalism. The transcendent light in the world issues from the subject, which is man and not God, although it includes a divine element within it, whereas social adjustment to the condition of this fallen world issues from the object. Knowledge may be understood not as dependence upon the object but as the universalizing of the subject, as the revelation of a universe within the subject. The epistemological subject is an abstraction; subject has before all else an existential meaning. Absolute knowledge about a thing, about an object, is impossible. That which is created by the subject itself can be absolutely known, Such is the metaphysical result of German idealism.

Thinking does not set itself over against something which is alien to it. It transcends itself and by so doing remains itself. This would be true if we were to speak not of thinking but of the whole subject as that which exists, as man. Behind man as a phenomenon stands man as noumenon. Hence the twofold character of human nature. An object changes, it depends upon the state of the subject, upon the correlation of the phenomenal and noumenal in man, of

[1] See Husserl: *Ideen zu einer reinen Phänomenologie und phänomenologischen Philosophie.*

54

the superficial and the profound. Dilthey says very rightly that the abstract relation of subject and object must be replaced by the vital relation of creature and environment. A metaphysics of the object is impossible, but a metaphysics of the subject is a possibility. We must not think of the totality of the world as an object: that totality is in the subject. Objectification, as we shall see, ought to have been replaced by the expressiveness of life, by the expression of it in the external. Only the whole man himself, the active human spirit should have been acknowledged as *a priori*.

Rickert makes an attempt to give precise meaning to the concept of object, and he makes it very complex. The first interpretation of object is spatial; it is the external world. My body also is an object. The subject is my mind and its content. The object, on the other hand, is that which is found outside my mind; this is the transcendent object. The object is also notions, impressions received, feelings, and desires; whereas the subject is that which produces the notions, receives the impressions, feels, and desires. This is the immanent object. The subject is my ego, my soul, my mind with its content, my mind as contrasted with its content.[1]

There is truth in Rickert's classification, but he takes his stand entirely on an epistemological interpretation of the problem. He is mistaken in allowing the existence of a transcendent object as what is outside my mind. But the transcendent is discovered on a path directly opposite to movement towards an object, directly opposite that is, to objectification.

Without explaining for the moment the concept of being, it must be said that the subject is not in opposition to being, as that which is outside being. The subject is itself being and intimately associated with it. Thinking and reason are immanent in being. The rational is submerged in the irrational or the supra-rational. This is admirably shown even by philosophers not of the existential type such as N. Hartmann and S. Frank. Kant himself still took an inadequate view of the transcendent aspect of the transcenden-

[1] Rickert: *Der Gegenstand der Erkenntnis.*

tal mind. Since the knowing subject is himself being, is himself in the highest degree existential, knowledge can be understood as an event in being itself, in existence, as a relation of being to being. In the existential sense, the subject is the correlative not of the object but of other subjects.

Prince S. Trubetskoy says with truth that in every act of his life man goes out from himself towards another. But he goes out from himself as one who exists. The subject is he who exists, he who is rooted in the noumenal world, and in that fact the existentiality of philosophy has its source. N. Hartmann says that being is the common sphere in which subject and object stand in antithesis to one another.[1] The subject, as it were, recognizes its dependence upon the object. In my view the subject itself introduces objectification and gives rise to the world of phenomena, and does so not only as he who knows, but above all as he who exists.

It is essential to grasp the mysterious process of objectification. I live in two worlds, in a subjective world which is my own proper world, and also in an objective world, the world of objects, which exists for my sake and at the same time is alien to me. This fact that I am cast into an objective world which acts forcefully upon me, has not merely an epistemological meaning, it has a metaphysical meaning also. Kant gave no explanation of why the world of appearances comes to be and why reason is limited to the knowledge of this world of appearances, which is not the true world. The true world of things-in-themselves is not open to perception. Does the thing-in-itself reveal itself in appearance? In the phraseology that I use this means that Kant did not explain the mystery of objectification. He leads up to the subject, but does not himself deal with it.

The objectification of the world takes place through our agency and for our sakes, and this is the fall of the world, this is its loss of freedom, and the alienation of its parts. It might be expressed by saying that the freedom of noumena passes into the necessity of

[1] See N. Hartmann: *Grundzüge einer Metaphysik der Erkenntnis.*

phenomena. The world of appearances acquires a grandiose empirical reality which exercises compulsion and force upon us.

According to Hegel 'objectivity is a real concept which has moved out from its own inwardness and passed into existence'. To him an idea is 'an objectively true concept, something which is true, as such'. Hegel makes the mistake of ascribing a sort of freedom to objectivity, whereas in fact it denotes the loss of freedom. He fails to understand that the self-alienation of spirit in objectivity is a fall. He is an optimist. He is mistaken in recognizing the existence of objective spirit instead of acknowledging only the objectification of spirit. It is along that line of thought that the Kantian dualism has been overcome and a transition made to monism. This comes near to St Thomas Aquinas and his ontologism again, though from the other direction.

In Hegel's view, objectivity having passed through the critical act of knowledge, issues from the subject. According to St Thomas Aquinas objectivity precedes this critical act. He teaches that the subject-matter of knowledge is real and objective, that it does not depend upon the subject, but that it does not exist in nature in a universal form; it is thought which adds that to it. The abstraction of the mind converts thought into act.

Both in Hegel and in St Thomas Aquinas there is in principle the same ontologism which is unwilling to see in objectification the fall of the world. There is in each of them the same erroneous elimination of that dualism which is a picture of the tragic position of man in his effort to know. But it was more naïvely expressed in St Thomas Aquinas. In Hegel it was put more critically and it moves to a greater extent through a dialectic of thought. The logic of St Thomas Aquinas is static; Hegel's logic in dynamic. Aquinas starts from objectivity as a datum provided by nature and it remains with him unimpaired right to the end. Hegel on the other hand begins with subjective spirit and arrives at objectivity and objective spirit as the result of a dialectical process. To St Thomas there is in fact nothing irrational; the Latin mind illuminates the life of the world without any oncoming of night. But to Hegel the irrational does exist. His panlogism is not to be identified with objective rationalism. With him the irrational is rationalized and the rational becomes irrational.

Schopenhauer, the most inconsistent of philosophers, left the Kantian dualism by another route. What he teaches about the objectification of the will contains a greater element of truth than there is in Hegel's objective spirit, for he does recognize that the objectified world is not the true world and that it is a world which 'lieth in evil'.

My inward spiritual experience is not an object. Spirit is never object: the existence of that which exists is never an object. It is thought which determines the objectified phenomenal world. The primacy of the mind over being can be asserted. But this is not the final truth. The mind itself is determined by the noumenal world, by the 'intelligible freedom' (in the Kantian sense) of that primary world. What also needs to be asserted is the supremacy of the primarily existent, of that which initially exists, over the mind. Idealism passes into realism.

Husserl remains within the limits of the conscious mind which in his view is more primary than subject and object. He should have arrived at a metaphysics of consciousness. But with him all consciousness is consciousness of something or other, the essence of consciousness is the transcending of self in 'intention'. Noesis is the subjective side of 'intentionality' and Noema is that which the conscious mind recognizes. Phenomenology is the sympathetic descriptive science of the working of the mind.[1] But this would not justify a belief in the metaphysical roots of the conscious mind. The 'intentional' character of consciousness is a doctrine which Brentano took over from scholasticism and it is obliged to give pre-eminence to objectivity over subjectivity. The transcending of the self in 'intention' must needs be objectification and an onrush towards the objective world. But in the phraseology which

[1] See his *Ideen*.

I propose, the act of transcending follows a path which is diametrically the opposite of objectification. It is the path towards the noumenal world, to that which truly exists. There are two 'intentions' of the conscious mind, one which leads to the enslaving world of objects and to the realm of necessity, the other which is directed towards the truly existent world, the realm of freedom.

The natural world of phenomena is symbolic in character. It is full of signs of another world and it is a symptom of division and alienation in the sphere of spirit. There is no natural objective world in the sense of a reality in itself; the only world there is is the world which is divinely and humanly free. The object world is enslavement and fall. But the whole cosmos enters into the true free world, whereas there is nothing of it in the world of appearances, the world of objects, How the two stand to each other may be put in this way; appearance is the objectified world, the natural and social world of necessity, servitude, enmity and dominance; whereas the noumenal world is spirit, freedom and creative power; it is the world of love and sympathy; it is the whole cosmos. What is called the other world is not an 'other' world to me it is pre-eminently my world.

There is a tendency in the reason to turn everything into an object from which existentiality disappears. The whole of Kant's critique is connected with this fact. The thing-in-itself is not an object or 'non-I', it is a subject, or 'Thou'. The subject is not, as in Fichte, the Absolute or the Deity. The subject, the human 'I' and 'Thou', are turned into objects and things as a result of a fall in the relations between us. That fall is a matter of importance in the theory of knowledge. Objectification and the unauthentic character of the phenomenal world are by no means to be taken as meaning that the world of men and women, animals, plants, minerals, stars, seas, forests and so on is unreal and that behind it is something entirely unlike it—the things-in-themselves. It means rather that this world is in a spiritual and moral condition in which it ought not to be, it

59

is in a state of servitude and loss of freedom, of enmity and alienation, of ejection into the external, of subjection to necessity.

Objectification is the ejection of man into the external, it is an
exteriorization of him, it is the subjecting of him to the conditions
of space, time, causality and rationalization. But in his existential
depth man is in communion with the spiritual world and with the
whole cosmos. The thing-in-itself can only be the thing-for-my-
sake, and it is only the thing-for-my-sake about which I can think.
Objectification is the uprising of an exteriorized 'not-I' in place of
the 'Thou' which exists interiorly. The subject matter of thought
is the creation of thought itself; and that is the objectifying act.

To Kant, the way out of this situation is simply through the
practical reason, which does not objectify and, therefore, breaks
through beyond the world of phenomena. There is nothing, no
things of the external world outside the subject which thinks them.
Thus the impress of thought lies upon reality. But 'things in-them-
selves' do exist and in them the spiritual element in thought is
inherent, and the irrational is inherent too. Objectification is not
only a creation of thought, of the reason and its categories. At a
deeper level than that is the fact that it is a result of a certain condition of the subject, with whom exteriorization and alienation are
taking place. The object depends above all upon the will of the
subject. There exists a transcendental will.

The most remarkable thing is that the objectification of the
constructions of the mind begins to live an independent life and
gives rise to pseudo-realities. In this respect the antidote should
have been Kant, who showed that the existence of an idea does not
imply the existence of a reality. This is a very strong point with
him. Objectification is rationalization. But it is not merely a perceptional process, it is still more an emotional process, the socialization of feelings and passions. And rationalization may itself be
a passion.

Lévy-Bruhl maintains that pre-logical, primitive thinking does
not objectify, it is subject to the *loi de participation*, that is to say the

person who thinks and apprehends is united with the subject-matter of his actual thought and knowledge.[1] Lévy-Bruhl himself is of opinion that at the summit of civilization, to apprehend means to objectify, that is, it makes the subject-matter of knowledge into something alien, it does not unite with it nor become a partner with it. This throws a light upon the nature of objectification.

What we may for the time being call existential philosophy marks a transition from the interpretation of knowledge as objectification, to understanding it as *participation*, union with the subject matter and entering into cooperation with it. The *loi de participation* among backward and pre-civilized peoples may denote a condition in which clear consciousness is not yet fully awake; it may denote the superstitious attitude to the world and the practice of magic, in which mankind was steeped at its origin.

The awakening and development of the conscious mind was accompanied by division and alienation. Man had to pass through a stage in which he subjected his thought and reason to a critique. To pass through objectification is the fate of spirit in this world. Moreover objectification has a positive significance also in a fallen world. It is capable of arming man and defending him. But at the summit of consciousness, where it comes into touch with the supra-conscious, the reverse process may be set on foot, and apprehension may become union and cooperation; yet in conjunction with all that has been gained by the conquests of criticism and enlightened reason.

German idealism marks an important stage along this road. But the word 'idealism' cannot be retained, because idea does not denote real existence, as was shown by Kant himself. The mystery of objectification has to be made clear. In it the mystery of this world lies hidden, and in it is the source of the evil and suffering which belong to the life of this world.

The problem of objectification, as I understand it, has nothing

[1]See Lévy-Bruhl: *Les fonctions mentales dans les sociétés inférieures.*

in common with the problem of perception, of sensation, or of the relation between the psychological and the physical, or even of the ordinary relation between the subjective and the objective. The problem of objectification lies in a different region from that of the criticism of naïve realism and the defence of idealism. It is an existential problem and it is concerned with the disintegration and the fettering of the world, with estrangement and the chains of servitude. It is a problem which arises as a result of the fall of the existential subject, for whom everything is exteriorized and subjected to necessity.

What are the marks of objectification, and the rise of object relations in the world? The following signs may be taken as established: (1) The estrangement of the object from the subject; (2) The absorption of the unrepeatably individual and personal in what is common and impersonally universal; (3) The rule of necessity, of determination from without, the crushing of freedom and the concealment of it; (4) Adjustment to the grandiose mien of the world and of history, to the average man, and the socialization of man and his opinions, which destroys distinctive character. In opposition to all this stand communion in sympathy and love, and the overcoming of estrangement; personalism and the expression of the individual and personal character of each existence; a transition to the realm of freedom and determination from within, with victory over enslaving necessity; and the predominance of quality over quantity, of creativeness over adaptation. This is at the same time a definition of the distinction between the noumenal and the phenomenal world. Phenomenon and noumenon are settled by the process of objectification. The fight against the power of objectification is a spiritual revolt of noumena against phenomena, it is a spiritual revolution.

Such an interpretation of the relation between the noumenal and phenomenal worlds is very different from Platonism, and moves out beyond the limits of Kantian dualism. The noumenon is spirit, personality, freedom; it is the creative energy which is active in this world. The task before man is to achieve liberation from his state of externality, and his subjection to necessity, from the violating power of 'objectiveness' in nature and history. It is to discover spirituality and freedom as being the plenitude of real existence, which, at its highest point is always personal: personal and at the same time experienced in common with other men. This is a sign of the transformation of enslaved nature by the power of the spirit. Spirit is the antithesis, not of nature, but of the enslaved state of nature which is in a disintegrated condition inwardly while outwardly it is fettered and bound. If this world is my objectification which sets up idols and illusions of consciousness, I can in that case create a new and better world. Victory over the sway of objectification is a messianic hope.

The thing-in-itself, the noumenon, is not a necessary cause of the appearance, of the phenomenon; the cause of the appearance may likewise be merely an appearance; necessary causal relations exist only in the phenomenal world. The noumenon, however, is freedom, and if causality is a possibility here at all, it is causality only through freedom, as Kant understood to some extent. But noumenal freedom operates in this phenomenal world as a creative power. Objectification enslaves man and it is from a world other than the phenomenal world that emancipation comes. Objective nature and objective society have no power to set themselves free, it is spirit alone that liberates

Objectification is above all exteriorization, the alienation of spirit from itself. And exteriorization gives rise to necessity, to determination from without, The horror which Pascal felt when confronted by the endless expanse of space is the horror of objectification, the horror of strangeness. Simmel has a good passage in which he speaks of the inhuman automatism of the objectification of culture, and of the conflict between life and form which makes for congealment.[1] But the source of evil is not in the apprehension of the world of phenomena—the world of the 'natural', nor in the

[1] See Simmel: *Lebensanschauung. Vier metaphysische Kapitel,*

epistemological subject himself, who has built up 'objective' science. It lies in the existential condition of man and the world, in alienation and the loss of freedom. Indeed, scientific knowledge itself has an emancipating value in this world, and it enslaves only when it is turned into scientism.

Kant brought to light the epistemological aspect of objectification. Idealist metaphysics went further, but objectified the subject, the ego, spirit, and concept. Thinking begins to present itself as something other than itself. The subject is converted into an object. Absolute idealism moves out beyond the confines of objectification, associated always with the division into subject and object, but it attains this by a premature and illusory monism.

The case is the same in Indian thought. The Absolute is neither subject, nor object. Subject and object are identified in Atman. Brahman is the subject in cognition. Indian thought has shown an insufficient appreciation of the whole burden of objectification and the whole difficulty of overcoming the breach. Its sense of the illusory nature of the world has been stronger than its sense of the world's evil and sin.

Three types of knowledge may be established: the knowledge of the subject by itself; that of the subject by another, qualified as object; and the knowledge of the subject by intuitive sympathy and love. We are much in the habit of calling what we apprehend an object. But this is conventional terminology, and we might call what we apprehend the subject, and apprehend the subject behind the object, we might apprehend outside objectification.

The weak side of the old 'spiritualist' metaphysics consisted in the fact that it naturalized spirit and interpreted it as substance. Traditional 'spiritualism' was a return to the philosophy which preceded Kant, Fichte and Hegel, it went back to the philosophy of Leibniz. But the reality of spirit is not merely a reality other than that of the natural world, it is reality in a different sense.[1] The 'spiritualist' metaphysicians of the nineteenth century, for instance

[1] See my *Spirit and Reality*.

Teichmüller and Koslov, set themselves the problem of the relation between noumenon and appearance. The recognizing and apprehending subject is a substance. It is that for which the appearance appears. Matter is only an outcome of the relation between substances. Material things are signs of spiritual substances.

At the same time a distinction is drawn between the simple recognition which precedes acts of thinking and the complex recognition which is knowledge. It all amounts to the traditional problem of the relation between spirit and matter, which is not an exact designation of the issue. The corporeal world possesses a sort of reality and we are in a very high degree dependent upon it. My body enters into the whole make-up of me, it is a constituent part of my personality, I am not a bodiless spirit. But the bodily constitution of man lies within that state of the natural world which is the outcome of objectification, that is, of exteriorization, alienation and enslavement.

The corporeal world is capable of issuing out of objectivity and entering into subjectivity, in other words of entering into spirit, into a spiritual condition. That is the path along which the transformation of the natural world takes place. It can be said that the whole material world, the whole natural world, is a symbol of the spiritual world, a sign of events which take place in the spiritual world, of division, alienation, and ejection into a state in which causality operates from without.

But the difficult and tormenting question remains: what sort of relation exists between the appearance and that which appears, that is to say, the noumenon? The very word 'appearance' points to the fact that somebody or something appears or reveals himself or itself. But is it the thing-in-itself, the noumenon, the noumenal essence which shows itself, and reveals itself in the 'appearance'? If the world of appearance, 'this world' is a world which is fallen and enslaved, there is a sort of viciousness in that appearance and self-revelation. The noumenon does not simply appear, merely reveal itself in the phenomenon, it also, so to speak, falls away from itself in the phenomenon, it is ejected into the external. And for that reason it may be said that the phenomenal world is not the true world of entities, of that which really exists, The noumenon not only reveals itself in the phenomenon, it also slips out of sight and hides itself away.

Another method of appearance is possible, a different way of self-revelation by the truly existent, one that is not in 'appearance' in the phenomenon. A method of finding expression for entities and existences which differs from objectification in the phenomenal world, is possible. The expression and revelation of freedom is a possibility without subjection to the power of necessity. This is a fundamental problem, and the problem of creativeness also is connected with it.

It may be put in this way. There is the possibility, not of symbolism, not of a symbolic embodiment of spirit in the natural world, but of realization, of a real embodiment of spirit in a world which is being set free and transformed. Objectification is not true realization, it is merely a process of symbolizing; it presents us with signs but not with realities. And that has a telling effect upon all human creativity and upon all that creativity produces.

The world of noumena, which is the world of creative entities, not the world of ideas, can express itself in a different world than the world of phenomena; but it is a mistake to imagine that the noumenal world and the phenomenal world are absolutely isolated and cut off from one another. There are no such frontiers that cannot be crossed just as there are no impassable frontiers to human consciousness. A break through of noumena into phenomena is possible, of the invisible world into the visible, of the world of freedom into the world of necessity. And all that is most significant in history is due to that fact. There are in the life of the world not only 'appearances', but noumena also; and the manifestation of these cannot be called merely an 'appearance'. It is from the noumenal world that the prophet and the creative genius enter into this world. They are ambassadors of the Spirit.

But there is no uninterrupted evolutionary process, the process is a creative one, and it is subject to interruptions and breaks. The new way of understanding the relation between noumenon and phenomenon is to interpret it from the eschatological point of view. But the interpretation of eschatology must also itself be a new one; it must become creatively-active and I shall deal with the basis of this in my last chapter.

Nicolas Hartmann, with his inclination for subtle distinctions, proposes that we should distinguish the trans-subjective from the transcendental, and from the trans-intelligible. One of these terms —'trans-subjective'—I should like to retain to replace 'objective'. The apprehending mind ought to issue out of the closed circle of itself, not into the objective, but into the trans-subjective. That is not objectification, but an act of transcending. While objectification is a movement outwards, the trans-subjective may mark a movement inwards and the discovery within of everything, of the whole, of the universe.

The creative subject expresses itself symbolically in the object and the objective, but it can express itself really in the trans-subjective. The doctrine of Brentano and Husserl about the 'intentionality' of the mind is still within the sphere of objectification and does not reveal the twofold nature of the outward movement of the mind towards an other.

2

The fundamental question is this: does the conversion of 'things-in-themselves' into 'appearances' take place in the process of knowledge and arise from it, or does it precede all cognition and occur within the actual 'things-in-themselves', in the primary reality itself, in existence itself, and is merely reflected in cognition? If the world is in a fallen state, the fault does not lie in men's apprehension of the world, as Shestov, for instance, would have it. The fault lies in the depths of the world's existence.

And there is a further question. When things-in-themselves

have been turned into appearances, have they then ceased to exist, has the noumenal world finally gone away into the phenomenal world? Such an exhaustion of noumena in the disclosure of phenomena is not to be supposed, it is certainly not an emanation or efflux. We could more easily picture it as the passage of the noumenal subject-entities through a process of splitting, division into two, alienation. This is a suggestion which implies a particular kind of cognition to correspond with it. Consciousness and cognition pass through the division into subject and object, but the primary reality does not on that account cease to exist and does not finally lose the possibility of a return to unity and relationship.

There remains in man the possibility of intuitive knowledge. Schelling thinks that in intellectual intuition subject and object are identified. But intuition cannot be intellectual only. It would in that case be the passive reflection of something, and that would mean that it would not overcome division and objectification. Intuition is also emotional and volitional, it is the activity, the intense effort of the spirit as a whole. Real contemplation is not directed upon an object. Philosophical apprehension presupposes a primary act, an act which precedes all rationalization, an existential act, and the measure of it is gauged by the depth and breadth of that act. Philosophical apprehension can be passion, it may be tears and exaltation, or suffering born of the awareness of the meaning of life. Such it was even to Spinoza himself. *Amor intellectualis Dei* is a cognitive passion.

The dispassionately intellectual is a figment of the imagination and a pretence. The results of knowledge are received emotionally and primary intuition itself is above all emotional. Emotional thinking exists (Heinrich Mayer is a case in point), but the emotional element is absolutely separable from the intellectual only in abstraction. The state of passion, emotional tension, is determined by the encounter with reality, with primary life. It is only thinking which is steeped in self and never emerges from self in any direction, which can be completely passionless and devoid of emotional intensity. In Hegel the concept is full of passion.

There is no reality without a creative attitude towards it on the part of the subject. Perception itself is creatively synthetic in character, spirit is active even in sensuous perceptions. The power of impression, without which there is no perceptional penetration assumes a condition of creative passion, a state of possession. That is why it is possible to say that true philosophy is an art. But even purely scientific discoveries presuppose passion, inspiration and power of imagination. In the early discoveries of science the emotional impulse played a much greater part than is commonly supposed.

Since knowledge is a part of life, and reason is a function of life, the appearance itself, the object of apprehension (objectification) is conditioned by the totality of life, by feeling, by the passions, by maladies of spirit. Primary life, the noumenal depth of existence determines the structure of the mind, and upon that the way in which the world presents itself to us depends. Upon a mind which had changed, the world would make a different impact. But this change presupposes a change in the character of existence, in primary life itself. Primary life (noumenon) itself, however, is not pre-eminently intellectual in character, which is the Greek point of view. It is to a greater degree passion, noumenal passion, which precedes the very distinction between good and evil.

Buddhist sympathy, Christian love, Schopenhauer's will to life and Nietzsche's will to power, are all noumenal. To the majority of men, the real world, 'reality' (in other words—that which acts upon them) is identified with the limits of the average and normal mind, that is, a mind which is already objectified and objectifying. And the average objectified mind is a matter of adjustment to the social conditions of existence.

Kant was disturbed by the problem of how to arrive at the universality, the general validity (*Allgemeingültigkeit*) of knowledge. But that is a matter which belongs to the sociology of knowledge, a theme which he did not develop. Kant did not acknowledge the mobility and variability of the transcendental mind as the sociology of knowledge has to acknowledge it. It is not only primary intuition which is socialized, The rationalized consciousness too is exposed to the process of socialization, the apprehension and the very perception of the world depends upon the social relations which hold good among men and the degree to which the spirit of community is attained.

No form of human creative power in the field of knowledge or in any other field is of a social character on the ground of its origin, even when it is directed towards social life. But it is liable to socialization in its dealings with men. Cognition has a social character in its products, as a means of communication among people. The realm of objectification is a social realm, it is made for the average person, for mankind in the mass, for the ordinary and hum-drum, for *das man*. The 'objectivity' of perception and representation is social in character. It might be said that man receives in a certain way a picture of the world which depends upon the forms assumed by his social relations with other people. There are for that reason particular worlds which disclose themselves to religious confessions, to nationalities, to professions, estates and classes. In this is to be found the measure of truth which belongs to the class ideologies of Marxism, but the way in which it is expressed is philosophically worthless. One can only speak of true creative inspiration when man is moved by the spirit and not by society, when he is determined from within and not from without, when he does not depend upon social suggestion and social imitation.[1]

The average man's picture of the world, as he takes his way through it along a middle path, does not present itself to him in an individual and personal manner but in a social and collective way. Thus the sin of human servitude is objectified. The extent of this includes not only people's opinions, which are always very

[1] See a book by Tarde which is in many respects remarkable: *Les Lois de l'imitation*.

70

much socialized (in public opinion, the opinion and honour of the nation, the class, regiment, profession and so on) but covers also the actual perception of the world, primary impressions received from it, which are conditioned by the family and environment. The most fundamental perception of the picture which the world presents, basic opinions and judgments formed of it, depend upon the degree of community that people have attained, or upon the extent to which they lack it. Even scholars who should, as a class, be bent upon the discovery of truth, have their own worlds and their own judgments upon them, which are settled by academic traditions, doctrinal prejudices and learned routine. There is much that is hidden so far as that class is concerned. Socialization sets up a process of fossilization in various degrees.

Different relations among men, a high degree of spiritual community among them and a lofty sense of their brotherhood would create a different world, another world would disclose itself to men. One single 'objective' world does not exist, it is nothing but social adjustment. Various worlds have already been revealed to various types of culture in the past and they have been revealed in various ways. The world presented itself in different ways to Hellenism, Judaism, to the Persians and the Indians. The criteria adopted by general consent for the establishment of truth, of which great use has been made by socialized religion and its armoury of theologies, are not criteria of truth, they are merely standards of what is useful for society.

Truth is aristocratic, it is revealed only to the few, the dissemination of it takes for granted a violent shock to the mind, it involves the melting and the burning up of the petrified and ossified state of mind, of a petrified and ossified world. This is not to say that truth exists only for the sake of the few, it exists for all men, for the very last one of them. But for the time being it is revealed only to the few and to them it administers a shock. The majority are too much conditioned by the limitations of their minds, by social imitation, by what they find of service in the struggle for life.

The most highly socialized thought is that of primitive, pre-civilized people; it is entirely group thought, the thought of the clan or the tribe. The primitive kindly and gracious 'nature' which Rousseau and Tolstoy regarded as the antithesis of the evils of civilization, is noumental nature, not phenomenal. Civilization creates new forms of social imitation and adjustment, and the processes of objectification are associated with it, but at the same time it reveals the possibility of growth in the conscious mind and of freedom of thought among the minority, and of raising personality to greater heights.

A new aeon will come in which truth will be revealed to all, when all will pass through the experience of shock, not only the living, but still more those who have died. But in this era of ours, in this objectified, objective world, philosophy in a universal and healthy sense, discovers, not truth, but the socialization of truth, it discovers the necessary thing, that which is needed and useful for the life of society. The objectified world, the world of phenomena, is not conditioned by the individual reason, nor by divine reason, nor by an individual, universal, general sensitiveness, but by socialized reason and socialized sensitiveness. The objectified world, which is regarded uncritically as the 'objective' world is conditioned by the transcendentally social.

It is a mistake to think that truth is revealed to the generic mind. Truth is revealed to spiritual awareness, which lies on the border line of the supra-conscious; spirit is freedom, an exaltingly creative impulse, it is personality and love. There is such a thing as the history of the conscious mind, of its stages and periods. This is a problem of which Hegel was better aware than anyone. Boldwin suggests the following periods of thought—pre-logical, logical and immediate, and supra-logical.[1]

But this supra-logical thought is possible at all times, it is intuitive thought, creatively original, it comes near to primary reality, it is not objectified. Pre-logical thought is very different

[1] See I. M. Boldwin: *Théorie génétique de la réalité.*

from supra-logical, for the primitive individual is not a distinguishable being who identifies himself; the social group constitutes the only 'ego'. This is what Lévy-Bruhl thinks also. The stage of growth of the mind contributes to the separating out of personality and its distinction from the social group. But as the conscious mind increases in strength, personality both becomes more isolated and at the same time subjected to new forms of the conscious spirit of community.

Knowledge takes two directions and has a twofold significance; it is on the one hand an active break-through towards meaning and truth, as it rises above the world, and on the other hand it is adjustment to the world as we are given it, to social dull routine. But even when it is of that second type, knowledge is a reflection of the Logos, it is a descent of the Logos into the world. In that fact the source of the high achievement of science, and of its independence is to be found.

Some of the greatest difficulties of knowledge are due to language and this is particularly telling in the case of philosophy, in which the problem of terminology has so vast a part to play. There is the interior logos, the inward word, which is in close proximity to the depth of one who exists, it is hard by the primary reality. And there is the exterior logos, the outward word which is orientated to this world and adjusted to its fallen state. In the first sense the word is not objectified, it is meaning. In the second sense, the word is objectified and alienated, remote from primordial meaning. Human language has its basis in the primordial un-objectified word and for that reason only it has meaning. But language is also a social fact and it is the chief means of communication among men. It is thanks to it that the existence of society is possible. Language is socialized, and the stamp of conventionality lies upon it; it bears the impress of enmity and of the limitations of all social organizations. The multitude of human tongues is the disintegrated, self-alienating primordial word—the Logos.

Language makes understanding and communication possible

73

among men. But language also estranges them and makes them incomprehensible to one another. There is also a single philosophical language associated with the Word, the Logos, and for that reason alone the history of philosophy is not merely a story of erroneous opinions, but even a revelation of truth. But philosophers also understand one another badly, because they often speak in different philosophical languages. I am speaking now of philosophical languages, not of the various tongues spoken by the nations and tribes of the earth.

All this leads to a trenchant statement of the problem of the sociology of knowledge, and with it the problem of logical general validity is also connected. The objectified world which is called objective is a world which has fallen into ruin and alienation and at the same time it is a world which is unified by compulsion, it is fettered and determined, it is a socialized world, a world of the commonplace. It is precisely in such a world that everything has the seal of the common upon it, everything is generalized. In spite of the assertion of Platonism, it is in the noumenal world that everything is individualized, the *principium individuationis* operates, and everything is linked with personality. Personalism is the basic property of a world which is not objectified. Objectification is above all depersonalization.

General-validity in knowledge, which is of so much interest to Kantians, is not only logical but also sociological in character. It means apprehending in common, a sense in the apprehending mind of community with others, with everyone. Its attention is turned not to the subject-matter of apprehension, but to other people, and it is concerned with what is convincing to them. But the degree of general-validity does not depend upon the apparatus of logic, it depends upon sharing the vision of reality in common. Logic is social. In the truth of his knowledge and in his primary perceptional acts the person who apprehends depends very little upon a logical process. He is not aiming at thinking consciously and knowing logically. It is a mistake to think that it is necessary

74

to prove anything to oneself, what is necessary is to prove it to someone else. Florensky very truly says that the law of identity $(A=A)$, that is to say the fundamental law of logic, is death, desert and nothingness. He also says that a concept is static whereas a judgment is dynamic. But to Florensky subjectivity is illusory, while objectivity is ontological, he is still under the sway of objectivism and ontologism.

Logic requires a new sociological clarification, but not on any account in the spirit of the sociologism of Dürckheim, but in a metaphysical spirit. The logical apparatus of knowledge is an outcome of objectification and corresponds to various degrees of the sense of community and of estrangement. The construction of a system of logic is an adjustment to the violent compulsion which the world as we have it exercises upon us. It is above all a means of protection in the struggle for life in this world of objects.

There is in this connection a certain amount of truth in pragmatism. But this truth which it contains is not about truth nor about a criterion of truth; it is concerned with something else. The objectified world, as I have said more than once, is a world in which things are strange and unknown, and this element of strangeness exists in varying degrees. Getting to know things has its place as a means of communication for an estranged world. Man struggles against this estrangement. He tries to establish an environment which is akin to him, a religious environment or a national, one formed by a social group, and by the family. For such environments there are different degrees of cognitive general-validity.

At the same time the degree in which man introduces the universal varies. General-validity has a different meaning in the case of a mind which is in the highest degree opened out to universal content, from the meaning it bears for a mind which is contracted and of small capacity. A medium degree of general validity holds for the consciousness of the narrow-minded and those with little space into which to receive. Man is a microcosm.

There is eternal truth in the teaching of Nicholas of Cusa that all is present in everything,[1] and of Leibniz on the monad as a universe. But man is a microcosm only potentially and as a possibility, in a deep-lying stratum of his being which is in the case of the majority of people covered up and compressed.

The cosmos as nature is disclosed outside the process of objectification and this disclosure presupposes the re-establishment of a sense of kinship and communion of man with nature, and of people among themselves. The secret of cosmic life remains hidden from the ordinary ways of knowledge and science has no interest in it. The revelation of the cosmos and the mystery of creation is still to come and is bound to come, and it is connected with a revelation of the sense of human community, with the overcoming of the estrangement which is an outcome of objectification.

The fundamental contradiction in human existence is that man is a finite being possessed of potential infinity and an ambition to strive towards infinity.[2] The empirical world is partial, not a whole, and it cannot without contradiction be thought of as either infinite or finitely consummated. So far as this world is concerned the insight of the physical and mathematical sciences is a possibility, and it is the most exact, it is of the greatest general-validity, and it is susceptible of verification. But this generally-valid insight does not penetrate into the mystery of cosmic life, it corresponds to the disintegrated and estranged condition of human beings from one another and from the cosmos. Spiritual insight on the other hand, knowledge of the things of the spirit, is not an activity in the world of extraneous objects.

I will not repeat what I have already written in *Solitude and Society* and other books. The empirical world is given to us not as a passive, reflected, experience, and not as one whole cosmos, but

[1] See M. de Gandillac: *La philosophie de Nicolas de Cues.*
[2] To Heidegger death is the last word in the finite existence of man, because he denies this element of infinity in man. See his *Sein und Zeit.*

as an evil infinity in which we are lost and have to find our bearings. 'Objective' scientific knowledge is itself such a taking of bearings. In that is to be found the meaning of the formation of concepts.

This is an opportune moment to amend the term 'thing-in-itself'. Existential reality always presupposes a relation, in other words, an impulse to issue out of the self in common with others in a community. The 'thing-in-itself' is real in so far as it is related to other things-in-themselves. In other words, it is not accurate to call it a thing in itself, or for itself; it is also for another, it issues out of itself. The knowledge of things in themselves, therefore, takes for granted a realized sense of spiritual community, and a 'melting-down' of the isolated mind. General-validity, which is always external and related to objectivity, is replaced by a sense of community, spiritual kinship, and reciprocal penetration of feeling. But spiritual intuition which comes from within is to the world of objects and the world of compulsion, the least generally valid and convincing in appearance, although it is the most universal. For this reason the position of metaphysics has always been precarious and open to suspicion.

The possibility of metaphysics is linked with the possibility of knowledge which is not objectified and not reached through the concept. Hegel turned being into concept and concept into being. But Hegel was a metaphysician of genius and his own metaphysics were certainly not knowledge through the concept. The Hegelian dialectic was not merely a logical dialectic of the spirit, that is to say, it was an existential dialectic. Such was the 'phenomenology of the spirit', the most notable thing his mind produced.

Concepts give us our bearings in the dark infinity of the object world which surrounds us. The concept is an intellectual defence, and at the same time a restraint which prevents us from upsetting the complex nature of the world. It rationalizes the subject-matter of knowledge and such rationalization is the application of reason to the world of phenomena. Such rationalization is of no use to the world of noumena. At the same time the concept generalizes, leads up to the universal and never lays hold upon individual reality. But its task is a different one, its task is pragmatically instrumental. The Logos acts in the concept, but it acts in application, in going out to the alienated object world. The concept does not get to know what is individual, nor does it apprehend freedom, and therefore it does not apprehend noumena, nor the secret of existence.

This has sometimes been expressed by saying that it is impossible to apprehend irrational reality through rational concepts (Rickert) or that intellect cannot apprehend life and movement (Bergson). But in so far as there is necessity and regularity in the world of phenomena, it displays the rational 'reality' which corresponds to the rationality of knowledge. Causal relations and regularities belong to generalizing thought and at the same time the phenomenal world is subordinated to causal relations and regularities. The difficulty of this problem which is encountered by epistemology, is due to the mystery of objectification.

It is a mistake to think that objectification occurs only in the sphere of knowledge. It takes place above all in 'being', in reality itself. The subject introduces it, and it does so not only as that which knows but also as that which exists. The fall into the object world took place in primary life itself. The effect of this was that only that which is secondary, rationalized and objectified was regarded as reality, and doubt was cast upon the reality of that which is primary, unobjectified, and not rationalized. Such is the structure of the mind which belongs to a fallen state, to alienation into the external.

Knowledge is an event which belongs to the intellectual sphere. How can something which is entirely non-intellectual, a material object, become an intellectual occurrence within the subject? How can a rational apprehension of the irrational be a possibility? The irrational itself has two different meanings. It can mean either the irrational in the phenomenal object world, or the irrational in the noumenal world, in the spiritual depth of the subject. The irrational of the first kind is regarded as a boundary line, but it functions as knowledge which gives men their bearings through a concept. A process of abstraction consists of this. It moves away from reality, but it also subordinates reality to itself. But this reality is by no means the primordially existent, the primary reality, which lies in the depth of the spirit, it is an exteriorization.

The object world is manifold, but personality is lost in it. It is infinite, but eternity is lost to sight in it; in it the commonplace is triumphant, but there is no unity; it is rationalized, but it is full of evil irrationality, which is the antithesis of meaning. It is such a world as that in which we live, and we are aware of it. But it is not a world which has perished beyond hope. The sun shines on it, albeit from without and not from within as it ought to have been. There is vigorous and growing life in it, although death brings that to an end. Flowers bloom in it, although they fade. The creative acts of man break through into it. The human face is here, and at times with a wonderful expression in the eyes. The heights of holiness and genius are attained, but so are the depths of moral ugliness and crime. Love, pity and self-sacrifice emerge, and yet how much cruelty and murder as well.

In this world, spirit has, as it were, fallen away from its own self, an estrangement has taken place, but the link with spirit has been preserved and spirit is active. This world is godless, but there is witness in it to the existence of God. If in objectivity there is a fall, there is in the concept a descent of reason towards that fallen state. The concept therefore has a limited application. It ought to yield place to unobjectified knowledge.

The critique of knowledge has brought to light a confusion of concept with being, with reality. It is a confusion which played an enormous part in the old metaphysics. Kant has done more than anybody in the service of criticism. We shall see that knowledge has left its mark upon 'being' itself and that 'being' is to a remarkable degree the outcome of the concept. The fallen state of the world has had its repercussion upon the conception of being. The socialization of knowledge in aiming at the establishment of general-validity for the average normal mind of the majority of men has a limiting effect upon both knowledge and reality itself. It is bent upon crowding out everything which demands a great spiritual effort and a sense of spiritual community. The average man, and human society especially, is always exercising violent pressure upon men. They find shelter from danger, they find self-preservation, in concepts and laws of logic in the field of cognition, in the laws of the State, in fossilized formulae of family life, of class, of the external life of the Church as a social institution. In these defensive measures, intuition, inspiration, love, humanity and living faith are crushed and stifled, the flame of the spirit is extinguished.

Feuerbach was right in his stress upon anthropology, in his revolt against the power exercised over man by all forms of objectification and estrangement which claim to be metaphysical reality. But Feuerbach was wrong in this respect, that in endeavouring to raise man, he took too low a view of him, and looked upon him as nothing more than a material, natural creature. Thus the whole existential dialectic of man and of his relation to God, was demolished and lost its meaning, for it makes sense only in relation to man as a spiritual being.

3

The mind must be given a line of direction, and be brought into correlation with the world environment. The conscious mind struggles against psychical chaos, an example of which we see in dreams; it synthetizes the life of the soul. But it is painful by nature, and it causes suffering, by dividing man into two parts within its own actual synthesis, even though man endeavours by great exertions of mind to free himself from suffering.[1] It is not only that the 'unhappy consciousness' of

[1] See J. Wahl: *Le malheur de la conscience dans la philosophie de Hegel.*

which Hegel wrote exists, but in fact all consciousness is unhappy.

The cause of this unhappiness lies in the fact that consciousness is linked with a division into two, with the falling apart into subject and object. And man, in order to get the better of his unhappiness and pain, sets himself either to rise to supra-consciousness or to sink down to the subconscious. Consciousness is a path along which man goes, and it lies between the subconscious and elemental, and the supra-conscious, the spiritual. Man is a suffering being because he is a divided being, one who lives both in the phenomenal world and in the noumenal. Man is an appearance, a creature of nature and subject to the laws of this world. At the same time man is also a 'thing-in-itself', a spiritual being, free from the power of this world. Consciousness is in an intermediate state, hence its twofold nature. But it accomplishes a great work and in it there is light.

To overcome the unhappiness of consciousness through the supra-conscious is not a rejection of consciousness. The positive acts of consciousness enter into the supra-conscious (this is, in fact, *Aufhebung* in the Hegelian sense).[1] But the structure of the supra-conscious corresponds to the noumenal world, just as the structure of consciousness answers to the phenomenal world, but not as a whole and not decisively. It is with a gap through which light from the other world is admitted, and it is with the possibility of a break-through. Consciousness recognizes as transcendent to itself that which would be immanent for the supra-conscious. For that reason I can say that the transcendent is not outside me but on the contrary within me. Mysticism, the very possibility of mysticism, is based upon that truth.

But in consequence of the fact that the structure of the mind is concerned with this phenomenal world, there takes place the exteriorization and objectification of that which is most inward

[1] On the relations between consciousness and the supra-conscious, see my book *The Destiny of Man.*

and spiritual. Primitive people make no distinction between this world and the other, to them everything is miraculous and supernatural. That is explained by the weakness of the conscious mind in its unawakened state. The supernatural and miraculous as distinct from the natural order, exists for a higher degree of consciousness. The very perception of the world of the senses has not always been one and the same. The forms and colours of the 'empirical' world depend upon the state of the mind, upon the direction it takes, and upon its weakness or strength.

Consciousness not only gives us our bearings in the world environment, not only gives us light; it also builds up a vast quantity of illusions. There are the illusions of the primitive mind which is still in a very feeble condition. Unhappy illusions are associated with them, and a large number of myths. And there are other illusions belonging to the higher and more civilized mind. There may be less falsity and more truth in the primitive mind than in the civilized mind. There may be more of reality in a myth, than in civilized reality. The societies into which people are grouped create a series of illusions which are necessary for their existence and development. And these are perhaps the most durable of illusions. Society objectifies human existence and inspires man with alarm as he faces its 'sanctity'. The English sociologist Kidd[1] developed the very piquant idea that society and the evolution of society, if they are to be maintained and flourish, require creeds and sanctities which by no means correspond with truth. Breed suggests to the individual person illusions of consciousness which are necessary to the breed. Schopenhauer also spoke of the illusions of love which made the individual the plaything of race. Social illusions take the form of class illusions, illusions of sectional prejudices, which distort the mind.

Hegel put forward a theory in which genius is displayed, the theory of the cunning of reason (*List der Vernunft*) in history. As a monist and an optimist he thought that the cunning of reason is

[1] See his *Social Evolution*.

82

an instrument in the revelation of spirit in history. But it ought, in fact, to be regarded as a source of bitter pessimism.

Breeding and birth create illusions which are necessary for the generative process, for the triumph of the common over what is individual, of species over the individual person, and of the collective over personality. And such illusions assume the forms of stable and established beliefs and sanctities which lead to the adoption of an idolatrous attitude towards them. This too is the objectification of human existence: it is to precipitate man into the world of constraining objects. The constraining power of socialization is exercised through the conventional lie, which is deep-rooted in the mind. Illusions and falsehood shape the structure of the mind to correspond with the object world.

But the lies of 'civilization', the falsehoods of society and history must be opposed not by 'nature' as Rousseau and Tolstoy inaccurately put it, but by spirit, by spirituality, by the noumenal world. This can produce changes in the mind and break into this world as a transforming power. Over against the conventional lie of the phenomenal world there is the rightness of instinct, but the roots of that instinct lie at a greater depth than what is commonly called 'nature'. Noumenal 'nature' in man is *a priori* in relation to external phenomenal nature.

The genius of Kant is most clearly displayed, not, as is usually thought, in his transcendental aesthetics, nor in his transcendental system of analysis, but in his transcendental dialectic, in his doctrine of the transcendental *Schein* and of antinomies. Reason, if it is used in the wrong way, gives rise to illusions. But Kant regards the whole dialectic of the reason as illusory. And he may be right if what is being discussed is reason apart from the whole life of the spirit, reason separated from existential experience. Where is the source of the transcendental illusions, *Schein*, which may arise from the dialectic of reason? Illusion arises as a result of accepting as real anything which can be thought of, and of transferring to noumena that which relates to phenomena. I should put it that illusions arise as an effect of objectification, of the projection into the object of that which has real existence only in the subject. This is a result of the power of the world of objects over human existence.

A concept gives rise to illusions if it is wrongly applied. It would not be true to say that reason is not qualified for a real existent dialectic. But it is distorted and loses its capacity in consequence of its fall. This fall, moreover, denotes a loss of completeness and of spirituality, division into subject and object, and thinking about the noumenal world in terms of adaptations to the world of phenomena.

It would be interesting to speculate upon how Kant would have criticized Hegel and his dialectic. Hegel at one time made his criticism of Kant, and it was his desire to get beyond him. He sought to communicate fullness of life to the concept and to convert the dialectic of the concept into an existential dialectic. He entirely parts company with Kant in the interpretation of the nature and the limits of logic. To Kant, dialectic is an imaginary organ of general logic, and its ability to convince is imaginary. Dialectic is the logic of illusions which extends the application of categories beyond the boundaries of the empirical. To Hegel logic is ontology and dialectic in logic is a dialectic of being. He seeks to overcome the Kantian antinomies.

Hegel's introduction of the dynamic into logic was a stroke of genius. He affirms self-movement in the concept, and the attainment of the identity of opposites. Truth is one whole thing. Hegel avoids the mistake of the old naturalistic metaphysics of accepting appearances as things-in-themselves. But the overcoming of antinomies is illusory, it is a new form of transcendental *Schein*. For Hegel remains within the circle of immanence, within a false monism, and an optimistic interpretation of the world process. With him there is no real transcending, and that is why it was possible for dialectical materialism to take its rise from him. The antinomy remains in force till the end of the world. If it is to be overcome, it can be by nothing but eschatology.

The mistake which Kant made, however, was to confuse and identify experience with that which relates only to appearances, which is to deny the possibility of spiritual experience. Illusion is not bound up with the transcendent but with the immanent. It is precisely the transcendent which is the least illusory. The antinomies of pure reason are connected with infinity. A third factor may be admitted, distinct from both thesis and antithesis, but this third factor is not revealed in dialectical development in this world: it is disclosed in transcending the confines of this object world. The objectified world is not presented to us as one whole thing, and, therefore, there is no truth in it in the Hegelian sense.

Since this world is not a thing-in-itself, not a noumenon, it does not exist either as an infinite or as a finite whole. The cosmological antinomy is overcome only by the fact that the world of appearances is not presented as a totality. But it is just in such a world that antinomies cannot be resolved. Kant was right in his dualism of two worlds and in recognizing that the antinomies involved in that dualism are unavoidable. But the explanation of this may be different from Kant's interpretation of it.

Consciousness is not to be thought of as static. It is only relatively stabilized. In principle change and a revolution in the mind are possibilities; consciousness can expand and it can also contract. It is possible to break through objectification which creates the lasting illusion of this unchangeable world. Images and pictures seen in dreams are connected with the loss of power on the part of the conscious mind, so also the shapes and pictures of the empirical world which presses upon our daytime awareness do not show us primary reality itself, but merely signs of it. Dreams have also a symbolical meaning. But at the same time the true, primordially real world of freedom, creativity and goodness does act within this deceptive and illusory world. We cannot make the decisive effort of the mind, and exertion of spirit to awaken ourselves from the deceptive, the illusory and the unreal which mark the empirical world of appearances. The structure of a mind adapted to the conditions of this world is too strong. But it is a mistake to regard movement and plurality as deceptive and illusory, as Zeno and the Eleatic philosophers did.

Indian philosophy has its own truth. It is more powerful than Greek and European philosophy in its recognition of the unreality and deceptiveness of the world of appearances. But it has not understood the meaning of man's passage through this world, nor has it been sensitive to the meaning of history. It is an interesting fact that Buddhist philosophy and European empirical philosophy alike acknowledge only fluid appearances, and, behind them, nothing. The former, however, is pessimistic whereas the latter is optimistic, and the former is more profound than the latter. Indian thought has created a remarkable metaphysics, but no science. Science is a creation of the European West. The creation of science presupposes not only the independence of reason and proficiency in the use of it, but also a special sort of attention to the phenomenal world. The mind is not only directed upon it and adjusted to it, but is also set free from that fear in the face of this world, which made scientific knowledge impossible for ancient man, tormented as he was by demonolatry. The original meaning of 'holy' was 'taboo', and panic the first sacred thing.

But as his conscious mind developed man ceased to venerate as sacred this objectified phenomenal world which menaces him. Thus fearless science and technical knowledge came into being. In this fearlessness, in this quest for incorruptible truth lies the majesty of science and its link with the Logos. Science recognizes no taboos at all; they were due to a diseased state of the mind. Henceforward, man has to search for the holy, he has to seek for God, in a different sphere, in the spiritual world, the world of interior existence, not in the object, but in the subject. The proud philosopher Fichte said that man must have an aim beyond the confines of this life.

But one must not think of the other world, the better world which lies beyond the confines of this life in naturalistic and objectivist terms, though traditional theology has not been free from that. One must think of it above all as a change in the direction taken by the conscious mind and in its structure. One must think of it as the world of spirit, which is not another and different 'nature'.

This world, which I call the world of objectification, denotes a self-estrangement and an exteriorization of spirit by which it is ejected into the external. There is no ontological dualism which gives rise to objectification in the same way that monism does. There is a dualism of modes of existence, of qualitative states in man and in the world. The distinction between the worlds does not make itself known through an objectifying concept, but through pure, integral intuition which penetrates into the secret of existence by an existential act of spirit. According to Descartes error is due to the will. But from the direction taken by the primordial will, not only errors in cognition occur, but errors also in the very perception of reality, in the very construction of worlds. Knowledge and science have their own worlds, religion has its own world, so have art and politics. This does not in the slightest degree mean that the world of science is a world of phantasy and is devoid of reality. It is of immense importance to man as he takes his way through life, and science plays an enormous part in the liberation of man and in the development of his powers. This is particularly so in the case of historical science which sets men free from the illusions and errors of the mind in its less developed stages.

But the seductive lures which enslave are always lying in wait for man. Such an enslaving lure which distorts and disfigures science is 'scientism', which is a conversion of the scientific attitude to the world into something unique which reigns supreme and alone. Scientific knowledge ought to be set free from the oppressive weight of 'scientism', in other words, from a false philosophy, the view of the world taken by materialism, naturalism and positivism. Such a liberating movement needs an understanding of the secret of objectification.

Is such a theory of knowledge to be called idealism or realism? It would be alike inaccurate to call this point of view either idealism or realism, because that would be to state the question wrongly and to express it in terms of the old categories of thought. It is idealism in one respect and eminently realism in another. Existential philosophy is the one authentically real philosophy. But it is not the realism of the old ontological school which was under the sway of objectification and was a form of naturalism. At the same time it surpasses the idealism of German philosophy at the beginning of the nineteenth century. But it does this in such a way that what was true in that idealism enters into it. We are now faced by the problem of being and existence.

PART TWO

The Problem of Being and Existence

CHAPTER III

1. Being as objectification. Being and the existent, that which exists. Being and non-being. Being as concept. Being and value. Being and spirit. 2. The supremacy of freedom over being. The determinism of being and freedom. Being and primary passion. Being as congealed freedom and congealed passion. Being as nature and being as history

I

From ancient times philosophers have sought for the knowledge of being (*ousia, essentia*). The construction of an ontology has been philosophy's highest claim. And at the same time the possibility of achieving this has raised doubts among the philosophers. At times it has appeared as though human thought was in this respect pursuing a phantom.

The transition from the many to the One, and from the One to the many was a fundamental theme in Greek philosophy. In a different way the same topic has been fundamental in Indian philosophy also. Indian thought has been disquieted by the question: how does being arise out of non-being? It has to a large extent been focussed upon the problem of nothingness, non-being and illusion. It has been occupied with the discovery of the Absolute and deliverance from the relative, which meant salvation. Indian thought has tried to place itself on the other side of being and non-being, and has revealed a dialectic of being and non-being. It is this that has made it important.[1]

The Greeks sought for ἀρχή—the primordial. They medi-

---

[1] See R. Grousset: *Les philosophies indiennes.* O. Strauss: *Indische Philosophie.* A. Schweitzer: *Les grands penseurs de l'Inde.*

91

tated upon the unchangeable; they were disquieted by the problem of the relation of the unchangeable to the changing; they desired to explain how becoming arises out of being. Philosophy has sought to rise above the deceptive world of the senses and to penetrate behind this world of plurality and change to the One. Doubts were felt even about the reality of movement. If man breaks through to the knowledge of being he will reach the summit of knowledge, and, it was sometimes thought, he will attain salvation through having achieved union with the primary source. Yet at the same time Hegel says that the concept of being is quite futile, while Lotze says that being is indefinable and can only be experienced.[1]

Heidegger, in claiming to construct a new ontology, says that the concept of being is very obscure. Pure being is an abstraction and it is in an abstraction that men seek to lay hold upon primary reality, primary life. Human thought is engaged in the pursuit of its own product. It is in this that the tragedy of philosophical learning lies, the tragedy, that is, of all abstract philosophy. The problem which faces us is this: is not being a product of objectification? Does it not turn the subject matter of philosophical knowledge into objects in which the noumenal world disappears? Is not the concept of being concerned with being quâ concept, does being possess existence?

Parmenides is the founder of the ontological tradition in philosophy, a highly significant and important tradition in connection with which the efforts of reason have reached the level of genius. To Parmenides being is one and unchanging. There is no nonbeing, there is only being. To Plato, who carried on this ontological tradition, true being is the realm of ideas which he sees behind the moving and multiple world of the senses. But at the same time Plato maintains the supremacy of the good and beneficent over being, and from that it is possible to go on to another tradition in philosophy. In Plato the unity of perfection is the

[1] See Lotze: *Metaphysik*.

highest idea, and the idea of being is being itself. Eckhardt held that *Esse* is *Deus*. Husserl, after passing through a phase of idealism and asserting the primacy of the mind, came to carry on the tradition of Platonism in the contemplation of ideal being, *Wesenheiten*.

In the processes of thought the human mind sought to rise above this world of sense which presents itself to us, and in which eveything is unstable, above a world which is a world of becoming, rather than of being. But by that very fact the search for being was made to depend upon thinking, and the impress of thought lay upon it. Being became an object of thought and thereby came to denote objectification. What reason finds is its own product. Reality is made to depend upon the fact that it becomes the subject matter of knowledge, in other words an object. But in actual fact the reverse is true, reality is not in front of the knowing subject but 'behind' him, in his existentiality.

The erroneous character of the old realism is particularly clear in the case of Thomism, the philosophy of the common or of sound common sense. It regards the products of thinking, the hypostatization of thought, as objective realities.[1] And so St Thomas Aquinas supposes that the intellect, and the intellect alone, comes into touch with being. Being is received from without. This is to make the average normal consciousness, which is also regarded as unchangeable human nature, absolute. That kind of ontology is a clear example of naturalistic metaphysics, and it does not recognize the antinomies to which the reason gives birth. The nature of the intellectual apprehension of being is settled by the fact that being was already beforehand the product of intellectualization. In the Thomist view being comes before thought; but this being was already fabricated by thought. Being is secondary not primary.

. In mediaeval philosophy the question of the relation between *essentia* and *existentia* played a great part. Being is *essentia*. But the question remains: does *essentia* possess an *existentia* of its own? In

[1] See Garrigou-Lagrange: *Le sens commun.*

present day philosophy, for example in Heidegger and Jaspers, this question assumes a new form, that of the relation between *Sein* and *Dasein*.[1] Aristotle and the scholastics admitted a classification in logic of the same sort as in zoology and in this classification the concept of being took its place as the broadest and highest. Brunschvicg points out with truth that it was Descartes who broke with this naturalism in logic and metaphysics.[2] But ontology has never been able to cut itself off entirely from the naturalistic spirit.

Hegel introduced a new element into the concept of being. He introduced the idea of non-being, nothingness, without which there is no becoming, no emergence of what is new. Being itself is empty and the equivalent of non-being. The initial fact is being-non-being, unity, being and nothingness. Being is nothingness, indeterminate and unqualified being. *Dasein* in Hegel is the union of being and nothingness, becoming, determinate being. Truth is in the transition from being to nothingness, and from nothingness to being. Hegel wants to put life into numbed and ossified being. He seeks to pass from the concept to concrete being. This is attained by way of recognizing the ontological nature of the concept itself, it is being which is filled with interior life. 'Identity', says Hegel, 'is a definition of only simple, immediate, dead being, whereas contradiction is the root of all movement and vitality. It is only in so far as nothingness has within itself its contradiction that it has movement and attains a state of wakefulness and activity.[3] Dialectic is real life.

But Hegel does not attain to real concreteness. He remains under the sway of object-ness. Vladimir Soloviëv, who was much under the influence of Hegel, makes a very valuable and important distinction between being and the existent. Being is the predicate of the existent, which is the subject. We

[1] Heidegger: *Sein und Zeit.* Jaspers: *Philosophie,* 3 Vols.
[2] See L. Brunschvicg: *Spinose et ses contemporains,* and *Le progrès de la conscience dans la philosophie occidentale.*
[3] See Hegel: *The Science of Logic.* Vol. II.

say: 'this creature is' and 'that sensation is'. A hypostatization of the predicate takes place.[1] Various kinds of being are formed through the abstraction and hypostatization of attributes and qualities. In this way ontologies have been built up which have constituted a doctrine of abstract being, rather than of the concrete existent. But the real subject-matter of philosophy ought to be, not being in general, but that to which and to whom being belongs, that is, the existent, that which exists. A concrete philosophy is an existential philosophy, and that Soloviëv did not arrive at, he remained an abstract metaphysician. The doctrine of the all-in-one is ontological monism.[2]

It is not true to say that being is: only the existent is, only that which exists. What being tells of a thing is that something is, it does not speak about *what* is. The subject of existence confers being. The concept of being is logically and grammatically ambiguous, two meanings are confused in it. Being means that something is, and it also means that which is. This second meaning of 'being' ought to have been discarded. Being appears as both a subject and a predicate, in the grammatical sense of those words. In point of fact, being is a predicate only. Being is the common, the universal. But the common has no existence and the universal is only within that which exists, in the subject of existence, not in the object. The world is multiple, everything in it is individual and single. The universally-common is nothing but the attainment of the quality of unity and commonness in this plurality of individualities. There is some degree of truth in what Rickert says, that being is a judgment of value, that the real is the subject-matter of judgment. From this the mistaken conclusion is drawn that truth is obligation, rather than being; the transcendent is only *Geltung*. *Geltung* refers to value not to reality.

When the primacy of obligation over being is asserted, this

[1] See Soloviëv: *Critique of Abstract Principles*, and *The Philosophical Principles of Pure Knowledge*.
[2] See S. Frank: *The Unfathomable*.

may seem like the Platonic primacy of the good over being. But Soloviëv says that that which obliges to be in this world is the eternally existent in another sphere. A fundamental question arises: does meaning, the ideal value, exist and if so in what sense does it exist? Does a subject of meaning, value, and idea exist? My answer to this question is that it does, it exists as spirit. Spirit moreover is not abstract being, it is that which concretely exists. Spirit is a reality of another order than the reality of 'objective' nature or the 'objectivity' which is born of reason. Ontology should be replaced by pneumatology. Existential philosophy departs from the 'ontological' tradition, in which it sees unconscious objectification. When Leibniz sees in the monad a simple substance which enters into a complex organization, his teaching is about the world harmony of monads, and what he is most interested in is the question of simplicity.and complexity, he is still in the power of naturalistic metaphysics and an objectified ontology.

It is essential to grasp the inter-relations of such concepts as truth, being, and reality. Of these terms, reality is the least open to doubt and the most independent of schools of philosophical terminology, in the meaning which it has acquired. But originally it was connected with *res*, a thing, and the impress of an objectified world has been stamped upon it. Truth again is not simply that which exists, it is an attained quality and value, truth is spiritual. That which is, is not to be venerated simply because it is. The error of ontologism leads to an idolatrous attitude towards being. It is Truth that must be venerated, not being. Truth moreover exists concretely not in the world but in the Spirit. The miracle of Christianity consists in the fact that in it the incarnation of Truth, of the Logos, of Meaning, appeared, the incarnation of that which is unique, singular and unrepeatable; and that incarnation was not objectification, but an abrupt break with objectification. It must be constantly reiterated that spirit is never an object and that there is no such thing as objective spirit. Being is only

96

one among the offspring of spirit. But only the trans-subjective is that which exists, the existent. Whereas being is merely a product of hypostatized existence.

Pure ontologism subordinates value to being. To put it in another way, it is compelled to regard being as a unique scale and criterion of value and of truth, of the good and the beautiful. Being, the nature of being, indeed *is* goodness, truth and beauty. The one and only meaning of goodness, truth and beauty is in this, that they are—being. And the reverse side of the matter is similar, the sole evil, falsehood and ugliness, is non-being, the denial of being. Ontologism has to recognize being as God, to deify being and to define God as being. And this is characteristic of the kataphatic doctrine of God, and distinguishes it in principle from the apophatic which regards God not as being, but as supra-being.

Schelling says that God is not being, but life.[1] 'Life'—it is a better word than 'being'. But ontological philosophy has a formal likeness to the philosophy of life, to which 'life' is the sole standard of truth, goodness and beauty; life at its maximum is to it the supreme value. The highest good, the highest value is defined as the maximum of being or the maximum of life. And there is no disputing the fact that one must be, one must live, before the question of value and good can be raised at all. There is nothing more sad and barren than that which the Greeks expressed by the phrase οὐκ ὄν, which is real nothingness. The words μὴ ὄν conceal a potentiality, and this therefore is only half being or being which is not realized.

Life is more concrete and nearer to us than being. But the inadequacy of the philosophy of life consists in this, that it always has a biological flavour: Nietzsche, Bergson and Klages illustrate the point. Being indeed is abstract and has no interior life. Being can possess the highest qualities, but it may also not possess them, it can be also the very lowest. And therefore being cannot be a

---

[1] See Schelling: *Philosophie der Offenbarung*.

standard of quality and value. The situation is always saved when the phrase 'real and true' is added. But then 'reality and truth' become the highest standard and appraisal. It is the attainment of 'real and true' being which is the aim, not the affirmation of being at its maximum. This only underlines the truth that ontologism is a hypostatization of predicates and qualities. Being acquires an axiological sense. Value, goodness, truth and beauty are a vision of quality in existence and rise above being.

But there is something else still more important in characterizing ontologism in philosophy. The recognition of being as the supreme good and value means the primacy of the common over what is individual and this is the philosophy of universals. Being is the world of ideas which crushes the world of the individual, the unique, the unrepeatable. The same thing happens when matter is regarded as the essence of being. Universalist ontologism cannot recognize the supreme value of personality: personality is a means, a tool of the universally common.

In the most living reality *essentia* is individual in its existentiality, while the universal is a creation of reason (Duns Scotus). The philosophy of ideal values is characterized by the same crushing of personality, nor has it any need to oppose the philosophy of abstract being. Real philosophy is the philosophy of the concrete living entity and entities and it is that which corresponds most closely to Christianity. It is also the philosophy of concrete spirit, for it is in spirit that value and idea are to be found. Meaning also is something which exists and by its existence is communicated to those that exist. Being and becoming must have a living carrier, a subject, a concrete living entity. That which concretely exists is more profound than value and comes before it, and existence goes deeper than being.

Ontologism has been the metaphysics of intellectualism. But the words 'ontology' and 'ontologism' are used in a broad sense and not rarely are identified with metaphysical realism as a whole. Hartmann says that the irrational in ontology lies deeper than the irrational in mysticism, for it is beyond the bounds not only of what can be known, but also of what can be experienced.[1] But in this way ontological depth is assigned a higher (or deeper) level than the possibility of experience, that is, than existence. This ontological depth is very like the Unknowable of Spencer. In Fichte being exists for the sake of reason and not the other way about. But being is the offspring of reason and reason moreover is a function of primary life or existence. Pascal goes deeper when he says that man is placed between nothingness and infinity. This is the existential position of man, and not an abstraction of thought.

Attempts have been made to stabilize being and strengthen its position between nothingness and infinity, between the lower abyss and the higher, but this has been merely an adjustment of reason and consciousness to the social conditions of existence in the objectified world. But infinity breaks through from below and from above, acts upon man, and overthrows stabilized being and established consciousness. It gives rise to the tragic feeling of life and to the eschatological outlook.

And this accounts for the fact that what I call eschatological metaphysics (which is also an existential metaphysics) is not ontology. It denies the stabilization of being and foresees the end of being, because it regards it as objectification. In this world indeed being is change, not rest. That is what is true in Bergson.[2] I have already said that the problem of the relation between thinking and being has been put in the wrong way. The actual statement of the problem has rested upon failure to understand the fact that knowledge is the kindling of light within being, not taking up a position in front of being as an object.

Apophatic theology is of immense importance for the understanding of the problem of being. It is to be seen in Indian religious philosophy and, in the West, principally in Plotinus, in the neo-platonists in pseudo-Dionysius the Areopagite, in Eckhardt, in

[1] N. Hartmann: *Grundzüge einer Metaphysik der Erkenntnis*.
[2] Bergson: *L'Évolution créatrice*.

Nicholas of Cusa and in German speculative mysticism. Kataphatic theology rationalized the idea of God. It applied to God the rational categories which were worked out in relation to the object world. And so it has been light-heartedly asserted, as a basic truth, that God is being. The kind of thinking which is adapted to the knowledge of being has been applied to him, the sort of thinking which is stamped with the indelible impress of the phenomenal, natural and historical world. This cosmomorphic and sociomorphic knowledge of God has led to the denial of the fundamental religious truth that God is mystery and that mystery lies at the heart of all things.

The teaching of kataphatic theology to the effect that God is being and that he is knowable in concepts is an expression of theological naturalism. God is interpreted as nature and the attributes of nature are transferred to him (almightiness, for example); just as in the same sociomorphic way the properties of power are communicated to him. But God is not nature, and not being, he is Spirit. Spirit is not being, it stands higher than being and is outside objectification. The God of kataphatic theology is a God who reveals himself in objectification. It is a doctrine about what is secondary not about what is primary. The important religious process in the world is one of spiritualizing the human idea of God.[1] The teaching of Eckhardt about *Gottheit* as of greater depth than *Gott* is profound. *Gottheit* is mystery and the concept of creator of the world is not applicable to *Gottheit*. God, as the first thing and the last, is the non-being which is supra-being.

Negative theology recognizes that there is something higher than being. God is not being. He is greater and higher, more mysterious than our rationalized concept of being. Knowledge of being is not the last thing, nor the first. The One in Plotinus is on the other side of being. The depth of the apophatic theology of Plotinus, however, is distorted by monism according to which the separate entity issues from the addition of non-being. This would

[1] See R. Otto: *Das Heilige*.

be true, if by 'non-being' we understood freedom as distinct from nature. Eckhardt's teaching is not pantheism, it cannot be turned into the language of rational theology, and those who propose to call it theo-pantheism have a better case. Otto is right when he speaks of the supra-theism not the anti-theism of Sankhara and Eckhardt.[1] One must rise higher than being.

The relation which subsists among God, the world and man is not to be thought of in terms of being and necessity. It must be conceived by thought which is integrated in the experience of spirit and freedom. In other words it must be thought of in a sphere which lies beyond all objectification, all object power, authority, cause, necessity and externality, outside all ejection into the external. The sun outside me denotes my fall, it ought to have been within me and to send out its rays from within me.

This is above all of cosmological significance, and it means that man is a microcosm.[2] But in the problem which concerns the relations which subsist between man and God, it certainly should not be taken to mean pantheistic identity. That is always evidence of rationalistic thinking about being in which everything is either relegated to a place outside, or identified with, something. God and man are not external to each other, nor outside one another; neither are they identified, the one nature does not disappear in the other. But it is impossible to work out adequate concepts about this, it can be expressed only in symbols. Symbolic knowledge which throws a bridge across from one world to the other, is apophatic.

Knowledge by concepts which are subject to the restraining laws of logic, is suitable only to being, which is a secondary objectified sphere, and does not meet the needs of the realm of the spirit, which is outside the sphere of being or of supra-being. The concept of being has been a confusion of the phenomenal world with the noumenal, or the secondary with the primary, and of

[1] See Otto: *West-Oestliche Mystik.*
[2] See my *The Meaning of the Creative Act.*

predicate with subject. Indian thought took the right view in asserting that being depends upon act. Fichte also maintains the existence of pure act. Being is postulated as an act of spirit, it is derivative. What is true does not mean what belongs to being, as mediaeval scholastic philosophy would have it. *Existentia* is not apprehended by the intellect, whereas *essentia* is so apprehended, simply because it is a product of the intellect. What is true does not mean what belongs to being, but what belongs to the spirit.

A matter of great importance in the question of the relation between kataphatic and apophatic theology, is the working out of the idea of the Absolute, and this has been in the main the business of philosophy, rather than of religion. The Absolute is the boundary of abstract thought, and what men wish is to impart a positive character to its negative character. The Absolute is that which is separate and self-sufficient, there is in the Absolute no relation to any other. In this sense God is not the Absolute, the Absolute cannot be the Creator, and knows no relation to anything else. The God of the Bible is not the Absolute. It might be put in a paradoxical way by saying that God is the Relative, because God has a relation to his other, that is to say to man and to the world, and he knows the relation of love. The perfection of God is the perfection of his relation; paradoxically speaking, it is the absolute perfection of that relation. Here the state of being absolute is the predicate not the subject. It is doubtful whether the distinction can be allowed which Soloviëv draws between the Absolute Existent and the Absolute which is becoming; there is no becoming in the Absolute. The Absolute is the unique, and the thinking mind can assert this of the *Gottheit*, though it says it very poorly.

A real, not verbal, proof of the being of God is in any case impossible because God is not being, because being is a term which belongs to naturalism, whereas the reality of God is a reality of spirit, of the spiritual sphere which is outside what belongs to being or to supra-being. God cannot in any sense whatever be conceived as an object, not even as the very highest object. God is not to be found in the world of objects. Ontological proof shares in the weakness of all ontologism. The service which Husserl rendered by his fight against all forms of naturalistic metaphysics must be acknowledged.[1] Naturalism understands the fullness of being in terms of the form of a material thing, the naturalization of the mind regards the mind as a part of nature. But existence bears different meanings in different spheres. Husserl draws a distinction between the being of a thing and the being of the mind. In his view the mind is the source of all being, and in this respect he is an idealist. It is the being of consciousness with which he is concerned.

It is rightly pointed out that there is a difference between Husserl and Descartes, in that the latter was not concerned with an investigation into the various meanings of existence. But Husserl is concerned with that, and seeks to pass on from a theory of knowledge to a theory of being. But he preserves the ontologism which comes down from Plato. It is upon being that he keeps his attention fixed. But there is this further to be said, that not only things but even *Wesenheiten* also exist for the mind only, and that means that they are exposed to the process of objectification. Behind this lies a different sphere, the sphere of the spirit. Spirit is not being, but the existent, that which exists and possesses true existence, and it is not subject to determination by any being at all. Spirit is not a principle, but personality, in other words the highest form of existence.

Those idealists who have taught that God is not being, but existence and value, have simply been teaching, though in a distorted and diminished form, the eschatological doctrine of God. God reveals himself in this world and he is apprehended eschatologically. This will become clearer in the last two chapters of this book. I stand by a philosophy of spirit, but it differs from the traditional 'spiritualist' metaphysics. Spirit is understood not as

[1] See Levinasse: *La théorie de l'intuition dans la phénoménologie de Husserl.*

substance, nor as another nature comparable with material nature. Spirit is freedom, not nature: spirit is act, creative act; nor is it being which is congealed and determined, albeit after a different fashion. To the existential philosophy of spirit the natural material world is a fall, it is the product of objectification, self-alienation within existence. But the form of the human body and the expression of the eyes belong to spiritual personality and are not opposed to spirit.

2

Ontological philosophy is not a philosophy of freedom. Freedom cannot have its source in being, nor be determined by being: it cannot enter into a system of ontological determinism. Freedom does not suffer the determining power of being, nor that of the reason. When Hegel says that the truth of necessity is freedom he denies the primary nature of freedom and entirely subordinates it to necessity. And in no degree does it help when Hegel asserts that the finite condition of the world is consciousness of freedom of the spirit, and the ultimate aim is the actualization of freedom. Freedom is represented as the outcome of a necessary world process—as a gift of necessity. But then, it has to be said that in Hegel even God is an outcome of the world process; he becomes within the world-order. The choice has to be made—either the primacy of being over freedom, or the primacy of freedom over being. The choice settles two types of philosophy. The acceptance of the primacy of being over freedom is inevitably either open or disguised determinism. Freedom cannot be a kind of effect of the determining and begetting agency of anything or anybody; it flees into the inexplicable depth, into the bottomless abyss. And this is acknowledged by a philosophy which takes as its starting point the primacy of freedom over being, freedom which precedes being and all that belongs to it.

But most of the schools of philosophical thought are under the sway of determined and determining being. And that kind of philosophizing is in the power of objectification, that is of the ejection of human existence into the external. 'In the beginning was the Logos.' But in the beginning also was freedom. The Logos was in freedom and freedom was in the Logos. That, however, is only one of the aspects of freedom. It has another aspect, one in which freedom is entirely external to the Logos and a clash between the Logos and Freedom takes place. Thus it is that the life of the world is a drama, it is full of the sense of tragedy, the antagonism of diametrically opposed principles occurs in it. There is an existential dialectic of freedom: it passes into necessity, freedom not only liberates, it also enslaves. There is no smooth development in the process of reaching perfection. The world lives in stresses of passion, and the basic theme of its life is freedom. The philosophical doctrines of freedom give little satisfaction for the most part. They shrink from coming into contact with the mystery of it, and fear to penetrate into that mystery.

There was real genius in Boehme's teaching about the *Ungrund*. It was a vision rather than a rational doctrine. Boehme was one of the first to break away from the intellectualism of Greek and scholastic philosophy, and his voluntarism is a revelation of the possibility of freedom for philosophy. He reveals an interior life and process within the Deity itself. It is an eternal birth of God, a self-begetting. The denial of this theogonic process is a denial of the life of the Godhead. Franz Baader also says the same.[1] It was Boehme's view, as it was that of Heraclitus, that the life of the world is embraced by fire, which is the fundamental element. Streams of fire flow through the cosmos: there is a conflict between light and darkness, between good and evil. The contradictory, suffering, and flamingly tragic character of the life of the world is accounted for by the fact that before being and deeper than being lies the *Ungrund*, the bottomless abyss, irrational mystery, primordial freedom, which is not derivable from being.

[1] See Franz von Baader's Complete works: Vol. XIII. *Vorlesungen und Erläuterungen zu Jacob Boehme's Lehre*. p. 65

I reproduce here what I wrote in my essay on 'The Doctrine of the *Ungrund* and Freedom in Jacob Boehme'. 'The doctrine of the *Ungrund* answers the need which Boehme felt to come to grips with the mystery of freedom, the emergence of evil, the conflict between light and darkness', Boehme says: 'Ausser der Natur ist Gott ein Mysterium, verstehet in dem Nichts; denn ausser der Natur ist das Nichts, das ist ein Auge der Ewigkeit, ein ungründlich Auge, das in Nichts stehet oder siehet, denn es ist der Ungrund und dasselbe Auge ist ein Wille, verstehet ein Sehen nach der Offenbarung, das Nichts zu finden.'[1]

The *Ungrund*, then, is nothingness, the groundless eye of eternity; and at the same time it is will, not grounded upon anything, bottomless, indeterminate will. But this is a nothingness which is '*Ein Hunger zum Etwas*'.[2] At the same time the *Ungrund* is freedom.[3] In the darkness of the *Ungrund* a fire flames up and this is freedom, meonic, potential freedom. According to Boehme freedom is opposed to nature, but nature emanated from freedom. Freedom is like nothingness, but from it something emanates. The hunger of freedom, of the baseless will for something, must be satisfied.

'Das Nichts macht sich in seiner Lust aus der Freiheit in der Finsternis des Todes offenbar, denn das Nichts will nicht ein Nichts sein, und kann nicht ein Nichts sein.'[4]

The freedom of the *Ungrund* is neither light nor darkness, it is neither good nor evil. Freedom lies in the darkness and thirsts for light; and freedom is the cause of light.

'Die Freiheit ist und stehet in der Finsternis, und gegen der finstern Begierde nach des Lichts Begierde, sie ergreifet mit dem ewigen Willen die Finsternis; und die Finsternis greifet nach dem Lichte der Freiheit und kann es nicht erreichen denn sie schliesst sich mit Begierde selber in sich zu, und macht sich in sich selber zur Finsternis.'[5]

[1] See Jacob Boehme's *Sämmtliche Werke* edited by Schiller. Vol. IV. pp. 284–5. *Vom dreifachen Leben des Menschen.*
[2] Ibid. Vol. IV. p. 286.   [3] Ibid. Vol. IV. pp. 287–9.
[4] Ibid. Vol. IV. p. 406.   [5] Ibid. p. 428.

Apophatically and by way of antinomy, Boehme describes the mystery which comes to pass within that depth of being which makes contact with the original nothingness. Fire flames up in the darkness and the light begins to dawn. Nothingness becomes something, groundless freedom gives birth to nature. For the first time perhaps in the history of human thought, Boehme saw that at the basis of being and superior to being lies groundless freedom, the passionate desire of nothing to become something, the darkness in which fire and light begin to kindle into flame. In other words he is the founder of metaphysical voluntarism which was unknown alike to mediaeval thought and to the thought of the ancient world.

Will, that is, freedom, is the beginning of everything. But Boehme's thought would seem to suggest that the *Ungrund*, the ungrounded will, lies in the depth of the Godhead and precedes the Godhead. The *Ungrund* is indeed the Godhead of apophatic theology and at the same time, the abyss, the free nothingness which precedes God and is outside God. Within God is nature, a principle distinct from him. The Primary Godhead, the Divine Nothingness is on the further side of good and evil, of light and darkness. The divine *Ungrund*, before its emergence, is in the eternity of the Divine Trinity. God gives birth to himself, realizes himself out of the Divine Nothingness. This is a way of thinking about God akin to that in which Meister Eckhardt draws a distinction between *Gottheit* and *Gott*. *Gott* as the Creator of the world and man is related to creation. He comes to birth out of the, depth of *Gottheit*, of the ineffable Nothingness. This idea lies deep in German mysticism.

Such a way of thinking about God is characteristic of apophatic theology. Nothingness is deeper down and more original than some-thing. Darkness, which is not in this case evil, is deeper down and more original than light, and freedom deeper and more original than all nature. The God of kataphatic theology, on the other hand, is already some-thing and means thinking about what is secondary.

'Und der Grund derselben Tinktur ist die göttliche Weisheit; und der Grund der Weisheit ist die Dreiheit der ungründlichen Gottheit, und der Grund der Dreiheit ist der einige unerforschliche Wille, und des Willens Grund is das Nichts.'[1]

Here indeed, we have the theogonic process, the process of the birth of God in eternity, in eternal mystery, and it is described according to the method of apophatic theology. Boehme's contemplation goes deeper than all the affirmations of secondary and rationalized kataphatic doctrines. Boehme establishes the path from the eternal basis of nature, from the free will of the *Ungrund,* that is groundlessness, to the natural basis of the soul.[2] Nature is secondary and derivative. Freedom, the will, is not nature. Freedom is not created. God is born everywhere and always, he is at once ground and groundlessness. The *Ungrund* must be understood above all as freedom, freedom in the darkness.

'Darum so hat sich der ewige frei Wille in Finsternis, und Qual, sowohl auch durch die Finsternis in Feuer und Lichte, und in ein Fremdenreich eingeführet, auf dass das Nichts in Etwas erkannt werde, und dass es ein Spiel habe in seinem Gegenwillen, dass ihm der freie Wille des Ungrundes im Grunde offenbar sei, denn ohne Böses mochte kein Grund sein.'[3]

Freedom has its roots in nothingness, in the meon, it is in fact the *Ungrund.* 'Der frei Wille ist aus keinem Anfange, auch aus keinem Grunden nichts gefasset, oder durch etwas geformet ... Sein rechter Urstand ist im Nichts.'[4] Here *Nichts* does not mean a void; it is more primary than being, since being is secondary. From this the primacy of freedom over being follows. The freedom of the will contains within it both good and evil, both love and wrath. Light and darkness alike are also contained in it. Free

[1] See Jacob Boehme's *Sämmtliche Werke* edited by Schiller. Vol. IV. *Von der Gnadenwahl.* p. 504.
[2] Ibid. Vol. IV. p. 607.   [3] Ibid. Vol. V. *Misterium Magnum.* p. 162.
[4] Ibid. Vol. V. p. 164.

will in God is the *Ungrund* in God, the nothingness in him. Boehme gives a profound exposition of the truth about the freedom of God, which traditional Christian theology also recognizes. His teaching about the freedom of God goes deeper than that of Duns Scotus.

'Der ewige Göttliche Verstand ist ein freier Wille, nicht von Etwas oder durch Etwas entstanden, er ist sein Selbst eigener Sitz und wohnet einig und allein in sich Selber; unergriffen von etwas, denn ausser und vor ihm ist Nichts, doch auch Selber als ein Nichts. Er ist ein einiger Wille des Ungrundes, und ist weder nahe noch ferne, weder hoch noch niedrig, sondern er ist Alles, und doch als ein Nichts'.[1]

To Boehme, chaos is the root of nature, chaos, that is to say, freedom. The *Ungrund,* the will, is an irrational principle. In the Godhead itself there is a groundless will, in other words, an irrational principle. Darkness and freedom in Boehme are always correlative and coinherent. Freedom even is God himself and it was in the beginning of all things. It would appear that Boehme was the first in the history of human thought to locate freedom in the primary foundation of being, at a greater and more original depth than any being, deeper and more primary than God himself. And this was pregnant with vast consequences in the history of thought. Such an understanding of the primordial nature of freedom would have filled both Greek philosophers and mediaeval scholastics with horror and alarm. It reveals the possibility of an entirely different theodicy and anthropodicy. The primordial mystery is the kindling of light within dark freedom, within nothingness, and the consolidation of the world out of that dark freedom. Boehme writes marvellously about this in *Psychologia vera*: 'Denn in der Finsternis ist der Blitz, und in der Freiheit das Licht mit der Majestät. Und ist dieses nur das Scheiden, dass die Finsternis materialisch macht, da doch auch kein Wesen einer Begreiflichkeit ist; sondern finster Geist und Kraft, eine Erfüllung

[1] Ibid. Vol. V. p. 193.

109

der Freiheit in sich selber, verstehe in Begehren, und nicht ausser: denn ausser ist die Freiheit.'[1]

There are two wills, one in the fire and the other in the light. Fire and light are basic symbols in Boehme. Fire is the beginning of everything, without it nothing would be, there would be only *Ungrund*. 'Und wäre Alles ein Nichts und Ungrund ohne Feuer'.[2] The transition from non-being to being is accomplished through the kindling of fire out of freedom. In eternity there is the original will of the *Ungrund* which is outside nature and before it. The philosophical ideas of Fichte and Hegel, Schopenhauer and E. Hartmann emanated from this, although they de-Christianized Boehme. German idealist metaphysics pass directly from the idea of *Ungrund*, of the unconscious, from the primordial act of freedom, to the world process, not to the Divine Trinity as in Boehme. The primary mystery of being, according to Boehme, consists in this, that nothingness seeks something.

'Der Ungrund ist ein ewig Nichts, und machet aber einen ewigen Anfang, als eine Sucht; denn das Nichts ist eine Sucht nach Etwas: und da doch auch Nichts ist, das Etwas gebe, sondern die Sucht ist selber das Geben dessen, das doch auch Nichts ist bloss eine begehrende Sucht.'[3]

In Boehme's teaching freedom is not the ground of moral responsibility in man. Nor is it freedom that controls his relations to God and his neighbour. Freedom is the explanation of the genesis of being and at the same time of the genesis of evil: it is a cosmological mystery. Boehme gives no rational doctrine expressed in pure concepts of the *Ungrund* and of freedom. He uses the language of symbol and myth, and it may be just for that reason that he succeeds in letting in some light upon that depth the knowledge of which is not attainable in rational philosophy. Boehme had a vision of the *Ungrund* and that vision became a

---

[1] See Jacob Boehme's *Sämmtliche Works* edited Schiller. Vol. VI. p. 14.
[2] Ibid. Vol. VI. p. 60.
[3] Ibid. Vol. VI. *Mysterium pansophicon*. p. 413.

fertilizing element in German metaphysics, which tried to rationalize it.

German metaphysics, as contrasted with Latin and Greek, was to see an irrational principle in the primary fount of being, not reason, which floods the world with light as the sun does, but will, act. This comes from Boehme, and beneath the surface his influence is to be traced in Kant, Fichte, Schelling, Hegel and Schopenhauer. The possibility of a philosophy of freedom was brought to light, a philosophy which rests upon the primacy of freedom over being. Hegel does not remain true to the philosophy of freedom, but in him also the principle enunciated by Boehme may be seen; he too is bent upon what lies beyond the boundaries of ontologism. Kant must be counted as a founder of the philosophy of freedom.

Everything leads us to the conclusion that being is not the ultimate depth, that there is a principle which precedes the emergence of being and that freedom is bound up with that principle. Freedom is not ontic but meonic. Being is a secondary product and it is always the case that in it freedom is already limited, and even disappears altogether. Being is congealed freedom, it is a fire which has been smothered and has cooled: but freedom at its fountain head is fiery. This cooling of the fire, this coagulation of freedom is in fact objectification. Being is brought to birth by the transcendental consciousness as it turns to the object. Whereas the mystery of primary existence with its freedom, with its creative fire, is revealed in the direction of the subject. Glimpses of the elements of a philosophy of freedom can already be seen in the greatest of the schoolmen, Duns Scotus, although he was still in chains. The influence of Boehme is of fundamental importance in Kant. It is also a basic theme in Dostoyevsky, whose creative work is of great significance in metaphysics.

The world and man are not in the least what they look like to the majority of professional metaphysicians, wholly concentrated

III

as these are upon the intellectual side of life and the process of knowing. It is only a few of them who have broken through towards the mystery of existence, and philosophers belonging to particular academic traditions least of all. Being has been understood as idea, thought, reason, *nous, ousia, essentia,* because it was indeed a product of reason, thought, idea. Spirit has seemed to philosophers to be *nous,* because out of it the primordial breath of life was drawn and upon it lay the stamp of objectifying thought. Kant did not bring to light the transcendental feelings, volitions and passions which condition the objective world of appearances. I am not referring to psychological passions nor psychological volitions, but to transcendental, which condition the world of phenomena from out of the noumenal world.

Transcendental will and passion are capable of being transformed, and turned into another direction, they can reveal a world within the depth of the subject, in the mind before it is rationalized and objectified. And then being itself may appear to us as cooled passion and congealed freedom. Primary passion lies in the depth of the world, but it is objectified, it grows cold, it becomes stabilized, and self-interest is substituted for it. The world as passion is turned into the world as a struggle for life.

Nicolas Hartmann, a typical academic philosopher, defines the irrational in a negatively epistemological manner, as that which became part of knowledge. But the irrational has also a different, an existential meaning. New passion is needed, a new passionate will, to melt down the congealed, determinate world and bring the world of freedom to light. And such a passion, such a passionate will can be set aflame on the summits of consciousness, after all the testing enquiries of reason. There is a primary, original passion, the passionate will, which is also the final and ultimate will. I call it messianic. It is only by messianic passion that the world can be transformed and freed from slavery.

Passion is by nature twofold, it can enslave and it can liberate. There is fire which destroys and reduces to ashes, and there is fire which purifies and creates. Jesus Christ said that he came to bring down fire from heaven and desired that it might be kindled. Fire is the great symbol of a primordial element in human life and in the life of the world. The contradictions of which the life of the world and of man is made up are akin to the fiery element, which is present even in our thinking. Creative thought, which experiences opposition and is set in motion by it, is fiery thought. Hegel understood this in the sphere of logic. But the flaming fiery basis of the world, to which men but rarely break through because of their dull prosaic everyday life and to which men of genius do break through, gives rise to suffering. Suffering may ruin men, but there is depth in it, and it can break through the congealed world of day-to-day routine.

Fire is a physical symbol of spirit. According to Heraclitus and Boehme the world is embraced by fire, and Dostoyevsky felt that the world was volcanic. And this fire is both in cosmic life and in the depth of man. Boehme revealed a longing, the longing of nothingness to become something, the primordial will out of the abyss. In Nietzsche, the dionysiac will to power, although it was expressed in an evil form, was the same fusing and flaming fire. Bergson's *élan vital,* although it is given too academic a form and smacks of biology, tells us that the metaphysical ground of the world is creative impulse and life. Frobenius, in the more restricted sphere of the philosophy of culture, speaks of alarm, the grip of emotion, and shock as creative springs of culture.[1] Shestov always speaks of a shock as a source of real philosophy. And in very truth shock is a source of strength in perceiving the mystery of human existence and of the existence of the world, the mystery of destiny. Pascal and Kierkegaard were people who had been subject to shocks of that kind. But their words were words of horror and almost of despair. But if it is in a state of horror and despair that man moves on his way, yet horror and despair are not a definition of what the world and man are in their primary

[1] See L. Frobenius: *Le Destin des civilisations.*

113

reality and original life. The primary reality, the original life is creative will, creative passion, creative fire. Out of this first source suffering, horror and despair do indeed arise. In the objective world and in appearances we already see the cooling process, and the realm of necessity and law. Man's answer to the call of God should have been creative act, in which the fire was still conserved. But the fall of man had as its result that the only possible response took the form of law.

In this the mystery of divine-human relations is hidden, and it is to be understood not in an objectified, but in an existential manner. But the creative passion is preserved in man even in his fallen state. It is most clearly seen in creative genius, and it remains unintelligible to the vast masses of mankind, submerged as they are in the daily dull routine. In the depth of man is hidden the creative passion of love and sympathy, the creative passion to know and give names to things (Adam gave names to things), the creative passion for beauty and power of expression. Deep down in man is a creative passion for justice, for taking control of nature: and there is a general creative passion for a vital exulting impulse, and ecstasy. On the other hand, the fall of the object world is the stifling of creative passion and a demand that it shall cool down.

The primary reality and original life shows itself to us in two forms: in the world of nature, and in the world of history. We shall see later on that these two forms of the world, as appearances, are linked with different sorts of time. While life in nature flows on in cosmic time, life in history moves forward in historical time. To metaphysics of the naturalistic type being is nature, not necessarily material, but also spiritual nature. Spirit is naturalized and understood as substance. That being so, history which is pre-eminently movement in time is subordinated to nature, and turned into a part of cosmic life. But the fundamental position of historiosophy, in opposition to the predominating naturalist philosophy, consists in just this, that it is not history which is a part of nature, but nature which is a part of history. In history the destiny and meaning of world life is brought to light.

It is not in the cycle of cosmic life that meaning can be revealed, but in movement within time, in the realization of the messianic hope. The sources of the philosophy of history are not to be found in Greek philosophy but in the Bible. Metaphysical naturalism, which regards spirit as nature and substance, is static ontologism. It makes use of the spatial symbolism of a hierarchical conception of the cosmos, not of symbols which are associated with time. But on the other hand to interpret the world as history, is to take a dynamic view of it, and this view understands the emergence of what is new.

Here there is a clash between two types of *Weltanschauung,* one of which may be described as cosmocentricism and the other as anthropocentricism. But nature and history are under the power of objectification. The only possible way out from this objectification is through history, through the self-revelation in it of meta-history. It is not found by submerging it in the cycle of nature. The way out is always bound up with a third kind of time, with existential time, the time of inward existence. It is only a non-objectified existential philosophy which can arrive at the mystery and meaning of the history of the world and of man. But when it is applied to history existential philosophy becomes eschatological.

The philosophy of history, which did not exist so far as Greek philosophy was concerned, cannot fail to be Christian. History has a meaning simply because meaning, the Logos, appeared in it; the God-man became incarnate, and it has meaning because it is moving towards the realm of God-Manhood. The theme of what in a derivative sense is called 'being' is concerned with the en-counter and the reciprocal action between primordial passionate will, primordial creative act, primordial freedom, and the Logos, Meaning. And these are flashes of freedom, will, longing and passion shining through by the power of the Logos-Meaning, through the acquisition of spirituality and a sense of spiritual freedom. Passion in cosmic life is irrational in character and sub-conscious, and it has to be transformed and become supra-rational and supra-conscious. We are told about the destructive nature of passion, and men assign a supremacy over the passion to reason and prudence. But the victory over evil and enslaving passions is also a passionate victory, it is the victory of radiant light, the light of a sun, not of objectifying reason. Is the absence of passion a mistake in nomenclature, or is it a mistaken idea? The spiritual sun is not dispassionate. The seed springs up out of the earth when the sun rays fall on it.

The latest attempt to construct an ontology is the work of Heidegger, and he claims that his ontology is existential.[1] It cannot be denied that Heidegger's thought displays great intensity of intellectual effort, concentration and originality. He is one of the most serious and interesting philosophers of our time. His chasing after new phrases and a new terminology is a little irritating, although he is a great master in this respect. In every metaphysical question he rightly takes the whole of metaphysics into view. One cannot but think it a revealing and astonishing thing that the latest ontology, at which this very gifted philosopher of the West has arrived, is not a theory of being, but of non-being, of nothing-ness. And the most up to date wisdom on the subject of the life of the world is expressed in the words 'Nichts nichtet'. The fact that Heidegger raises the problem of nothingness, of non-being, and that as contrasted with Bergson, he recognizes its existence, must be regarded as a service which we owe to him. In this respect a kinship with Boehme's teaching about the Ungrund may be noted.[2] Without nothingness there would be neither personal existence nor freedom.

But Heidegger is perhaps the most extreme pessimist in the history of philosophical thought in the West. In any case his pessimism is more extreme and more thorough-going than Schopenhauer's, for the latter was aware of many things which

[1] See his Sein und Zeit.   [2] See Heidegger: Was ist Metaphysik?

were a consolation to him. Moreover, he does not in actual fact give us either a philosophy of being, or a philosophy of *Existenz*, but merely a philosophy of *Dasein*. He is entirely concerned with the fact that human existence is cast out into the world. But this being cast out into the world, into *das man*, is the fall. In Heidegger's view the fall belongs to the structure of being, being strikes its very roots into commonplace existence. He says that anxiety is the structure of being. Anxiety brings being into time.

But from what elevation can all this be seen? What intelligible meaning can one give it? Heidegger does not explain whence the power of getting to know things is acquired. He looks upon man and the world exclusively from below, and sees nothing but the lowest part of them. As a man he is deeply troubled by this world of care, fear, death and daily dullness. His philosophy, in which he has succeeded in seeing a certain bitter truth, albeit not the final truth, is not existential philosophy, and the depth of existence does not make itself felt in it.

This philosophy remains under the sway of objectification. The state of being cast out into the world, into *das man*, is in fact objectification. But in any case this essay in ontology has almost nothing in common with the ontological tradition which descends from Parmenides and Plato. Nor is it a matter of chance, it is indeed full of significance, that this latest of ontologies finds its support in nothingness which reduces to nothing.

Does this not mean that it is necessary to reject ontological philosophy and go over to an existential philosophy of the spirit, which is not being but which is not non-being either?

In the next chapter we go on to discuss the problem of the individual and the universal, perhaps the most difficult problem of all.

CHAPTER IV

*1. The reality of the individual and the reality of the 'common'.
The controversy about universals. The common and the universal. The common as objectification. 2. Collective realities
and individual realities. Genus, individual, and personality.
3. The mistakes of German idealism. Personalism*

I

The controversy between the realists and the nominalists
on the subject of universals is regarded as characteristic of
mediaeval philosophy. But it is an everlasting controversy and is constantly being revived in new forms. It is being
renewed even in existential and personalist philosophy. In this dispute the issue cannot be decided in the sphere of logic, and each
side can bring plenty of arguments to the support of its position.
The process of thinking has in itself a tendency towards the
realism of concepts and readily comes under the sway of the
'common' which is established by itself. That which the subject
alienates from itself begins to appear to it as an objective reality.
To find a way out of the controversy which thus arises is possible
only through an egress beyond the bounds of abstract thought;
that is, by way of an integral act of the spirit which makes a
choice, and establishes values. Thought sets up a wrong statement
of the problem; it is, so to speak, in bondage to itself. The exteriorization which is brought about by thought is in fact an act of
self-absorption. There is here a paradox of pure thought which
has ceased to be a function of existence. It is only existentialist and
voluntarist thought which can acknowledge the primacy of the

118

individual over the common, and the sovereign value of personality as the existential centre.

Duns Scotus thought that the single and individual was the sole end of creation and the most important of things. But this cannot be discovered by abstract thought. As a matter of fact the three leading scholastic trends in the controversy about universals state the question in the wrong way. Some say *universalia sunt ante rem*, or, *universalia sunt realia*. The product of thought is projected into things. This is a typical result of objectification. Others say: *universalia in re*. This is an interior degree of objectification. But it must be admitted that conceptualism contains a greater measure of truth than realism and nominalism. A third group say: *universalia sunt post rem*. In this case thought regards itself as entirely dependent upon the empirical object world and speaks of what takes place as the result of the objectification of human existence. The fundamental error is the confusion of the universal with the common.

This confusion of the universal and the common already exists in Aristotle. In consequence of it, universals assume the character of being, which dominates over what is individual, although it has no concrete existence. The universal is quite certainly not the common, it is not the product of abstracting thought and by no means stands in opposition to what is individual. There may be an antithesis between universalism and individualism as philosophical trends of thought, but not between the universal and the individual. The concrete universal may be individual and individuality. The individual can include the universal.

The common, the generic, suppresses the individual and cannot impart any content to it. But the universal certainly does not suppress the individual. On the contrary it raises it to the fullness of existential content. The common is abstract and exists only in thought, which tends to self-alienation. The universal is concrete and is within actual existence as that which gives it qualitative value and fulfilment.

God is the most exalted of universals and at the same time He is the concretely individual. He is personal. God is the one true and admissible hypostatization of the universal. It is false to admit an ideal being outside creatures, and to make the creatures subject to this ideal being.[1] The concept is common and abstract, and to the concept the common and abstract is the primary reality, while the individual acquires a secondary, derivative significance. This view is characteristic of objectifying thought. Hence it is that for the theory of knowledge the problem is ever posed anew—how is the apprehension of reality possible through a concept, seeing that in reality everything is individual and unique? Do the abstract and universal concepts of the subject correspond with objective reality?

Hegel aimed at knowledge of the concrete universal (not of the common) but he does not provide it. His philosophy only brings to light the complexity of the problem and points to a new way of stating it. The realism of concepts which goes back to Greek philosophy, and which took control of the philosophy of the Middle Ages, was indeed the real source of rationalism, in spite of the fact that the reverse is usually supposed to be the case, as a result of the illusions of consciousness, the illusions of objectification.

Another side of this rationalism was the empiricism which was born of nominalism and recognized only rationalized and secondary experience. Consistent nominalism has never been thought out to the end. It ought to analyze not only the universal, but the individual also, and it cannot make a halt at any sort of concrete reality. No kind of concrete wholeness exists for nominalism, no concrete unity or concrete image. It is opposed to personalism no less than the realism of concepts when this latter is transferred to the collective entities. Nominalism and empiricism give rise to a false atomism. The antithesis of nominal-

[1] Festugière: *Contemplation et vie contemplative selon Platon,* a most remarkable book on Plato.

ism is integral intuition, the intuition of wholeness, thinking in terms of images, in which the intellectual is combined with the emotional.

Realism and nominalism, rationalism and empiricism are products of one and the same direction of the spirit towards self-alienation in the sphere of objectifying thought. What is in actual fact real, is the individual image, even to think about which individual images are necessary. Aristotle has been considered the source of moderate realism (by Thomas Aquinas, for example). But this moderate realism, which endeavours to rescue the individual, has all the same been based upon the deduction of the partial from the general, and has postulated the identity of rational thought with the forms of reality. To thought which issues from the fundamental conceptions of Greek philosophy the species has been more primary than the individual, man in general has been more primary than the concrete man, than Socrates, for instance. The partial exists through the species. Thus, for Platonism it is knowledge of the common only that is possible. In opposition to this stands the theory of knowledge according to which that which is individual is known, not by perception through the senses, which are common to all, but by spiritual intuition, which is unique and personal.

The realism of concepts gave rise to the reaction of extreme nominalism, which recognized the existence of universals only in words (Roscelin), the verbalism of Occam. But Occam was obliged to deny even the reality of the individual. It is existential personalism alone which can be set over against the erroneous and illusory solutions of the problem of the relation between the universal and the individual. According to existential personalism, the universal exists, but it exists as a qualification of personality. At the same time personalism breaks open the closed circle of individual consciousness in empiricism. In that case, the ontological method of deducing the truth of a thing from its concept is rejected. Ontologism in reality means not the primacy of being but the primacy of concept. This is one of the paradoxes which arise from the illusions of consciousness.

As opposed to Platonism and scholastic realism, as opposed to all forms of rationalism, what is true is not that the world of the senses is individual and unique, while the world of ideas, the noumenal world is the world of the common and the universal; the truth is that in the phenomenal world of the senses everything is brought into subjection to the common, to the species, to law, whereas in the noumenal world everything is individual and personal. Pantheism was the logical conclusion of the realism of concepts. Personalism ought to be the logical conclusion of the theory of knowledge which unmasks the illusions of objectification and of the dominance of the 'common'. According to Spinoza, God loves not individuals but eternal entities. But it is impossible to love eternal entities. It is precisely individual people who are loved by the Christian God.

Philosophical thought, having passed through Kant, ought to have arrived at a statement of the problem of the irrational and at a limitation of the application of concepts in knowledge. That which is individual is irrational, and the concept, whose attention is always directed towards the common, fails to grasp it. Kant himself had a notable doctrine of the specification of nature, which has been left in obscurity. Kant discloses a law of specification. Capacity for judgment is the possibility of thinking of the partial through the common.[1] The principle of teleology specifies general laws. In this way the possibility of getting to know what is individual is opened up. But all the same it is above all the tragedy of human knowledge which is revealed in Kant's philosophy. Knowledge rationalizes its subject matter and turns it into the common'. But the actual reality itself is individual and irrational. This means also that rational knowledge objectifies, and in objectification the truly existent thing and the truly existent person disappear.

[1] See Kant: *Kritik der Urteilskraft*.

Neo-Kantians of the type of Windelband and Rickert rely upon the problem of the irrational. Müller-Freienfells, a representative of the philosophy of life, says that the common is a product of the rationalization of what is individual.[1] Bergson, who follows a different path from that of Kant and the Kantians, arrives at the conclusion that reason does not take knowledge of life, and movement is unattainable by it. The intellect fabricates.[2] Bergson is here enunciating the same theme that I express in terms of objectification, though he makes use of a different terminology. He finds a way out towards reality. His thought is interesting: the same things which were discovered by the ancient Greeks as species are discovered by present day Europeans as laws. This may throw light upon the shackling of generic being by laws.

And what is intuition? Is it a vision of essential substances or a vision of individualities? The schools of philosophy are divided on the question. To Husserl, as to the Platonists, intuition is the vision of essential substances. This raises the age-long question, is the noumenal world individual, multiple and susceptible of movement, or is it single and immovable; do multiplicity and movement belong only to the phenomenal world? But if the phenomenal world, as the subject-matter of knowledge, is born of rationalization and conceptualization of a generalizing kind, it is precisely in it that what is individual and creatively free disappears, and the common is left supreme. The real problem of knowledge, however, consists in this: is it possible to arrive at universal knowledge of the individual, or does such knowledge refer only to the common?

Thinking about the individual is of a different character from thinking about the common, and what distinguishes it is precisely the fact that in it there is none of that division and of that loss of wholeness which accompany all objectifying knowledge. It is existential thinking, it reveals the apprehended reality as subject

[1] See Müller-Freienfells: *Philosophie der Individualität.*
[2] See *L'Évolution créatrice.*

not as object. This, in turn, is bound up with the relevance of intuitive images in knowledge. Intuition, however, must be understood not passively, as for instance in Lossky, to whom objective reality is immediately present in the process of cognition, but creatively and actively. Intuition is not only intellectual in character, an element which is emotional and volitional also enters into it. It is a passionate break-through of the will towards the light, towards truth as a whole. Then the universal is revealed in the concrete and individual without crushing it and turning it into a means. Truth is not common and abstract, truth is concrete, it is individually personal. Indeed, the whole pure Truth is a living Personal Being, it is the incarnate Logos.

Genus has two meanings; it is used in a natural and biological sense, and also in a logical sense. The two meanings are connected with each other. The generic in the field of logic is adjusted to the generic in the sphere of nature and corresponds to it. The genus crushes the individual, although it is from the bosom of the genus that the individual emerges. In the logical scheme, the generic crushes what is individual. Life in the phenomenal world is a generic process, it is life shared in common. We shall see that human personality is a break-through and a rupture in this natural world, in which the generic and the common play a dominating part.

There is a dualism running through the life of the world, it is not continuous and all of a piece. Present-day physics and notably the quantum theory, give a special meaning to discontinuity. Neither the philosophy nor the science of our day recognizes that evolutionary monistic philosophy of the nineteenth century which was bound up with the idea of continuity. The individual person is a discontinuity, an interruption. Number is already an interruption. But the generic process of life which subordinates individuality to itself and crushes it, points to a tendency towards continuity, and in the sphere of logic this finds expression in the power of the common. As I have said many times, the common is the offspring of objectification and finds both biological and logical expression. The individual becomes a part of the genus, while personality is given a normative character.

Simmel speaks of the dualism of the stream of life and of individual form; and Jaspers refers to the position of spirit between chaos and form. This is one and the same theme, expressed in different ways. The danger of the philosophy of life lies in the fact that it may regard the stream of life as the primary reality; that is to say, it may regard the generic and the common as primary, while it looks upon what is individual as secondary and derivative. Existential and personalist philosophy, on the other hand, does not acquiesce in thinking of what is individual as a part of the universal. It does not consent to the subordination of the personal to the common. In its view the individual includes the universal.

In actual fact, being is always a generic principle; there is for being no primogeniture, no primordial status assigned to personality. And in the apprehension of being the logos is adjusted to the generic and the common; it finds itself in difficulties in apprehending the individual and personal. Consciousness itself is understood as a generic process. Such is the 'consciousness in general' of German idealism. Prince S. Trubetzkoy uses the expression 'metaphysical socialism' to indicate the generic character of consciousness.

Reality has a logical ideal foundation, that is to say a foundation which is generic, universally common, 'objective'. But in reality, the universally common, the ideal, the generic, the 'objective' proceeds from the subjective work of the reason, from a process of objectification. Deeper than the ideal logical foundations of world reality, lies the act through which all reality exists. The generic logical process is a process of socialization and the form of social relations among men sets its stamp upon the very categories of logical thought. The compelling power of logic is a social compulsion. A conflict goes on in the world between freedom and generic being, between spirit and necessity. Man ought to be dependent not upon generic nature, not upon the object, but upon spirit. But the paradoxical and conflicting character of the relations between the individually personal and the generic, objective nature of the world, cannot be resolved within the confines of this world and the limits of conceptual logical thought.

2

The question of what are known as collective, suprapersonal realities and communities, or collective 'symphonic' personalities, is one of great difficulty and it still remains an unsolved problem. It is, of course, connected with the controversy about realism and nominalism, but present-day thought, which is steeped in sociology, raises the question from entirely new angles. The conflict is carried on not so much in the sphere of logic as it was in mediaeval philosophy, as in the sphere of sociology. And it is quite understandable that the question should become particularly acute in the realm of sociology.

The question of the sense in which collective communities exist and represent realities, and whether it is possible to recognize the existence of collective personalities cannot be decided by rational, conceptual knowledge. The decision presupposes a choice, a line taken by the will, an act of moral appraisal.[1] The choice of the will and the establishment of a hierarchy of values create realities. The act of volition is objectified, the chosen qualities are hypostatized. Man lives in the midst of realities which are created by himself. What presents itself to him as most objectively actual and in the highest degree real, is the objectification of the subject's intention, the hypostatization of its qualitative states.

Man's inclination for self-alienation and self-enslavement

---

[1] N. Mikhailovsky, a sociologist of the seventies of the last century, expressed some very true thoughts about the subjective method in sociology; he fought for individuality, and exposed the organic theory of society which is hostile to the individual. But his mind was not trained in philosophy; he was a positivist, and was unable to provide a basis for his point of view.

is one of the most astonishing things in the life of the world. To the man who has made for himself an idol out of the nation or the State, the nation and the State are realities immeasurably greater and more 'objective' than man, than personality; in any case realities which are more primary and more dominant. All nationalists and étatists are like that. The nation and the State do, of course, represent a certain degree of reality in world life, but their overwhelming grandiose and compelling 'objectivity' is created by the 'subjective' state of society, by the beliefs of the people, by the objectification of a state of mind.

The supremacy of society over the human person is a fact which is both not open to doubt and objectively coercive to those who are overwhelmed by a view of human existence from outside, or by an idolatrous attitude towards society as the highest thing in their scale of values. Such is the point of view of sociologists of the type of Dürkheim. In exactly the same way one might assert the absolute supremacy and dominance of the world as a whole, the cosmos, over man and his interior life, and thus fall into an idolatrous attitude to the cosmos.[1]

In all these cases the nation, the State, society or the cosmos are regarded as primary totalities and realities in relation to which man is nothing but a subordinate part. The genus is a greater and more primary reality than the individual, and this alike in the sphere of logic and in the realm of biology. Such is the 'objective' 'eccentric' way of regarding the world, society and man. It is impossible to confute those who have taken a firm stand upon such a point of view and solidly established themselves in projected realities. The cosmic whole, society, the nation and the State are linked with powerful human emotions. And the most difficult thing of all is to refute judgments which are born of such emotions when they are exteriorized and turned into objective realities. The realism of concepts when transferred to sociology is protected by the emotions, passions and wills of men and women and of

[1] See my *Slavery and Freedom*. An Essay in Personalist Philosophy.

social groups. A radical change of thought is needed if judgments in this field of thought are to be changed.

The way in which Marx (who naïvely considered himself a materialist) applied logical realism in the mediaeval sense to his conception of class as a primary reality on a deeper level than society or than man, is astounding. The idea of the proletariat in Marx is not a scientific but a messianic idea. He fought passionately and with indignation for the liberation of the working class from the oppression and slavery which is its lot in capitalist society. And he objectified his passionate emotions, he hypostatized the oppression and the revolt of labouring men, he turned moral judgments into ontological judgment. The labouring class exists as an empirical reality within capitalist societies and Marx said a great deal that is true about its position. But it certainly does not exist as a reality that can be apprehended by the mind; in the Marxist sense it does not exist as a universal. In the same way there exist no similar realities of the cosmic whole, society, the nation or the State; they are objectifications and hypostatizations of ancient emotions, desires and passions.

Collective realities are the outcome of objectification in various degrees, of the projection into the external of states of consciousness and the arranging of them in hierarchical order. Existentially, at the deeper, subjective level, which does not belong to the objective natural and social world, I do not accept the mastery and dominance of the genus over the individual, or of the nation, State or society over human personality. I do not want to make a corresponding objectification; I take my stand upon a different scale of values, one in which human personality, unique, unrepeatable and irreplaceable is the highest value of all. Spirit, which reveals itself in the depth of the subject, makes its judgments in a different way, and establishes realities in another fashion, than nature and society, which have revealed themselves in the object. The collective group mind, which always objectifies, distorts human judgments about realities.

Logical realism may be a form of social suggestion and a state of hypnosis. And human personality is called upon to wage a heroic struggle for its emancipation. The fight for personality is a fight on behalf of the spirit. Nor is there a greater foe of spirit and spiritual freedom than objectified collective realities. And this foe is so much the more terrible in that it pretends to be spirit. It is an astonishing thing that again nominalism, having reached its triumph in positivism, has led to new forms of the realism of concepts, for example, in sociology. At the present time man experiences real social slavery. The socialization and nationalization of slavery is taking place.

Collective realities may be regarded as individualities, but not by any means as personalities; they have no existential centre and are not capable of experiencing suffering and joy. The existential subject, whether of the cosmos, of society, of the nation or of the State, can be sought only in existing man, in the qualitative character of personality. The universal is found in what is individual, the suprapersonal in the person. Man is a microcosmos and a microtheos. It is in the depth of man that world history works itself out and society is assembled and dissolved. But the microcosmic nature of man undergoes a process of exteriorization, it is projected into the external, its qualities are hypostatized, and realities are objectified which have no existential centre.

There are no such things as nations, States and societies existing as collective common realities which stand on a higher level than personality and turn it into a part of themselves. But there is such a thing as, for instance, 'Russianness' which exists as a qualitative factor uniting like to like among people and charging the life of personality to the full with concrete content. There is that community and communion among men and women without which personality is unable to realize itself, and there are functions of the State which are necessary to the corporate life of men.

Man is both a cosmic being and a social being. Personality realizes itself in both cosmic and social relations. But projection into the external, and alienation from self, the state of affairs in which nature and society are represented as acting upon man from without, and with compelling force, are evidence of the Fall of Man. There is nothing universal outside human personality and above it, but the universal does exist within it. And when this universal is transcendent, it is still all the while within man and not outside him.

Leibniz would not allow the action of monad upon monad, acting from without. There was a measure of truth in this. But a solution of the problem of interaction in the spirit of occasionalism is external and unsatisfying. The monad is not bottled up in itself, it does not lack windows and doors.

But the fall of the monads at once finds expression in their seclusion from true communion and unity and in their excessive exposure to coercive action from without. The monad loses its character of a microcosm as a result of alienation, the projection into the external of that which ought to be within, and is subjected to the forcible action of nature and society in their capacity of forces established as external things. The sun no longer shines from within man. Nature has become the object of external technical activity on the part of man. Nature as subject is to him a hidden thing. Personality is empty unless it is filled with suprapersonal values and qualities, unless by means of creative acts it moves outwards and upwards beyond its own confines, unless it triumphs over itself and in so doing realizes itself.

But man has an unconquerable disposition to idolatry and servitude; he inclines to alienate the depth of his own proper nature and to turn it into a reality which stands over him and issues its orders to him. A certain element of truth about the alienation of human nature and its projection into the external was revealed to Feuerbach, but it is truth which is related not to God, but to human powers and qualities which are represented as realities external to man.[1] In objectification, in the self-alienation of spirit, the genus

[1] There are flashes of genius in Feuerbach's *Das Wesen des Christentums*.

and the generic dominate over what is individual and personal. Sham universals and a false 'common' are accepted not by way of abstraction from sensuous experience as the empiricists suppose, but by way of exiling into the external that which is interior and a datum in the spiritual experience of man.

As part of the problem of collective realities the question of the Church is one of especial difficulty. In what sense is the Church a reality? The Church as an objective reality which stands at a higher level than man is a social institution, and in that sense is the objectification of religious life; it is an adaptation of spirit to social conditions. But in its depth the Church is the life of the spirit, it is spiritual life. It is a miraculous life which is not subject to social laws; it is a community, a brotherhood of men in Christ. It is the mysterious life of Christ within a human communion, it is a mysterious entering into communion with Christ. In this sense the Church is freedom and love, and there is no external authority in it, there is no necessity and no coercive force. What is in it is freedom enlightened by grace. And this is what Khomyakov calls *sobornost*. *Sobornost* is not a collective reality which stands higher than man and issues its orders to him. It is the highest spiritual qualitative power in men; it is entering into the communion of the living and the dead. This *sobornost* can have no rational juridical expression. Each must take upon himself responsibility for all. No one may separate himself from the world whole, although at the same time he ought not to regard himself as part of a whole.

The whole tragic character of the history of the Church lies in this its two-sided nature. The Church is not a personality, it is not an ontological reality in relation to which human personality would be a subordinate part. The Church as an ontological reality which stands above man, is the objectification of inward *sobornost*; it is a projection of it into the external. There is no existential centre of the Church except Christ himself. The expression 'Church consciousness' is merely a metaphorical phrase like the expression 'national consciousness' or 'class consciousness'. The objectification of the Church has been a source of slavery; it has also given rise to the clericalism which has been so destructive to spiritual life.

The traditional way of putting the problem about the visible and the invisible Church which arises in course of disputes between the Orthodox and Roman Catholics on the one hand and the Protestants on the other, is mistaken. The distinction between 'visible' and 'invisible' is a relative one, and the marks of visibility and invisibility change in accordance with the volitional acts of those who form the judgment. In the celebration of the Mystery of the Eucharist there are signs which are outward and visible to sensuous perception. But at the same time there is no doubt that the sacrament of the Eucharist is invisible, and is accomplished in a mysterious sphere which is hidden from the phenomenal world, a sphere which is accessible to faith alone, which draws aside the veil from things which are invisible. The Church is visible, it has a whole series of visible marks: the sacred building constructed of stone, the act of worship which is expressed in human words and action, the parochial meetings, the authority of the hierarchy which is very similar to hierarchical authority in the State. But the mysterious presence of Christ in the Church is invisible, it is not offered to the perception of the senses, it is discovered only by faith.

The Church is a visible reality, but this visible reality has a symbolic character and in it there are given only signs of a different reality, which is spiritual. The noumenal side of the Church is real spirit, not nature and society; it is the Kingdom of God which cometh not with observation. The phenomenal side of the Church, however, is the objectification and symbolization of spirit. The Church as spirit is a reality which exists within human beings, not outside them and not above them as objective universals do. In this sense the Church is an illuminated and transfigured world, an illuminated and transfigured society.

I repeat, the question of the supreme value of personality, of the supremacy of what is personal and individual over the common, and the controversy about universals, are not open to intellectual and rational solution; a solution is to be found only through the moral will which establishes values, only through volitional choice. The secret of personality, the existential mystery, is revealed only in the creative life of the spirit as a whole. It is a spiritual conflict. False objectified universals, false collective realities must be overthrown in the combat which the spirit wages.

3

The establishment of value is of the first importance in the matter of judgments about reality. People regard such and such a thing as a reality, and even as the highest value, because they had already chosen it as a value beforehand. The State is accepted as an ontological reality because people see a high value in it, because they love the principle of authority. This phenomenal natural world, this 'objective' world they look upon as absolutely real. They bow with reverent submission before the grandiose scale of it, before its coercive power, because they are tied to it and adjusted to it by the whole structure of their minds. Man always lives not only in the 'empirical' world but also in the world of 'ideas', and the ideas by which it is determined are of a character which is above all concerned with value.

Up to the time of birth the soul has been united with the universal mind. The union of soul and body gives rise to a relation with the world of sense, but the recollection of ideas remains. Philosophy does not know what this particular man here is, but only what man in general is. Such was the doctrine of Platonism. It was not a doctrine of achieved personality, but of achieved race, achieved society. The individual soul emanates from the universal soul.

Plato's influence upon European thought has been enormous and decisive. The distinction between the world of ideas, the noumenal world, and the phenomenal world of the senses was a great discovery. But the secret of personality was not revealed. It was not revealed in Indian philosophy either, to which the existence of the separate soul is an illusion.[1] In Atman the individual ego loses itself. There is an identification of all souls with the universal soul. Such is the meaning of *tat twam asi*. It is true that Jainism admits the existence of a plurality of souls and gives an appearance of preserving individuality, but the prevalent teaching is otherwise.

Mediaeval scholastic philosophy, and Thomist philosophy in particular, found great difficulty in the problem of individuality. The individualization of matter in reality indicated the denial of the individual. As a matter of philosophy Avveroes was in the right. The quarrel with him was on religious grounds, since the Christian faith demanded individual immortality. Form was universal. This meant that only what is universal could be founded on the basis of spirit; what is individual could not be so grounded. Plurality and, therefore, individuality were regarded as belonging to the world of the senses only.

The most astonishing thing is the fate of German metaphysics in regard to this question. It began as a philosophy of the ego, of the subject, and arrived at the denial of the individual ego, it arrived at a monism in which personality disappears. In Fichte the individual ego is merely a part of the great whole. Personality disappears in the contemplation of the end. The ego from which Fichte starts on his philosophical journey is not an individual ego. To him the individual man is an instrument of reason. This constitutes the difference between Fichte and Kant who alone among the great idealists in German philosophy came close to personalism. Hegel was a most extreme anti-personalist. To him to think

[1] The reservation must be made that not all the theories of Indian philosophy have been monistic and denied what is individual. Vaiseshika is a pluralist ontology. Ramanuja came near to theism. But a monistic interpretation of the identity of Atman and Brahman and of the illusory character of a pluralist world has been predominant.

meant to bring the universal into form.[1] Religion was to Hegel the self-consciousness of the absolute spirit in the finite. Religion was not a relation of man to God but the self-consciousness of God in man. It might be said that the philosophy of Hegel enhances man immeasurably in making him the source of the self-consciousness of God, and at the same time completely degrades him by denying all independence to human nature. This is characteristic of monism. Schopenhauer was also an anti-personalist, though in a different way.

German idealism sacrificed the soul in the interests of absolute spirit. The absolute spirit crushes the personal spirit, it devours man. And there ought to be a revolt of man, a rebellion of the human soul against the absolute spirit. The philosophy of absolute spirit began with the proclamation of the autonomy of human reason. It ended in the denial of human personality, in its subjugation to collective communities and objectified universals. Philosophical thought has disclosed a very complex dialectic in the relations between the individual and the common, between personality and universals. A dialectic in the relations between personality and society is to be found in Plato, Rousseau, Hegel, Feuerbach, Max Stirner, Marx, Nietzsche, Dostoyevsky, K. Leontiev and Kierkegaard. The political theorists, Rousseau and Marx, who were inspirers of revolution, constructed ideologies which are highly unfavourable to personality, to the very statement of the problem of personality. Dostoyevsky and Kierkegaard enunciated the problem of personality and personal destiny more trenchantly than anyone else.

I have already written enough about the distinction between the individual and personality.[2] I repeat that the individual is a naturalistic and sociological category. The individual is born within the generic process and belongs to the natural world.

[1] See Hegel's small logic in his *Enzyclopädie* and the great *Science of Logic*.
[2] See a book by Ch. Baudouin which has recently been published, *Découverte de la Personne*.

Personality, on the other hand, is a spiritual and ethical category. It is not born of a father and mother, it is created spiritually and gives actual effect to the divine idea of man. Personality is not nature, it is freedom, and it is spirit. It might be said that personality is not man as phenomenon, but man as noumenon, if such terminology had not too much of an epistemological flavour about it.

Of the individual it may be said that he is part of the race and of society, but an inseparable part of it; whereas personality is not to be thought of as a part of any whole whatever. It is outside the world, it is spiritual and it invades the natural and social order with a claim to be its own end and the supreme value, with a claim to be a whole and not a part. Human personality is a break with the world order. It is an integral form, it is not constituted from parts, and it has mutual relations with other forms, social and physical. But man is spiritual personality, whereas other forms may not be personalities. Totality, wholeness, the supremacy of the whole over the parts—such ideas have reference to personality only.

The natural world, society, the State, the nation and the rest are partial, and their claim to totality is an enslaving lie, which is born of the idolatry of men. Collective substances (aggregates) are not real. The fact is that the soul within its own thought imparts a unity to them. The soul of man consolidates realities which bring it into subjection to necessity and into a state of servitude. It is true that such a whole as, for instance, society, is not only the sum of its parts and a social union of human beings, it also possesses properties which do not exist in men and women taken separately. The atomic doctrine of society is an error. But this truth has no sort of bearing upon our subject of personality. The universal, the cosmic, the social, are within human personality. The separate man is a cosmic and social being to start with; he is already a whole world.

Human personality is not to be thought of in the abstract and

136

in isolation. It is a cosmic and social being, not because it is determined by nature and society in the sense of having a cosmic and social content bestowed upon it from outside, but because man bears within him the image of God and is summoned to the Kingdom of God. In the process of its self-realization personality ought to carry on a campaign against the objectification which enslaves it, against the estrangement and exteriorization which creates the order of nature and brings men into subjection to itself as part of it.

The existence of personality with its infinite aspirations, with its unique and unrepeatable destiny is a paradox in the objectified world of nature. It is placed face to face with a world environment which is alien to it, and it has tried to accept that world as a world harmony. The conflict of human personality with the world harmony, the challenge of the world harmony, is a fundamental theme in personalist philosophy. No one has stated it with such power and trenchancy as Dostoyevsky. The world and world harmony must be brought to an end for the very reason that the theme of personality is insoluble within the confines of the world and history, and because the world harmony in this æon of the world is a mockery of the tragic fate of man.

The supreme value of personality, the supreme truth of personalism cannot be demonstrated as a proposition of objective ontology, it is affirmed by the moral will which assumes that value is a choice on the part of freedom. The supremacy of freedom over being is the supremacy of ethics over ontology. Personality is an exception. The apprehension of personality is the apprehension of an exception. But the exceptional apprehension of the individual may be unconditional and absolute. It is a passionate apprehension and the revelation which is granted to it is not of an object but of the subject.

137

PART THREE

Being and Creativity
The Mystery of Newness

CHAPTER V

1. Being is distorted and compressed by evil. The inconsistency of monism and of the philosophy of all-in-one. 2. Weakness of rational explanations of the origin of evil. Criticism of the traditional doctrines of the Providence of God in the world. Personality and world harmony. 3. There is no objective world as one whole. The mysterious nature of freedom.

I

S. Frank who professed the philosophy of the all-in-one was constrained to say that the fact of the existence of evil is a scandal in that philosophy.[1] I should say that the problem of evil is a scandal to all monistic philosophy and so it is also to the traditional doctrine of Divine Providence. The world 'lieth in evil', in the life of the world evil predominates over good. But the origin of evil remains a most mysterious and inexplicable thing. Being is twisted out of shape by evil. How can an optimistic monist ontology be maintained in face of the immensity of this distortion?

Ontological philosophy regards being as the highest value and good, it accepts it as truth, goodness and beauty. Ontology says its yes to being and to non-being its no. The element of appraisal enters into the very formation of the concept of being. Plato affirmed the supremacy of the good over being. But those who recognized the supremacy of being, have by that very fact acknowledged being as good, as both the source and the criterion of the good. An appraising moral element cannot be dissociated even from purely ontological philosophy. Being is regarded as the highest idea, the supreme idea, and the existence of evil being

[1] See his *The Unfathomable.*

141

is denied. The antithesis of the supreme good of being is not a different being, but non-being, nothingness, the absence of good, a deficiency.

Some of the doctors of the Church, St. Gregory of Nyssa, for instance, and St Augustine, have been of the opinion that evil is non-being. The philosophy of life replaces being by life, and sees the highest good in life, in life at its maximum, and the diminution of life and the absence of it, is what it sees as evil. But alike for ontological philosophy and for the philosophy of life the existence of evil in the world, the immense scale of it and its triumph remain a scandal. Why have this beneficent being and this beneficent life been disfigured by evil? From whence has evil made its appearance—from being itself or from life itself, or does it come from some other source? Why do not the goodness of being and the goodness of life rule decisively in the world, why is the intrusion of non-being and death possible, where does the power of nothingness come from?

In order to save the philosophy of the all-in-one and uphold the world harmony, a theory has been concocted according to which evil exists only in the parts, and is disconcerting only to such people as devote their attention to the parts. But so far as the whole is concerned evil does not exist; for those who contemplate the whole, it disappears. Evil is only the shadow which belongs of necessity to the light. Even such people as St Augustine have held to this anti-Christian and unethical view. The theodicy of Leibniz is permeated with it.

But such a denial of the existence of evil in the world is a mockery of the measureless suffering of man and of all created things. All those who uphold the traditional doctrine of Providence are obliged to maintain an attitude of unconcern in the face of the injustice and wrong of the world, and they have contrived to turn even hell into a good. It is essential not only to the recognition and explanation of the fact that evil exists, but for the very existence of man and the world as a possibility at all, that a dualistic movement should be taken for granted. But this dualistic movement must be thought of dialectically. It must not be converted into a dualistic ontology, which is just as much a mistake as a monistic ontology. Human thought has an unconquerable tendency to turn either towards monism (pantheism) or towards dualism. It tends to turn the dialectical movements of thought into a static ontology. But both the one theory and the other are nothing but a limited form of rationalism which is liable to be superseded.

Every system of identity inclines to the denial of evil and of freedom, or else it is obliged to betray itself, as was the case with Schelling. It is an interesting fact that both the actively negative and the actively positive attitude to the world may alike be associated with a strong ethical sense. Ethics, which are especially sensitive to evil and suffering do not deny the world in general, but they deny this world, they repudiate this present state of the world.

Everything insists upon our admitting the existence not only of being, but also of non-being, of the dark abyss which precedes the very identification of being and the very distinction between good and evil. This non-being is both lower than being and higher than being. Or rather, it would be more exact to say that non-being does not exist, but that it has an existential significance. Dualism, polarity, the conflict between opposed principles is an existential fact. It is not the case that we are obliged to say that evil is non-being, but that the emergence of evil presupposes the existence of non-being and that it is inexplicable on the assumption that being is a system which is locked up in itself.

2

I have already said that all attempts at a rational explanation of evil are frustrated by inconsistency. An ontology of evil is impossible and it is a very good thing that it is impossible, for it would be a justification of evil. It was an ontology of evil that gave rise to an ontology of hell, and that was represented as a triumph of good. But evil and hell may be regarded as merely human experience as it moves on its way, and they may be described in terms of spiritual experience.

Here we meet with a paradoxical corollary. Out of a false ontological monism arose a false ontological and eschatological dualism—heaven which is the Kingdom of God, and hell, the kingdom of the devil. Admittedly, the acceptance of the principle of dualism in relation to the world is primarily ethical and may lead to eschatological monism, to the transformation of all things and to salvation. This world 'lieth in evil', but it can be overcome, the evil of it can be conquered, victory over it can be achieved beyond its own confines. 'I have overcome the world.' Further, the victory over evil and over evil men is not punishment, it is not the casting of them into the eternal flames of hell. It is transformation and enlightenment, the dispersal of the phantom world of evil as a dreadful nightmare.

Perhaps the most profound of all thought on this subject was that of Jacob Boehme when he said that the Fall arose from evil imagination. It may be that a deepening of Boehme's thought is the one and only path to a solution of the problem of evil. It was a very difficult matter for Plato and also for Plotinus, in view of their intellectualism, to explain whence evil arose. Greek metaphysics saw the source of evil in matter. But this was merely an indication of the limitations of Greek thought. Socrates regarded ignorance as the source of evil. Knowledge disperses it. Man is by nature disposed towards the good. There is no choice by the will. The Greeks did not understand metaphysical freedom. The Socratic solution remains classical for all forms of intellectualism. It is to be found in Leo Tolstoy. It is enough to be conscious of what the good is, for the evil to disappear. Boehme's voluntarism is the antithesis of this. A dark will exists at the basis of world life and victory over it cannot be attained by intellectual means, by the power of the mind alone.

St Augustine was one of the first to part company with Greek intellectualism in the interpretation of evil and freedom. But he turned right in the opposite direction. In his view there is freedom to act in the direction of evil, but not in the direction of good. Evil is to be conquered only by grace. But the reprobate, according to him, serve the order of this world. From St Augustine a dialectic of freedom and grace has derived which has completely occupied all Christian thought in the West, both Catholic and Protestant. In Boehme, however, something new is opened up both in relation to the thought of the ancient world and in relation to St Augustine.

A great step forward was taken by German idealism at the beginning of the nineteenth century. It disclosed a dialectic which not only belonged to the sphere of logic, but was also an ontic dialectic. Spirit does not act without antithesis and without a limit. 'No' belongs to the ego. The negative is a moment of the positive. Absolute spirit makes an antithesis for itself, evil is the surmounted moment of its own self. This has not proved a solution of the problem of evil owing to the monism of that philosophy. But the possibility was revealed of a dialectical instead of a static interpretation of evil, of evil in process. Relativism was a danger which lay in wait for Hegel, but he understood the dynamic of spiritual and historical life better than other philosophers.

Hegel's philosophy is not a static philosophy of unity, it is a dynamic philosophy. He does not disclose evil from the point of view of world order and harmony, he sees in it the impelling forces of world history, envisaging everywhere a dialectical conflict of opposites. But this is not a conflict which is waged by human beings, nor a struggle of freedom with necessity. It is a conflict in which human beings are moved by universal forces, by the universal Spirit, and freedom is the child of necessity. The question of evil is put in other terms by personalist philosophy and its solution sought in a different way. The subject is developed through a dualistic movement of spiritual conflict, of freedom striving with necessity, the personal with the common, the subjective with the objective.

The problem of evil exposes the fundamental mistake of the evolutionary monistic interpretation of the world process (such an interpretation may be spiritual just as it may be naturalistic). It takes the erroneous view that there is in the world as a whole, in its historical process a progressive 'furbishing', which is the direct expression of spirit or the direct operation of God. This is a mistaken interpretation of objectification as a disclosure of noumena in phenomena, as a realization of spirit in history. Subjective spirit becomes objective spirit and behind it absolute spirit stands and acts.

Such is the optimistic monism of Hegel. In the same way he mistakenly sees in the world process a continuous teleological process. This idea of teleology, whether immanent in the world or transcending it, has been put to very bad use, and by means of it many things have been justified which ought not to have received justification. The ancient Greeks had more right on their side in thinking that *Moira* reigns over world life. But that is the realm of fatalism, not of teleology. An enormous part is played in the world not only by inevitable necessity but also by unforeseeable and inexplicable chance. Chance will be recognized more and more by science, which is freeing itself from the idea of hypostatized regularity, which is due to a false outlook upon the world.[1]

There was no chance to primitive minds, but neither was there to the enlightened people of the nineteenth century in the pride of their scientific outlook. They have, however, to move on to a still higher degree of enlightenment. Darwinism was still under the control of optimistic teleology. Those adaptations survive most which are also the best. But the real fact is that in this world the worst are the most adaptable. They possess the greatest aptitude to survive and triumph, whereas the best are exposed to persecution, and perish. There is in the world a partial teleology,

[1] See Borel: *Le Hasard*, and M. Bole: *Les certitudes du hasard.*

146

that is to say in regard to the separate parts of the world, to separate groups, but there is no teleology as a universal principle. The idea of teleology was due to a mistaken confusion of the ethical with the ontological, of obligation with being.

In Fichte's view an absolutely good world was the only possible world, because he regarded an absolutely good world as a matter of obligation. Fichte taught that man ought to free himself from fear in the face of necessity, which was created by himself. But this is evidence of a conflict of the spirit. This world inspires fear in the face of necessity, and at the same time an attitude of submissiveness towards it. There is in it no immanent progressive revelation of spirit; no regular development which must lead on to the highest goal. Hopes of that kind cannot be made to rest upon processes of objectification, upon the ejection of man into the objective world.

In actual fact a conflict goes on between spirit and natural necessity, a striving of personality with the objective world, a conflict which God in man wages with the 'world', which in its fallen state has lost its freedom. Real development and progress in the world are the result not of a regularly-working and necessary process, but of creative acts, of the invasion of the realm of necessity by the realm of freedom. There is nothing more untrue and enslaving than to invest with a sacrosanct character all those concrete forms which have found embodiment in history, those solid bodies of history, in which men are wont to see either the direct action of the Divine Spirit or a manifestation of objective spirit.

The truth is that all these ' sacred ' historical embodiments have been relative forms of objectification, an adjustment of the spirit to the weighty burden of the world in its disintegrated and at the same time shackled condition.

The theme of a tragic conflict between personality and 'world harmony', between personality and the world process remains the fundamental theme. It is the theme of Ivan Karamazov. To Dostoyevsky this was a matter of his own experience, it was like a violent shock in which something was revealed. The theme is very Russian, and it enters to a small extent into the highly socialized thought of the West. It is *par excellence* a theme of existential philosophy, for no solution of it is to be found within the bounds of history and it requires an end to history. History ought to come to a conclusion, because it turns human personality into a means to an end, because in it every living generation merely manures the soil for the benefit of the generation which follows, and for which the same fate awaits. History must have an end also because it is based upon a terrible breach between ends and means.

The end of history is not only a truth of religious revelation but also a moral postulate of existential philosophy. That is why it is so important to grasp the fact that the objective world does not exist as a whole, as a cosmos; it is partial. The cosmos is a regulative idea. The cosmos is still to be created, and it must be created; it will make its appearance as a result of the transformation of the world. The phrase 'world harmony' is quite certainly not applicable to this world; it is a false idea which acts as a palliative to evil and is at variance with truth and right.

This world is tortured by rancorous hatred and cruel animosity. Human history presents a hideous spectacle of pitiless wars among people, nations and classes. A state of peace among men exists for a mere brief moment, as a breathing space, even the *pax Romana* did not last long. The vision of world harmony is the image of a world which can be grasped by the mind, and which anticipates the transformation of the world. The beauty of this world, the beauty of man, of nature and of works of art, all this is a mark of the partial transformation of the world; it is a creative breakthrough towards the other world.

The only possible way of thinking about a world harmony and a world order is by making it part of eschatology, by regarding it as the coming of the Kingdom of God, which is not a 'world', not an objective order. Monism and the philosophy of the all-in-one are possibilities only as an end of this world, as an end of objectification. For this world, on the other hand, dualism remains in power. The idea of 'being' has been a compromise between two worlds and has hidden the eschatological mystery from view. But dualism indicates not a transcendent breach between two worlds; it points to a conflict and it is a summons to creative action.

The motive which led to investing kingship and other historical institutions with a sacred character is plainly sociological. In order to force the masses of mankind into submission, discipline and order, it was necessary to inspire them with a belief in the sanctity of authority, of the State, of the nation, of war, to make them believe that the subordination of the individual to the common, of the person to the race, was sacrosanct. A fiction and a lie were required for the government of men and peoples. And fear lest this lie should be exposed has risen to an insane degree, men were in dread lest the disclosure of the truth should lead to the collapse of society. How great a value the Roman Catholic Church has set upon such a lie, as, for instance, the Donation of Constantine and the False Decretals, already exposed as it was!

Nations cannot exist without myths nor can even the power to govern human societies exist without them. Myths unite, reduce to submission, and inspire. Society is protected by them, and by means of them revolutions are brought about. Such myths are those of the sacrosanct character of kingly power and of papal authority, or of the sanctity of the *volonté générale*, of popular sovereignty in a democracy, of the sacrosanct character of a chosen class or a chosen race, of the sanctity of the Leader, and all the rest. All these are fictions which are built up in the collective social process. They are of enormous strength even in the life of the Churches and tradition is to some extent filled with them.

This investing with a sacrosanct character is a social act on the part of the collective and is brought about in the name of the collective. Could societies and peoples exist by pure truth, without an alloy of falsehood, without fictions which are practically useful in social life, without the sanctions, the inspiration and the safeguards which the myths supply? Theologians recognize the existence of economy in the life of the Church. This category of economy has been extended even to the relation of the Holy Trinity to the world. In economy relativity reigns, and compromise with the state of the world. In every system of teaching there is this element of relativity.

I may be told that I am denying the right of the relative, which answers to the condition of the world of men, and that I am demanding the absolute. But this is not the case. It is precisely the giving of a sacred character to the relative which is a process of making it absolute. It is suggesting to people that phenomena which are entirely relative and acts which are far from sacred, are endowed with a sacred authority and spring from a sacred source. But people and nations ought to have been re-educated into recognizing the significance of the relative, as relative, without any enslaving sacred sanctions. Authority, any form of authority, is in essence a relative thing, it is not sacred, there is nothing noumenal in it, it has merely a transitional and functional importance in the life of society. There is nothing that is sacred in politics, and much that is criminal. To deprive them of their supposed sacred character is the real process of setting man free. Political revolutions do not as a rule accomplish this, they create their own process of sanctifying the relative. The proclamation of pure truth, the overthrow of the conventional social lie does not mean a denial of what is relative, but to remove from it its halo of sanctity, that is to say, it means putting a stop to the process of making the relative absolute. A noumenal significance ought not to be ascribed to that which is entirely phenomenal in character.

The most essential thing is to get free from enslaving sociomorphism in the knowledge of God. And, having arrived at monotheism people have continued to live not by the reality of God, but by a sociomorphic myth about God, which was necessary for the consolidation of power in this world. There exists a socially useful lie about God and the only thing that can withstand it is a purified spiritual religion. It is only the crowning revelation of the Holy Spirit and the era of the Paraclete that will lead to this. At a certain stage of development this ascription of a sacrosanct character to institutions was a matter of necessity.

When faced by the importance and the disquieting nature of the problem of evil, the inconsistency of all the traditional theological and metaphysical doctrines about the Providence of God in the world is exposed. It is even the case that these doctrines constitute the chief hindrance to belief in God. The feebleness of, for in-instance, Malebranche's or Leibniz's teaching about divine Providence is astonishing and what is so striking about the official theological doctrine on this matter is its naïve rationalism, the pitiable arguments it adduces, its insensitiveness to mystery and its involuntary immorality.

God does not act everywhere in this objectified world. He was not the Creator of this fallen world. He does not act and he is not present in plague and cholera, in the hatred which torments the world, or in murder, war and violence, in the trampling down of freedom or in the darkness of the ignorant boor. Doctrines of that sort have even led men to atheism. The more sensitive kind of conscience has found itself unable to accept him. This type of doctrine of the divine Providence either denies evil altogether or is constrained to throw the responsibility for it upon God. The projection of theological doctrines of this sort upon eternal life leads to an apology for Hell, on the ground that it represents the triumph of justice and is thus a good thing. In the writings of St Gregory the Great and St Thomas Aquinas, the just rejoice in the eternal pains of sinners in Hell as in a triumphant vindication of God's truth and right.[1] In the earthly sphere in like manner, executions, tortures and penal servitude have provided grounds for rejoicing.

All this simply testifies to the truth of the enormous importance of this problem of evil and suffering in the sphere of the know-

[1] See Addison: *La vie après la mort dans les croyances de l'humanité*.

ledge of God. It draws attention to the distortions which exist in the human mind in regard to this subject and which have taken shape as a result of social servitude. To bring belief in God within the bounds of possibility and to make it morally possible to accept him, can only be done by recognizing the truth that God reveals himself in this world. He reveals himself in the prophets, in his Son, in the breath of the Spirit and in the uplifting spiritual aspirations of men. But God does not govern this world, the world of objectivity which is under the power of its own Prince—the 'Prince of this world'. God is not 'the world', and the revelation of God in the world is an eschatological revelation. God is not in the world, that is, not in its given factuality and its necessity, but in its setting of a task and in its freedom.

God is present and God acts only in freedom. He is not present nor does he act in necessity. God is to be found in Truth, in Goodness, Beauty and Love, but not in the world order. God shows himself in the world in truth and right, but he does not dominate over it in virtue of his power. God is Spirit and he can operate only in Spirit and through Spirit. Our ideas about power, about authority and causality are entirely inapplicable to God. The mystery of God's operation in the world and in man usually finds expression in the doctrine of grace, and grace bears no resemblance to what we understand by necessity, power, authority and causality; our conception of these is derived from the world. For this reason alone grace cannot be set in antithesis to freedom—it is combined with freedom. But the doctrines of theology have rationalized grace and have imparted a sociomorphic character even to it.

Thus it is that atheism, in its higher, not in its base form, may be a dialectical cleansing of the human idea of God. When men have risen in revolt against God on the ground of the evil and wrong of the world, they have, by the very fact of so doing, presupposed the existence of a higher truth, that is to say in the last resort, of God. They rebel against God in the name of God; for the sake of purging men's understanding of God they revolt against a conception of him which has been besmirched by the mire of this world. But as he treads this path of conflict and anguish man may pass through an experience which brings him moments not only of absolute Godforsakenness but even of the death of God. ('They have killed God'—said Nietzsche.)

The dreadfully strained and artificial explanations in the Doctrine of Providence, and the application to the noumenal of that which refers only to the phenomenal lead to rebellion. Belief in God is lost, because evil is triumphant, the immeasurable extent of suffering among created things cannot be reconciled with what people have been taught about the presence and activity of God in the world. A loftier sort of belief in God may come about as it becomes more spiritual and frees itself from the false cosmomorphic and sociomorphic myths about God with which the traditional doctrine of Providence is permeated,

The biblical doctrine of God is still more steeped in sociomorphic mythological elements and an idolatrous attitude to power. Yahwe was a tribal God and a God of war. It is of interest to note that Yahwe had no authority over *sheol*. In the prophets the knowledge of God is made spiritual and universal, but not finally and decisively so. It is only in the Son of God that he is revealed as love. Yet historical Christianity has not yet entirely freed itself from sociomorphism arising out of the conception of God as power, from myth and from idolatry. We believe that the last word belongs to God but this we can conceive only in terms of eschatology. It can be brought home to us only by the final and definitive revelation of the Spirit. Then everything will appear in a new guise.

3

It is eschatology, based upon existential experience, which must be adopted in opposition to monistic ontology. Freedom must be opposed to being, and creativity to the objective order.

There is in this world no objective order of which there could be, in the commonly accepted phraseology, ontological, metaphysical and noumenal knowledge. There is no eternal and unchangeable 'natural' order side by side with which the theologians recognize a 'supernatural' order as a supplement to the 'natural'. The 'natural' order to which only a relative and temporary stability belongs is simply a concatenation of phenomena which are open to scientific explanation. It is always an empirical, not a metaphysical order. Spirit can upset and change the 'natural' order.

In phenomena of the 'natural' order it is possible to find signs and symbols of what is being achieved in the spiritual world. But this is in principle a different attitude towards the 'natural' order from that which invests it with a metaphysical character. There is no harmonious whole in this object world of phenomena, there is no 'world harmony'. 'World harmony' does not reign in this world nor settle an eternal order in it. But it is being sought, to achieve it is a creative task, and its coming means the end of objectification and the transformation of the fallen world. No sort of eternal, objective, or 'natural' principles exist in nature and society. To suppose that they do is an illusion of the mind which arises from objectification and social adjustment. The very laws of nature are not eternal, they merely correspond to a certain condition of the natural world, and given a different state of the world, would be superseded.

Only the eternal spiritual principles of life exist—freedom, love, creativeness, the value of personality. The eternal image of personality exists, whereas everything generic is transient. And all that is transient is but a symbol. This does not mean that the transient and the relative are devoid of all reality, but their reality is secondary, not primary. Spirit is not an epiphenomenon of the material world, the material world is an epiphenomenon of spirit. Moreover, the primary reality of spirit is different from all realities of the objectified world. What Heidegger calls *in-der-Welt-sein,* is the rule of the humdrum and commonplace, of *das*

Man. So is everything that has become objectified. The power of the objective is indeed the power of the commonplace, it is the law of the realm of dull and petty philistinism.

When the tormenting problem of evil is seen in another light, it ceases to be an argument against the existence of God. This world into which we are thrown is not God's world and in it the divine order and divine harmony cannot hold sway. God's world only breaks through into this world, the light of it shines through only in that which really exists, in living beings and in their existence. But it does not shape an order and a harmony of the whole; such order and harmony can only be thought of eschatologically. What is of God in life is revealed in creative acts, in the creative life of the spirit, which penetrates even the life of nature.

The most important task which the mind has to face is that of ceasing to objectify God, to give up thinking of him in naturalistic terms after the analogy of the things of this world and their relation with one another. God is a mystery but he is a mystery with which it is possible to enter into communion. There is nothing of God in the dull and prosaic normality of the objective world order. It is only in a disruptive act which breaks through that commonplace normality that he is to be found.

A supremacy over being belongs to freedom: and to spirit there belongs a supremacy over the whole of congealed nature. But freedom too is a mystery, it is not open to rationalization. The mysterious nature of freedom is expressed in the fact that while it creates a new and better life, it gives rise at the same time to evil, in other words, it possesses a capacity for self-destruction. Freedom desires unending freedom, it seeks the creative flight into infinity. Yet, on the other hand, it may display a desire even for slavery, and this one sees in the history of human societies.

There would be no freedom if appearances were the very things-in-themselves, if the noumenal exhausted itself in the phenomena. Nor would there be any freedom if there were absolutely no activity of the noumenal in phenomena. But man is not a two-dimensional being, there is depth in him, and this depth goes deeper than three dimensions, it issues in ever new dimensions. Kant taught a doctrine of causality through freedom. But he left unexplained in what manner the intelligible cause, that is to say noumenal freedom, is able to break in upon the causal sequence of appearances. His conception was of two worlds which are, so to speak, entirely sundered from one another, and each shut up in itself.

But the one world can invade the other and act creatively within it. Man, as a creatively active and free being, as a spiritual being, is not merely a phenomenon. That is the main question. At the risk of repetition it must again be said that the philosophy of freedom is not a teleological philosophy. Subordination to an end, for the sake of which man is compelled to come to terms with the most unfitting and improper means, is opposed to the freedom of man. What is important is not the aim, but the creative energy, the nobility of human beings who are creating life. And again what is important is radiation out of the depth, which illumines the life of men.

CHAPTER VI

*1. The emergence of newness within being. Newness and time.
Newness and evolution. Progress. 2. Newness and history.
Necessity, fate and freedom. 3. Newness and the causal link.
Creative newness overthrows objective being.*

I

It is not only the fact of evil having made its appearance which
presents a difficutly for monistic ontology. It also has to meet
the difficulty to which the appearance of what is new gives
rise. How does non-being enter into being and become that which
happens? Hellenic philosophy was ontological *par excellence,* and
the difficulty it found in the idea of movement is well-known, it
was indeed forced to deny it. Hence Zeno's paradox about
Achilles and the tortoise. Neither did Plato find the problem an
easy one. Aristotle tried to find a way out of the difficulty by the
theory of potency and act, a theory which for a long while remained classical. But there is a deep-rooted obscurity in it. What
is the source of movement and of change? Is it potency or act?
Pure act is unmoved and unchanged, for it is a completed condition, whereas movement and change indicate incompleteness.
Garrigou-Lagrange, who is a Thomist, lays particular stress upon
the idea that there is something more in immovability than there
is in motion, for there is in immovability that which in movement
only becomes.[1] This too is a philosophy which maintains the
supremacy of being over freedom; according to it freedom is
incompleteness, and creative movement is incompleteness.

But it is possible to adopt a point of view which differs in

[1] See his *Le sens commun.*

principle from the Aristotelian and scholastic position. It is possible to take the view that there is more in potency than in act, more in movement than in immovability and that there are greater riches in freedom than in being. The noumenal spiritual world discloses itself in creativeness, in movement, in freedom, not in congealed, self-enlocked, motionless being. To Greek idealism the multiple world of the senses was all in movement, it was a world of genesis and becoming, a world in which things happen. It was in this that its incompleteness lay, and for this reason it could not be regarded as being. The world of ideas, the noumenal world, knows nothing of growth, change and move ment.

Greek ontologism had a stifling influence upon Christian theology. It was a victory of the spatial interpretation of the world. Order exists in space, movement and creativity exist in time. The interpretation of the phenomenal world in terms of causality, which is a condition of getting to know it, does not in fact allow of the emergence of what is new, of what has not been before, of what is not derived from that which has already been. Creative newness is causeless.

When you describe the cause of a thing, you embark upon a series which is infinite, and you never reach the primordial creative act in which a new thing in being was for the first time disclosed. It is true that causality has two sides to it, it is also causative in consequence of a force to which attempts have from time to time been made to reduce freedom.[1] But it is better to think of freedom as outside the causal sequence, and as belonging to another order. If we make use of the Aristotelian phraseology, we may put it that our world is full of potencies, possibilities and energies, but the sources of these potencies reach back into the noumenal world to which our causal relations are not applicable. And the question of the relation of the creative act in which a new

[1] L. Lopatin developed a doctrine of freedom on these grounds. See his *The Positive Tasks of Philosophy*. Vol. 2.

thing emerges, to reality remains highly complex. If being, shut in on itself and finished off, being in which no movement or change of any kind is possible be regarded as reality, then the possibility of creative action must inevitably be denied. There is no creative act whatever except the one by which God made the world.

The official theology which regards itself as orthodox denies that man is a being with a capacity to create. Capacity for creation belongs to the Creator alone who is pure act, and the creature is incapable of it. But if the existence of potency, and that means of all movement, in God, the Creator, is denied, we are obliged to deny to God the possibility of creativeness, for the creation of what is new is due to potency. But man, on the contrary, creature as he is, is capable of creation, since there is potency in him, he is not actualized to the point of losing the possibility of movement and change. The possibility of accomplishing a creative act, of disclosing change and newness, is due to imperfection. Thus we reach a paradox.

That which reveals the image and likeness of the Creator in man, and is the most perfect thing in him, is, it would appear, the outcome of imperfection, of incompleteness, of potentiality, of the presence of non-being within him. A doctrine of God as pure act in which there is no potency, in actual fact makes the idea of the creation of the world meaningless and absurd. The creation of the world and of man becomes a matter of chance, and serves no necessary purpose at all to God. And the creature as a mere fortuitous happening has no vocation to the inner life of the Divine, he is summoned merely to blind submission. He is asked for no creative response to the call of God. The emergence of the created world was not a new thing in the inner life of the Deity, and in the creation of the world itself no sort of newness can make its appearance. Consistent and thorough-going ontologism is obliged to deny the possibility of newness, creativity and freedom, for these are things which denote a break through in the closed system of being. To avoid misunderstanding it must be said that if the possibility of creativity and, therefore, of movement, in God is conceded, it must be recognized that such creativeness and movement do not take place in time in our sense of the word.

In the nineteenth century theories of evolution were a safeguard to the possibility of newness. They allowed change in the world, the appearance of what had not been; they envisaged development, as movement which promises amelioration and a process of reaching perfection. But it is a great misunderstanding to see in the theory of evolution a defence of creativeness. Bergson's phrase 'creative evolution' must be regarded as open to misunderstanding. The doctrine of evolution is entirely under the control of determinism and causal relations. In evolution, as the naturalistic theory of evolution understands it, newness cannot make its appearance in any real sense, for there is no creative act, which always ascends towards freedom, and breaks the causal link. It is only the consequences of creative acts which are accessible to the theory of evolution, it seeks no knowledge of the active subject in development.

Evolution is objectification. What takes place in it is the shifting and redistribution of the parts of the world, of the matter of the world, which fashion new forms out of the old material. But evolution is essentially conservative on principle and takes no cognizance of what is in actual fact new, that is, of the creative. What is true in the theory is its recognition of the fact that there is evolution in the world, but the evolutionary theory is under the ascendancy of a limited naturalism. Evolution tells merely of that which passes through a new experience.

In the case of every experience which is passed through, whether in thinking or in living, and after it has been surmounted, there is something positive that remains from it. In this lies the meaning of Hegel's *Aufhebung*. There is newness in every strong gripping experience, and this experience lived through is in-

160

delible. '*Souffrir passe, avoir souffert ne passe jamais*', said Léon Bloy. Out of suffering which is passed through as a deeply felt experience, something new emerges. But this means that there was a creative impulse in the experience, there was a creative attitude towards the suffering. And this cannot be explained by an objective series of causal relations. If in the course of evolution something new makes its appearance, this means that everything was not determined, everything was not fixed and settled by the preceding series. In creative newness there is always an element of the miraculous. The causal explanation of newness in the world speaks always of that which is secondary, not of what is primary, it deals with what surrounds the core, not with the core itself. The causal determinist explanation is conspicuously worthless as an elucidation of the emergence of creative genius.

Boehme would seem to be the first to make use of the word *Auswicklung* to express the development, and emergence into view of that which reveals itself anew. The evolutionary thought of German metaphysics goes back to him. From him is derived the metaphysical evolutionism of Hegel, who was the first to interpret the world process as dynamic, as development and not as a static system. Hegel's evolutionary thought goes much deeper than the naturalistic evolutionism of the second half of the nineteenth century. The process of becoming, and the dialectic of world development are possibilities only because non-being exists. If we concede being only, there will be no becoming or development of any sort. Newness in the process of becoming emerges from the heart of non-being.

But does a heart of non-being exist? This is a different interpretation of potency from the way in which Aristotle understood it. In the heart of potency, which is not being, and which we are constrained apophatically to call non-being, is lodged that primordial freedom which precedes being, and without which there can be no creation of what is new, of what has not been before. Hegel turned becoming and dialectical development into a necessary logical process, and in so doing was false to the idea of freedom as the source of creative newness. But Hegel's discovery remains true, that becoming, development, the appearance of what is new, are impossible and inexplicable if we remain within the confines of being and fail to introduce non-being into our dialectic.

Hegel was under the sway not of determinism only but also of teleology. The teleological outlook upon the world is, however, inimical to the emergence of what is new. There is a determining power in it, which works from the opposite end, that is from the final goal. In the last resort freedom in Hegel's view is born of necessity. The creative act which issues from freedom stands opposed to this. It is by this act that movement is decreed, the movement which is in origin outside objectified being and is merely projected in it. Apophatically speaking, it may be said that the noumenon is non-being, because the noumenon is freedom. Whereas being is determination; being is not freedom.

Newness presupposes time; it makes its appearance in time. Without time there is no change. But time is not a form into which the world process is packed and which communicates movements to the world. Time exists because movement and newness exist. A motionless and unchanging world would have no knowledge of time. The creation of what is new presupposes that that which is created was not before, it had not been within time, and it discloses itself within time. And this means that creativeness presupposes non-being, something other than being. But time which brings new life with it has also a death-dealing pity, it mercilessly crowds out what was, it bestows at one and the same time the presentiment of life and of death. Youth and old age are alike brought about by time. It gives rise alike to change, which is good, and to betrayal, which is evil. I shall say more later about its various meanings.

The fact that the world exists in time and not only in space means that the world is not completed, that its creation has not yet reached its crowning consummation, that it continues to be created. If the creation of the world were closed, newness would not be possible. Finished and closed reality does not exist. The empirical world as one whole thing does not exist. Reality may expand or contract for us. The recognition of the subjectivity of time by no means leads to a static understanding of reality as conditioned by time. On the contrary, it means that time depends upon existential experience and that there is a time which depends upon objectification, which occurs in the events of existence itself. To the subject, as he who exists, time is of different sorts, and is decided by the state he is in and the direction he is taking. Our existence is steeped not only in reality which has realized itself in the forms of the object world, but also in reality which is potential and which is deeper and wider. It is for that reason alone that change, creativeness and newness are possible. But potentiality itself is steeped in freedom and for that reason can be distinguished from being.

It is not only the present which is reality, but also the past and the future, but this reality is disrupted and shattered into pieces by fallen time. It is in fallen time that the life of nature and historical life flow on. But everything that happens in time which has broken up into past, present and future, that is to say in time which is sick, is but a projection on to the external of what is being accomplished in depth. True creative newness is achieved in existential time, time which is not objectified, that is to say it happens in the vertical and not in the horizontal. But creative acts which are accomplished in the vertical are projected upon a plane and are accepted as accomplished in historical time. Thus it is that meta-history enters into history.

But the same thing already happens in the life of nature. Creative acts in depth which bring newness with them, when projected upon a plane as a rearrangement of points which indicate those creative acts, are taken as determined evolution, as an objective natural process. But, as I have already said, evolution is not the source of newness but an effect which follows from it. Evolution belongs to the system of objectification. In relation to the future no task can be placed before evolution. It is possible to set a task for creativeness only. Bergson set thing and action in antithesis and he recognizes the creation of what is new. But he understands creativeness in too naturalistic a way. He brings it too much into the biological process.

Further, it is necessary to draw a distinction between evolution and progress. Evolution is a naturalistic term, whereas progress belongs to the spiritual category. It is axiological; it presupposes appraisal from the point of view of a principle which ranks higher than the natural process of change. The idea of progress is of Christian origin and was born in the Christian messianic hope, in the expectation of the Kingdom of God as the consummation of history and there is an eschatological impulse in it. But in the mind of the nineteenth century the idea of progress was secularized and naturalized. It was brought into subjection to the power of disrupted time. In the world of objectification progress treats the present as a means to serve the interests of the future. One generation is a means which serves the interests of the next, progress carries with it not only life but death also. In the natural and historical world birth is pregnant with death.

The eschatological conception of the resurrection of the dead, of the restoration and transfiguration of the whole world and of man is entirely alien to progress, which is subordinated to a determined objective world. It has for this reason been regarded as possible to speak of the law of progress, of the necessity of progress. In actual fact no such law exists. Progress presupposes creative freedom. There is no progress in a direct line upwards in the world. There is progress only in relation to the parts and to groups of phenomena, not in relation to the whole. Progress in one respect may be accompanied by regress in another. There may be intellectual progress and moral regress, technical progress and regress in general culture; there may be progress in culture and social regress, and so forth. Progress is a task, not a law, and the idea of progress inevitably finds its support in a messianic and eschatological expectation, but it is an expectation which requires the creative activity of man. Fate operates in history, but so does human freedom also.[1]

In the nineteenth and twentieth centuries the ideas of development and progress were distorted. There is development in the world but necessary development does not unfailingly mean amelioration and enrichment, nor raising the intensity of life to a higher level. The freshness of creative youth, the initial force of self-giving in expression may be lost in development. In the course of what is called development a process of cooling, ageing, may enter upon the scene and it may bring with it the disappearance of genuine wholehearted faith, intuition and enthusiasm. Love grows cold, faith grows cold, creative enthusiasm grows cold, and maturity and old age set in. The exalting impulse of life has been left behind. Such is fallen time. But in the triumph over objectified time, the past and future are united. Creative power fixes its gaze upon eternity, upon that which lies outside time. Within time, however, it is objectified.

2

Newness does appear in historical time. The singleness and unrepeatability of historical events have been pointed out many times and this has been seen as the quality which distinguishes them from the phenomena of nature in which repeatability occurs. This difference is a relative one because the phenomena of the physical world are also single, even in spite of the fact that they can be produced by means of experiment, and, on the other hand, historical events show traits of family likeness, for example,

---

[1] In his curious book: *Histoire philosophique du genre humain ou l'Homme,* Fabre d'Olivet says that three principles operate in history—Providence, fate and the freedom of man. The book exhibits the usual defects of occult literature.

revolutions, wars, the foundation of powerful States and their dissolution, the clashes between social classes and so on. There is even a painful tedium about the well-known course of revolution and reaction. There is a poignant sense of comedy about world history as a whole. As I see it the main distinction is this, that the events of history take place in another sort of time from that in which the events of nature occur. They happen in historical time, whereas the events of nature occur in cosmic time.

Cosmic time is cyclic. Historical time is a line stretching out forwards. Once more Spring and Autumn come; the trees are covered with leaves again, and again the leaves fall. But a given historical epoch, such as, for instance, that of early Christianity or the Renaissance, the Reformation, the French Revolution, or the industrial development of the nineteenth century, is never in its concrete expression repeated, although some features of likeness to it may occur in a new epoch. History issues out of the cosmic cycle and stretches out towards what is coming. There is a crushing necessity in history and the power of grandiose solidity. There is suppression of what is individual by the generic. Yet all the same history is pregnant with newness which enters into the eschatology of history and is an influence which exerts a pull towards an end by which everything is resolved. It is for this reason alone that history is not in the final count just a repellent and meaningless comedy.

It is not only that the events of historical time invade the cycle of events belonging to cosmic time and point to a way out from the cycle, but the events which take place in existential time and which are not susceptible of mathematical calculation also intrude upon the events of historical time, and interrupting the determined series of historical events, impart to them a higher meaning and throw light upon the destiny of man. To this process we may give the name meta-historical and it comes to pass out of the existential depth. The meta-historical breaks up not only the cosmic cycle but also the determinism of the historical process, it breaks up objectification. Thus the appearance of Jesus Christ is the meta-historical event *par excellence*. It took place in existential time, but it broke through into the historical, and here it is received with all the limitations which history imposes, those which belong to particular periods of history and those which are due to the limitations of human nature. But meta-history is always there as the background behind history, and the existential design throws light upon the objectified order.

The creative acts of man in which new life springs up and which ought to lead on to the end by which all is resolved, proceed from that design. In the plane of objectification real creativeness and real newness are impossible. What is possible is merely a redistribution of the material of the past. No sort of creative newness can emanate from 'being'. It can take its rise from 'freedom' only. The soil of history is volcanic, and it is possible that volcanic eruptions may break out in it. It is only the topmost layer of history which belongs to a stabilized order and puts a brake on movements towards the end.

The world is not only the cosmic cycle which the Greeks and the people of the Middle Ages after them were inclined to accept as a cosmic harmony. The world is also history with its catastrophes and its liability to interruption. History is a combination of traditions; it is the preservation of continuity together with the incidence of catastrophe and discontinuity, history is both conservative and revolutionary. New aeons are a possibility in the life of the world. We do not live in an aeon which is absolutely shut in on itself. It is possible for the world to enter into an eschatological era, into the times of the Paraclete, and then the face of the world and the character of history will be essentially changed.[1]

3

Real newness which is not merely a redistribution of parts always arrives, as it were, from another world, from another

[1] There are some remarkable thoughts on this subject in *Notre Père* by Cieszkovsky, the philosopher of Polish messianism.

scheme of things. It issues from freedom, from what we think of as 'non-being' in comparison with the 'being' of this world era, and so we say that the mystery of newness is not a mystery of being, it is a mystery of freedom which cannot be derived from being. To monistic philosophy creative newness is unthinkable. James was right in associating newness with pluralism. But a more important matter in principle is that creative newness presupposes dualism, a break through in this objective world, and not the evolution of this objective world. Newness cannot be explained with the object as the point of departure. It is only when we start from the subject that it becomes explicable.

Determinist science explains all newness in the world causally. It finds the explanation in the past and it makes it a point of honour to demonstrate that newness is a result of necessity and that in newness there is nothing new in principle. In this manner science discovers many things. It throws light upon the processes which take place in the world. It investigates the environment in which creative acts are achieved and the way prepared for the appearance of what is new. But the primary thing, the most important thing of all escapes it. Determinism and the naturalistic theory of evolution, in investigating the world setting and historical environment in which the creative act breaks through and enters, imagine that they are explaining the creative act itself.

It is not to be disputed that the very greatest of creative minds are dependent upon the world environment, upon the period of history in which they live and upon the historical forces which are at work in it. But the main problem arises from the fact that they introduced something new in principle, something which had not been in the life of the world and history hitherto. The important thing is not that they receive but that they bring, that something comes from them not that something enters into them.

It is impossible to explain the appearance of Jesus Christ in the world, and the light which He brought into it, by processes which had their origin in Judaism and Hellenism, but one can so explain the reception given to Christianity by its human environment Thorough-going determinism, as it enters upon the vicious infinity of the causal series, is obliged to accept it as the fact that in man and in every act of his, everything is received from without, that there is nothing within him, no kernel, which is not capable of derivation from outside him. And more than that, it must believe that there is nothing in the world in general which possesses an inner core, or interior power; everything is capable of explanation in terms of the action of outside forces, and these outside forces are themselves to be explained in like manner by the operation of forces which are external to them.

All this means that there is no such thing as freedom. In the last resort objective being is turned into non-being. But this non-being is not freedom. It is nothing but the limit of movement into the external. To such a degree is the dialectic of being and non-being tangled and complicated.

The fundamental error is the explanation of creative newness in terms of the past, in spite of the fact that it is capable of explanation only from the standpoint of the future. In this lies the mystery of creativeness and the emergence of what is new. In this lies the mystery of freedom. It is the paradox of time. The original first-born creative act certainly does not issue from the past. It is not accomplished within cosmic and historical time; it is achieved in existential time which knows no system of causal links.

But in historical time the creative act has the paradoxical appearance of coming from the future. In this sense it can be called prophetic. The very distinction between past and future exists only for the time of the objectified world. People of conservative minds accuse the creative act which raises up something new, of being unfaithful to the past. But it does have faith in the future. It is not only the past which is associated with faith, the future is linked with it too. And the past can be false to eternity, just as the future can be true to it. But neither should the future be idolized as divine, any more than the past should be. It is only eternity which is good and to be loved. '*Denn ich liebe dich in Ewigkeit*' says Zarathustra in Nietzsche. But we cannot think of eternity itself as a final completeness and consummation in the meaning we ascribe to the words here and now. Eternity is eternal newness, eternal creative ecstasy, the dissolving of being, in divine freedom.

I have already said that the creative imagination which demands what is new, issues from existential eternity, to which our categories of thought are not applicable. To enter into union with the mystery is not only the frontier of knowledge. It is knowledge, a different sort of knowledge. History is heavily encumbered not only with natural necessity, but also with fate, which is a more mysterious thing than necessity. But behind this intolerable burden, the conflict which freedom wages with fate is concealed. In history, therefore, in which determinism, that is, the series of causal links, is in power, another scheme of things opens out and lets its light shine through. At a deeper level creative subjects are in action and freedom breaks through.

But the acts of the creative subject meet with the opposition of the objective world, and the strength of freedom measures itself against the power of this resistance. Freedom in this world is conflict, not a thing to be enjoyed. According to Fichte, the 'I' postulates the 'not I', and this is the opposition which has to be overcome.

But this is not the final truth. The final truth is that the 'not I', the crushing burden of the objective world, is the child of objectification, of a fall which hides other egos, other existential subjects from view. In Fichte there is no understanding of this fall.

The drama of the world lies in the fact that creative newness is subjected to the laws of this objectified world. Thus a vicious infinity is disclosed in history. The creative act of man lives through its tragic destiny in history. And this makes it possible to affirm perpetual determinism, and to deny the very possibility of creativeness on the part of man. We meet with this denial both in the doctrines of theology, and in positive science.

CHAPTER VII

1. Being and continued creation of the world. Imagination, inspiration, ecstasy. Depression and exultation. The victory over congealed being. 2. Ascent and descent in creativeness. The creative act and the product of creation. Objectification and embodiment. 3. Subjective and objective creativity. The 'classical' and the 'romantic' in creativity.

I

To be aware of the fact that man does not exist within a finished and stabilized system of being is fundamental to the philosophy of creativeness, and it is only on that understanding that the creative act of man is possible and intelligible. Another fundamental position consists in the realization that the creative act of man is not simply a regrouping and redistribution of the matter of the world. Nor is it merely an emanation, an outflowing of the primary matter of the world. Nor again is it just a shaping of the material in the sense of imposing ideal forms upon it. In the creative act of man, a new element is introduced, something which was not there before, which is not contained in the given world, and is not part of its make-up, but which breaks through from another scheme of the world, not out of the eternally given ideal forms, but out of freedom; and not out of a dark freedom, but out of an illuminated freedom.

The fact that creativity is possible in the world testifies to the inadequacy of this world, to a continual overcoming of it and to the existence of a power to achieve that purpose which issues from another world, or from a deeper level than this flat world. At the same time the creativeness of man is evidence of the fact that he belongs to two worlds and that he is called to assume a ruling position in the world. Pascal made the very profound observation that man's awareness of his insignificance is a sign of his greatness.

I have already said that the appearance of men of great creative power is not to be attributed to their environment nor to be explained by causal relations. The environment of the times in which he lived was incapable of giving birth to Pushkin; from that point of view his appearance must be regarded as a miracle. And this is true of every act of creativeness that is conceived, in it the old world always comes to an end.

Nor is it only that which the ego creates, but the very existence of the ego itself is a creative effort, a synthetizing creative act. Hundolph says with truth that creative power is an expression of the whole life of a man. Man creates his personality and in the act of doing so expresses his personality. In the self-creation of the ego, of the personality, the human spirit accomplishes a creative act of synthesis. A creative effort is needed in order to avoid any disintegration of the ego, any division of the personality, to prevent its breaking up into parts. Man is not only called to creativeness, as an activity which operates in the world and is exerted upon the world, but he is himself creative power and without that creative power his human countenance is lacking.

Man is a microcosmos and a microtheos. And it is only when he refuses to acquiesce in being part of anything whatever or in being himself made up of parts, that he is a person. The true image and form of man is a creative unity. It is difficult to understand Gilson's assertion, in terms of traditional Thomism, that it is impossible to imagine creative activity in man.[1] To my mind that amounts to the same thing as saying that it is impossible to imagine man. Man is a being who masters and surmounts himself and overcomes the world; it is in that that his value and dignity consist. But this securing of the mastery is creative power. The mystery of creativeness is the mystery of achieving the mastery

[1] See E. Gilson: *L'Esprit de la philosophie médiévale.*

172

over given reality, over the determinism of the world, over the locking of its closed circle. In this sense creative activity is an act of transcending; in a deeper sense it is the victory over non-being.

The philosophy of creativeness is not a philosophy of finitism, which, as Bergson justly observes, is based upon the assumption that everything is included in the datum. In regard to creativeness what needs to be established is a doctrine analogous to the teaching of Kant and Fichte, that is to say we must assert the creative activity of the subject, a creative activity which is not deducible from objective being. Fichte calls contemplation the productive power of imagination. But this is to recognize the character of intuition as creative and not passive. It is commonly said of art that it is concrete creative power as compared with the abstract nature of philosophy. But this may give rise to misunderstanding and requires elucidation.

Creativeness in art, like every other form of creative activity, consists in triumph over given, determined, concrete life, it is a victory over the world. Objectification knows a humdrum day-to-day concreteness of its own, but creative power finds its way out from this imposed concreteness, into concreteness of another kind. Creative activity does not consist merely in the bestowal of a more perfect form upon this world; it is also liberation from the burden and bondage of this world. Creativeness cannot be merely creation out of nothing, it presupposes the material which the world supplies. But the element of 'out of nothing' does enter into creative activity. For it is creativeness out of the freedom of the other world. This means that what is most important, most mysterious and most creatively new, comes not from 'the world' but from spirit.

There is something miraculous about the transformation of matter which takes place in art. This miraculous element exists also in images of beauty in nature, that nature in which the forces of enmity, ruin and chaos are at work. From a shapeless stone or lump of clay the beautiful form of a statue is given to us;

173

out of a chaos of sounds we have one of Beethoven's symphonies; out of a chaos of words, the verses of Pushkin with all their power to charm. From sensations and impressions all unaware of meaning, knowledge is derived, from elemental subconscious instincts and attractions the beauty of moral form takes shape, out of an ugly world beauty is captured. In all this there is something miraculous from the point of view of the world, this given empirical world. Creative power anticipates the transfiguration of the world. This is the meaning of art, of art of any kind. And creative power has an eschatological element in it. It is an end of this world and a beginning of the new world. The world is created not by God only, but also by man. Creation is a divine-human work. And the crowning point of world creation is the end of this world. The world must be turned into an image of beauty, it must be dissolved in creative ecstasy.

The creative act is by its very nature ecstatic; it involves movement out beyond the boundaries; there is an act of transcendence in it. Creativeness is not an immanent process, nor susceptible of explanation in terms of immanence. There is always more in it than in any of the clauses by which it is sought to explain creative power; that is to say, the forcing of a way through within the realm of fettering determinism. Creative activity will not come to terms with the given state of the world, it desires another. The creative act always calls up the image of something different; it imagines something higher, better and more beautiful than this —than the 'given'. This evoking of the image of something different, something better and more beautiful, is a mysterious power in man and it cannot be explained by the action of the world environment. The world environment is full of the results of creative power in the past, which have grown cold and rigid. How is the rekindling of a new creative fire out of them to be explained?

Creative fancy and the rise of images of something better are of fundamental significance in human life. The relation between the real and what can be imagined is more complex than is commonly thought. That which appears to be a solid reality in the realm of things might be the stabilized, lignified, petrified, ossified result of very ancient imagination. I have already pointed out that Jacob Boehme regarded evil as a result of vicious imagination. A bright serene imagination, directed towards divine beauty can create a bright serene world. It is interesting to note that positivists, agnostics, materialists and sceptics ascribe extraordinary power to human imagination and thereby deny the primary foundation of their own *Weltanschauung*. Man, a pitiful product of his natural environment, and wholly determined from without, has, it would appear, discovered within himself the power to invent a spiritual world, God, and eternity! There is something wildly improbable about this.

Productive imagination is a metaphysical force which wages war against the objective and determinate world, against the realm of the commonplace and dull. The creative imagination builds up realities. The forms which are constructed by the creators of works of art lead a real existence and they are active in the world. Imagination is a way out from an unendurable reality. But a lying imagination, and it is not rare for it to be lying, precipitates a man into a reality which is a nightmare. It is always to be remembered that the imagination can be creative of falsehood, it can cast man into a world which, for all that it is a world of things, is fictitious. Present day psychopathology reveals much truth in this connection. Books on the spiritual life had formerly a great deal to say on this same subject. The creative imagination may construct a true idealization and a false; it can be an act of real love or an act which is unreal and brings terrible disillusionment with it. This is a source of the deep sense of.tragedy in human existence.

It is possible for man to become the victim of his own imagination, despite the fact that the imagination is capable of being a way out towards a higher world. The antithesis between image and thing is fundamental. The primary reality is not the thing, it belongs to the image. Man finds it intolerable to live in the midst of things which have no image or which have lost it. Imagination brings feeling and thought to bear upon the complete image. The concrete reality which has an image is apprehended through the imagination, not through sensation. The imagination has played an enormous part in the very creation of objects which appear to be stable realities and exert their force from without. But the image is an act not a thing.[1]

The theme of creative power leads to a question which is fundamental in metaphysics: what is the primary reality, the thing, the object, including even spirit if it be understood in that way, or the act, the subject, the creative life? If the former is the case, the world cannot be changed and the situation of man in the world is hopeless. If the latter is the truth, then the world can be changed and man can find a way out from the realm of necessity into the realm of freedom. It is, therefore, necessary to draw a distinction between rational metaphysics and the metaphysics of images. The philosophy of the Spirit is the metaphysics of images.

Ribot, who has a positivist frame of mind, says that the creative imagination corresponds to the will, that it moves from the internal to the external and that images are the material of creative imagination.[2] In Ribot's view creative activity depends upon the power of the images to incite and prompt. The myth-creating process which belongs to the fountain head of human nature and from which human nature has not emancipated itself even today, is a product of imagination and personification. And there has been a greater element of truth in mythology than in the undivided power of concept and thing. Beauty is connected with the image, not with concepts. Kant says that if objects are regarded through concepts, every presentment of beauty disappears.[3]

[1] See Sarte: *L'imagination*, Husserl's influence is to be seen in the fact that the image is regarded as the recognition of whatever it may be.

[2] See Ribot : *Essai sur l'imagination créatrice*.

[3] See *Kritik der Urteilskraft*.

The image of something different, something better, the image of beauty is brought into being out of the mysterious depth, out of freedom, not out of necessity, it arises from the noumenon, not from the phenomenon. And the creative act is, as it were, a link between the noumenal and phenomenal worlds, a way out beyond the confines of the phenomenal world, it is ecstasy, an experience of transcendence. The choice between the two orientations of metaphysics depends upon the line of direction which the spirit takes. The recognition of things and objects as the primary reality, has a very great deal behind it in which it can find a basis, and the metaphysics which correspond to this is movement in the line of least resistance.

On the other hand, to regard the act, the subject, and spirit as the primary reality requires an effort of spirit and the exercise of faith, it means a fight against the power of necessity. What is in question is not merely two ways of cognition, but also two ways of existence. It would be absurd to say—is there any meaning in making an effort of the spirit, if there is even a possibility that spirit, as a reality, does not exist? If I am able to make an effort of spirit, then spirit does exist. It is in this that the particular reality of the spirit lies, and it is not the same sort of reality as that of the world of things.[1]

To picture oneself as a free spirit in a consistent and thorough-going manner, and to act as a free spirit, means to *be* a free spirit. Creative fancy is capable of producing real and vital consequences. Creative ecstasy is a way out from the time of this world, historical time and cosmic time, it takes place in existential time. Those who have experienced creative ecstasy are well aware that in it man is, as it were, in the grip of a higher power. It is possession by a god, by a daemon (in the Greek sense of the word). In Plato's *Phaedrus* there is an amazing story about the growth of wings on a man. Ecstasy is akin to delirium. Genius is a daemon which has taken up its abode in a man and assumed control of him. Creative power

[1] See my *Spirit and Reality*.

is always of an individually personal character, but the man is not alone in it. Human creative power is not human only, it is divine-human. The mystery of creative power lies in that fact. An act of transcending takes place in it, in it the closed circle of human existence is broken open. The creative act is an act which is achieved by man, and in achieving it man has a feeling within that he is going beyond his strength. The genius of Pushkin has put this into words. There is a kinship between the poet and the prophet.

There is an element of gracious beneficence in creative activity. It is bound up with the nature of all gifts which are freely bestowed—*gratia gratis data*. The creative act is gracious and beneficent, creative freedom is clarified and serene. This does not hinder the fact that man can put his gift to evil use. The contradictory and paradoxical aspect of the creative condition consists in this that man at the moment of creative impulse feels himself, as it were, possessed by a higher power, by a daemon, and yet at the same time has a sense of extraordinary freedom, of scope for the expression of his own will. In creative activity, and especially in art and poetry, there is a suggestion of the remembrance of a lost Paradise. The poetry of Pushkin in particular calls up such memories. But the memory of a lost Paradise, a memory which never abandons man, and to which the most gracious moments of creative power draw his attention, is no mere turning to the past, which has withdrawn beyond the boundaries of this empirical world. Such reminiscences of a lost Paradise are also a turning to the future which likewise lies beyond the bounds of this empirical world. The creative act cannot but turn to face the future. But beyond the confines of the objectified time of our world, the distinction and the opposition we make between past and future are taken away. It is a distinction which holds good only for the intervening state, not for the boundaries, or to put it more exactly, not for what lies beyond the confines of world life.

Messianic thought was characteristic of the ancient Hebrews,

178

and it faced towards the future. The ancient Greeks also faced their Golden Age, but in their case it meant looking to the past. Still, there is a sphere in which the messianic kingdom of the future and the Golden Age of the past draw together and are compressed into a single hope. Thus if one looks more deeply into creative activity we can say that there is a prophetic element in it. It speaks prophetically of a different world, of another, a transformed state of the world. But that means that the creative act is eschatological. In it the impossibility of resting content with this given world is proclaimed, in it this world comes to an end, and another world begins.

This is true in every case of the creative condition in man, even though no creative product should result from it. The significance of the creative state for the inner life of man lies in this, that it shows he is overcoming the state of subjection and humiliation which is imposed by the burden of this world; it shows he has attained the experience of an exalting impulse. Creative power, therefore, proclaims that this world is superable, that congealed being can be overcome. It tells of the possibility of setting it free from its chains, it speaks of liberation and transformation.

The romantics have been fond of connecting the creative artistic process with the fruitful imagination experienced in dreams.[1] This cannot be accepted in the form in which the romantics assert it, but it does contain a certain amount of truth. The images which arise in dreams are not called up by impressions received from the external empirical world immediately, but are due to those that have been preserved in the depth of the subconscious.[2] The state of dreaming is not dependent upon the perception of images of the world of sense at the given moment, it is a passive condition, not active. Consciousness is suppressed and almost paralyzed. When a man is dreaming he may be absolutely overwhelmed by the past. In creative activity, on the other hand,

[1] See A. Beguin: *L'Ame romantique et le rêve*.
[2] See Lafargue: *Le Rêve et la psychanalyse*.

179

images arise which are not determined by the empirical world, or if they are determined by it, it is through the medium of creative transformation. And they bring with them liberation from subjection to the past, from impressions and injuries which have accumulated in the subconscious, and from the wounds which the past has inflicted. There occur, it is true, radiant, luminous visions, and there are dreams which are prophetic, (though such conditions are comparatively rare), and in them the creative exalting impulse has a place. It is not only the subconscious which is operating in creative activity but the supra-conscious also; there is a movement upwards.

2

There are two sides and two meanings to the creative impulse. There is an inward creative act, and there is the created product, the outward disclosure of the creative act. I have written a great deal on this subject.[1] Here I shall say what is necessary on a new aspect of the matter. It is most important to elucidate the question whether the created embodiment is an objectification or whether we ought to distinguish between embodiment and objectification. It is necessary also to draw a distinction between embodiment and materialization, for bodily form and materiality are not one and the same: the bodily form may be illuminated, whereas the material thing is to be overcome. The creative impulse is realized along a line which ascends, and along a line which descends. The primary creative act is a flight upwards, towards another world. But within the matter of this world it meets with difficulty and opposition, from its formlessness, its solidity and its weight, from its evil infinitude which surrounds the creator on all sides. Man is a demiurge, he creates, working upon the matter of this world, shaping it and illuminating it. There is in the creative state much that is easy, wings grow ready for the flight, but there is much difficulty also, much suffering, and much that hinders and hampers

[1] See as especially important my *The Meaning of the Creative Act*.

the flight. The creative subject stands face to face with a world of objectification, and the results of the creative act have to enter into that world of objectification. It is in this that the tragedy of creative activity consists.

The primary creative impulse takes place outside the objectified world, outside the time of this world; it happens in existential time, in a flash of the present; it knows neither past nor future. A creative act is a noumenal act, but the product which is created by it belongs to the phenomenal world. Beethoven makes a symphony and thereupon in this creation of his people discover 'objective' regulating principles. But the creative activity of Beethoven ought to have led to the whole world's breaking into sound like a symphony. And in the same way the creative power of a genuine philosopher should have led to the changing of the world and not merely to the enrichment of it by new and expensive books.

The Greeks already drew a distinction between acting ($\pi\rho\hat{a}\xi\iota\varsigma$), the aim of which is the activity of the acting subject itself, and making ($\pi o\acute{\iota}\eta\sigma\iota\varsigma$) the aim of which is in the object which has been made and possesses being.[1] The creating mind which is in a state of creative upward flight is in actual fact not bent upon the realization of an end, but of expressing the condition it is in. Benedetto Croce is to a notable degree right when he sees the essence of art in self-expression.[2] But in any case the creating mind cannot remain within itself, it must issue out of itself. This going out from the self is usually called embodiment and a character in the highest degree objective is ascribed to it. It is precisely in such embodiment that the creating mind strives after perfection of form. In creativeness there is no matter and no content without form. The creative act is bent upon the infinite, whereas the form of the created product is always finite. And the whole matter in question is this: does the infinite shine through in the finite image?

[1] See Jacques Maritain: *L'art et la scholastique*.
[2] See Benedetto Croce: *Esthétique comme science de l'expression et linguistique générale*.

The whole creative process takes place between the infinite and the finite, between the flight and the image which enters into this objectified world. The initial creative act along an ascending line is creative ecstasy, an upward flight, primary intuition, discovery. It is a marvellous evocation of images, a great project, a great love; it is an attraction which draws upward to the heights, an ascent into the mount, creative fire. At such a time the creating mind stands before God, face to face with Mystery, before the primordial source of all life.

Knowledge, for example, is not a written book, not a system, nor a body of proof, nor the objectification into the external world of what has been discovered. It is the dawn of inward light, entry into communion, an experience of transcending. One must speak in exactly the same way about a projected purpose in the sphere of art or about a design for a new social order; and, in absolutely the same way again, about the love which has taken fire and constitutes the creative condition of a man.

But creative activity is not only all this, it is also a turning towards men and women, towards society, towards this world, it is the attraction of the creative act downwards. And here a man must display dexterity, he must be a master of artistry in every respect, not merely in 'art' in the strict sense of the word, but in science as well, and in creativeness in the social and moral spheres, and again in the technical side of life. Art strives after perfection, but it is a movement which goes downwards, not in an ascending line. The art of a man comes to light as a result of the resistance which the creative act meets with in the world, in the matter of the world. It is the duty of art to convert this force which resists man into an instrument for the use of the creative power which produces results. There is a paradox in this, and it consists in the fact that creative power and art (not merely that of the painter) are inseparably linked with each other, and at the same time find themselves, so to speak, in conflict and not rarely hostile to one another. In methodically elaborated scientific knowledge creative intuition may vanish, in the finished classical form of works of art the creative fire of the artist may have cooled down, in elaborated social forms of human community the initial thirst for righteousness and the brotherhood of men may disappear. There are forms of family life which have become cold and rigid and from which the flame of love may have vanished away. Faith and the prophetic spirit may become weak and disappear in traditional ecclesiastical institutions. The embodiment of spirit may be an objectification of spirit and in that case it is impossible to recognize the spirit in its embodiments. Objective spirit is a *contradictio in adjecto,* it is the exhaustion of spirit, spirit which is drained of its life.[1] And this holds good for the organizations of human society and civilization. And every time that the will to power lays its grip upon a man in this world he enters upon the path which means that spirit is chilled and drained of life, upon the way of servitude to this world. It is essential to underline the truth that the bestowal of form, with which all creative power is connected, is an absolutely different thing from objectification, that is to say, it quite certainly does not denote alienation from the core of existence, a process of cooling, or subjugation to the power of determinism.

Creative impulse is at its first beginning connected with dissatisfaction with this world. It is an end of this world and in its original outburst, it desires the end of this world, it is the beginning of a different world. Creative activity is, therefore, eschatological. It is a matter for surprise that no attention has been given to the eschatological side of creative activity. The explanation of this may be in the fact that there are two views which open out before the creative act. The first is the end of this world and the beginning of a new; and the second is the process of strengthening and perfecting this world. They are respectively the outlook of revolutionary eschatology and that of evolutionary construction. The creative act, both initially and finally, is eschatological, it is an upward flight towards a different world. But in its medial

[1] See N. Hartmann: *Das Problem des geistigen Seins.*

aspect it produces works which count upon a long continued existence in this world.

The embodiment achieved by creative power is not the same thing as objectification, but the results of creative power may equally well be objectified, just as the whole of human existence may be in this world of objects. The very possibility of creation presupposes an infusion of the Spirit into man, and that we call inspiration. And this raises the action of creative power above the world. But the world demands that the creating mind should conform to it, the world seeks to make its own use of creative acts which count upon the end of this world.

Great creators produce great works. And this success is at the same time a failure of creative power. What does the world do with what is made in the world, what happens to all the creative acts which are for ever flaming up from their source? The creative fire cools down, and the load of the world bears heavily upon it. A new life does not advance to meet us. The transformation of the world does not take place, nor a new heaven and a new earth appear. Every act of love, of eros-love and of the love which is compassion is a creative act. In it something which is new arrives in the world, that which had not been comes to light, and in it there is hope of the transformation of the world. A genuine act of love is eschatological, it marks an end of this world, this world of hatred and enmity, and the beginning of a new world. But within its existence in the world love grows cold, it becomes objectified and it is robbed of its eschatological character. And so it is with everything.

The creative act of knowing has an eschatological character; it points to the coming of an end, the end of this world of darkness and the rise of the world of light. But knowledge also in its existence in this world cools down and is objectified in just the same way. Every creative moral act, which always presupposes its own mental images, is an end of this world (which is founded upon the abuse of the good and the persecution of good men) and the beginning of a world of true godlike humanity. But moral acts, in their existence in the world are objectified and turned into an oppressive realm of legalism and an inhuman systematization of virtue.[1]

Every creative act, whether moral or social, whether in the sphere of art or in the realm of knowledge, is an act which has its share in the coming of the end of the world, it is a flight upwards towards a different world, it makes a new plan for existence. But for the sake of the world and in the interests of other men the creating mind must give bodily form to its images of the other world, to its ecstasy, its fire, its transcending experience, its communion with another life; and it is obliged to do this in accordance with the laws of this world. The creative freedom of man is strengthened and tempered by the resistance of this world and by the weight of it. Man is sometimes a victor and at times he suffers defeat. Freedom which is too easily won has a demoralizing effect. Creative power is noumenal in its origin but it is in the phenomenal world that it reveals itself. The product of creative power belongs to phenomena, but the noumenal also shines through in those phenomena, the eternal also is in them.

The embodiment has a noumenal significance, it reveals the ideal image, it is disclosed in an experience shared with others, with other subjects, that is to say, but it is distorted by objectification in which the initial fire of its life is spent. This world does not come to an end. It is held back from doing so. But it ought to come to an end. The creative act of man is an answer to the call of God, it ought to prepare the way for the end of this world and the beginning of another. It is very important to establish the truth that there is an antithesis between teleology and eschatology, as there is between teleology and creativeness. A consistent teleological view of the world recognizes a definite aim to which everything is subordinated, but it excludes an end, it makes an

[1] See my *Slavery and Freedom*, and *The Destiny of Man*, An Essay in Paradoxical Ethics.

end unnecessary. The world ought to come to an end precisely because there is in the world no perfect conformity of purpose, in other words there is no complete conformity with the Kingdom of God.

Creative genius is rarely content with its own creations. Eternal discontent of spirit is indeed one of the marks of genius. The inward fire of natural genius is not completely transferred to the work it produces. The perfection of created work is something different from creative fire. The fate of a genius is tragic. He is frequently not recognized in his lifetime, he is dissatisfied with himself and he is misrepresented after his death, the productions of his genius are utilized for purposes which are alien to him.

There is something prophetic in creative power, in the genius which creates. But there is nothing more painful and tragic than the fate of prophets. The voice of God which is heard through them arouses the hatred which is felt for an inconvenient and un-welcome reminder. The prophets are stoned to death. It has been said of the genius, that he focuses within him the spirit of his time and expresses it. This is a most inaccurate saying and one which distorts the truth. The genius is a man who does not belong to his own day, he is one who is not adjusted to his own time and throws out a challenge to it.

But the genius is a vehicle of the Spirit which moves within him. He looks forward into ages that are coming in the future. He plucks off the mask from the falsehood of his own day. In this respect the spirit of genius comes close to the spirit of prophecy. For the rest there are several types of genius. A creative man who has produced a most perfect work is called a genius. But even the most perfect production does not reach the same high level as the creative genius himself.

It must emphatically be recognized that failure is the fate that awaits all embodiments of the creative fire, in consequence of the fact that it is in the objective world that it is given effective realization. Which stands at the higher level, St Francis of Assisi

186

himself, the actual appearance of his religious genius which is unique in the history of Christianity, or the Franciscan Order which he founded and in which his spirit has been extinguished and the dull commonplace routine has triumphed? Which reaches the higher level, Luther and the flaming religious drama which was his experience, or the Lutheran Church which he founded, with its pastors and theologians of the eighteenth and nineteenth centuries among whom rationalism and moralism flourished victoriously? Which is the higher, the new emotional experience revealed in J. J. Rousseau, or the doings of his followers, the Jacobins? Once again, which is the higher, Nietzsche himself with that human tragedy experienced by his burning genius, or the men and the movements which so shamefully exploit him? The answers are all too clear.

But the history of the world knows of one most terrible creative failure, the failure of Christianity, of the work of Christ in the world. All too often the history of Christianity has amounted to a crucifixion of Christ. There is nothing more horrifying and more gloomy than the objectification in history of that fire which Christ brought down from heaven. Supreme failure has defeated all the great constructive efforts of history, and all designs which planned the social ordering of men. Athenian democracy did not succeed, nor did the world-wide empire of Alexander the Great. The Roman Empire did not achieve success, and the same is true of the Christian theocracies. The Reformation, the French Revolution, Communism, all alike met with failure.

This is not to say that it was all without meaning and pure loss. But it does mean that the result of every flaming creative effort and every creative design makes itself known as a true image not within this phenomenal world of objects, but in a different world, in another order of existence. Creative failure in this world is a sad and tragic thing. But there is success on the grand scale in the fact that the results of every true creative act of man enter into the Kingdom of God.

This then is the eschatology of creative energy. The failure of the creative act consists in this, that it does not achieve its purpose of bringing this world to an end, of overcoming its objectivity. Its success, on the other hand, lies in the preparation it makes for the transformation of the world, for the Kingdom of God. Sin is burnt up in the creative fire. All the great creative works of man enter into the Kingdom of God. It follows, therefore, that the creative embodiments which man produces are twofold in their nature, the conflict between two worlds is, so to speak, reflected in them. But for all that, there is nothing more terrible, more hopeless, nothing more tragic than every act of realization.

3

The theme of creative activity and its embodiments has its connections with the long-standing controversy between the classical and the romantic. Here the point at issue is not one which concerns different tendencies in art. It is a matter rather of various ways of perceiving the world, of differing types of *Weltanschauung*, and of different attitudes which are adopted to creative power in every field.

The distinction between the classicists and the romantics and the contrast between them are to a large extent relative and are often exaggerated. Of the greatest creative minds, for example, of Shakespeare and Goethe or of Dostoyevsky and Tolstoy, it is certainly impossible to enquire whether they were classical or romantic. Creative geniuses have always stood outside the quarrelling schools, and above them, although the disputing tendencies dragged them into their controversies. The Bible, for instance, which contains writing of most moving artistic power, stands entirely apart from any question of classical or romantic.

Second class works of art are sometimes called 'romantic' in the narrower sense of the word, such, for instance, as the productions of many German romantics. Other works which reach a greater degree of perfection and are completely successful, are called

188

'classical'. But none the less, the distinction itself and the anti-thesis do raise a serious problem in connection with creative activity.

In the first place, in what relation does creative power stand to the 'subjective', and the 'objective', what is its bearing upon the finite and the infinite, and what does the perfection of a created product mean? Creative power is in its essential nature subjective, the creating mind is a subject and it is in the subjective sphere that the creative process takes place. To speak of 'objective' creativeness is inaccurate and refers merely to the course taken by the creating subject.

But the results of the creating act, its embodiments, fall under the sway of the world's laws of objectification. Three principles may be said to operate in creative activity, and the three principles are those of freedom, grace and law. And it may be that there are various degrees in the predominance of one or another of the principles. 'Classicism' in creative action has its truth and it has its falsehood, and so also has 'romanticism'.

The truth of classicism lies in its striving after perfection and harmony, in its effort to control matter by form. But what is false in classicism is precisely due to that. For perfection of form, and harmony, are attained within the finite. Infinity in the objective world, the world of phenomena, is formlessness, an evil infinity, and therefore the effort to reach perfection in the product of creative activity falls into the power of the finite. The subjective is aiming at a transition into the objective.

Classicism falls a prey to the illusion that perfection can be attained in the finite, in the object. Having created beauty, classicism would leave us in this world for ever. On this basis great things may be achieved, they were to be seen in the culture of Greece. Greece had its romanticism as well, of course, But classical creative activity displays a ready liability to lose the freshness of its life and to become withered and numbed. This again is the process of objectification which moves further and further away from the springs of life. And then the creative re-action of romanticism becomes inevitable.

Romanticism aims at expressing the life of the creator in what he creates. The truth of romanticism lies in its striving towards the infinite, in its dissatisfaction with all that is finite. In romanticism the truth of the 'subjective' is opposed to the falsity of the 'objective'. Romanticism does not believe that perfection is attainable in this world of objects. In this world there can only be signs, symbols of the perfection of the other world. This holds good alike in knowledge and in art.[1]

Pure classicism seeks no knowledge of the transcendent. A yearning after the transcendent is, however, in the highest degree a property of romanticism, although it is usually accompanied by a sense of impossibility of attaining it. To romanticism, creative activity is before all else the way of life of the subject himself, it is his experience of uplifting impulse and ecstasy, of an interior act of transcendence, and it may lead him out beyond the limits of romanticism.

To classicism, on the other hand, everything is concentrated upon perfection of form in the created product, upon the object. But romanticism also gives rise to illusions though they are of a different kind from the classical. There has been not a little falsity, uncleanness, and stirring up of mud in the creative work of the romantics. There is a form of falsity in romantic subjectivity; it is revealed in the inadequacy of the outlet it provides for escape from the closed circle of the self and from submersion in self. There is also a lack of capacity for real acts of transcendence. The ego has been split into two by the romantics and their expression of personality is weak. Pretentiousness and a sense of failure have

[1] The French ,who are hostile to romanticism, are inclined to reduce it to what E. Seillière, the author of numerous books on romanticism and imperialism, calls 'mystical naturalism'. See his *Le mal romantique*, an essay on 'irrational imperialism'. It all goes back to Rousseau and the recognition of the goodness of human nature. See also P. Lasserra: *Le romantisme français*. All this has little application to German romanticism and in general is not true.

readily assumed the form of romanticism and have sought in this way to justify themselves.

The sense of value is not merely a psychological experience of the subject, there is also a value in the reality upon which the subject is engaged. Romanticism may indicate a loss of the sense of reality, while classicism, on the other hand, is inclined to interpret reality exclusively in terms of objects. In point of fact both classical and romantic elements are brought concretely together in creative action. Classical and romantic tendencies are already revealed in the world of objectification. But it is in a different world that the whole truth lies.

There were some remarkable and far-reaching ideas about beauty and art in Kant's *Critique of Judgment*. That is beautiful which, without a concept, pleases *allgemein*. Beauty is adaptability to an end without bringing the end into notice. The beautiful pleases, without serving any interest. The beautiful pleases, not in its reception by the senses, not in a concept, but in an act of judgment, in appraisal. The beauty of nature is a beautiful thing. The beauty of art is a beautiful representation of a thing.

This stresses the significance of the creative subject. A judgment of taste does not depend upon reality in the sphere of things. Art, as indeed all creative expression, rises above the commonplace, that is to say above the reality which belongs to the objective world, the world of things. It is usual to say that art depicts only what is essential, significant and intense, that it is not an imitation or a reflection of nature considered as an assembly of objects. But that is to say that the creative act breaks through to a deeper reality, to the noumenal which lies behind the phenomenal.

The problem of creative power raises the question of true and false realism. The romantics from Rousseau onwards have defended the truth and rightness of 'nature' against rationalization and mechanization, which follow in the train of civilization. There was some truth in their position, but the actual concept of 'nature' was left ambiguous. Confusion arose between the objectified nature of this phenomenal world, the nature of the mechanical way of looking at things, nature in Darwin's sense, on the one hand, and the nature of the noumenal, ideal cosmos, on the other.

Beyond the dispute between the classical and the romantic (in which there is a great deal which is a matter of convention) stands genuine realism or realistic symbolism, and that is what actually characterizes the greatest creative minds. Human creative power is realist to the extent that it is theurgic, that is to say, in proportion as it is directed towards the transformation of the world, towards a new heaven and a new earth. Truly creative realism is eschatological realism. It takes the line not of reflecting the natural world and not of adjustment to it, but of changing and transforming the world.

Creative knowledge, creative art, in the same way are not a reflection and expression of the eternal world of ideas (in the Platonic sense) in this world of the senses. They are the activity of free spirit which continues to carry on the creation of the world, and prepares for its transformation. The limits of human creative activity, of human art, are imposed by this objective world. They make it symbolical, although this symbolism is realist, not idealist. But the final transformation of the world will be the passing of the symbols into reality. Human creative power will create life itself, another world, and not things, in which the breach between subject and object always remains. Then no sacrifice will be offered by life and love for the sake of creative power, such as for instance those of Goethe, Ibsen and others, but creative power and life will be made one and the same.

Creative power will then be neither classical nor romantic. Then thought, perfected after its own kind, whether in Greece or in China, will not be characterized as classical and rationalist. At that time it will not be enough to combine (as it was said that Hegel did) the values of protestant theology and those of classical antiquity. At that time there will be a unity of nature and freedom, the thing that is true and good will be the thing that is beautiful.[1] Creative power must be theurgic, the cooperation of God and man; it must be divine-human. It is the answer of man to the call of God.

The religious difficulty of this problem lies in the fact that the will of God concerning the creative vocation of man, the need of God for the creative activity of man, could not be revealed to man by God, it had to be brought to light by the daring of man himself. Otherwise there would be no freedom of creative power, there would be no answer made by man.[2] Redemption comes from God, from the fact of the Crucified and Sacrificed God, whereas creative activity derives from man. To oppose creativity and redemption, however, is to succumb to the rules of objectified and fallen consciousness.

Man finds an outlet from the closed circle of subjectivity in the creative act of spirit by two routes, that is, by the way of objectification and by the way of transcendence. By the way of objectification the creative act is adjusted to the circumstances of this world and does not reach its final state, it is cut off short. By the way of transcendence the creative act breaks through to noumenal reality and sets its bearing upon the final transformation of the world.

In reality what actually happens is that both ways are combined in human creative activity with some preponderance of one or the other. It would be a mistake to conclude that objectified creative power is devoid of importance and meaning. Without it man would be unable to endure the conditions of his existence in this world, or to improve those conditions. Man is called upon to expend his labour upon the material of this world and to subjugate it to spirit. But the limits of this way of objectification must be understood, and so must the danger of its exclusive use, for it clinches and strengthens the wrong state of the world. This is a

[1] Boldwin asserts this as already attained. See his *Théorie génétique de la réalité*.
[2] See *The Meaning of the Creative Act*.

matter of the correlation of law with freedom and grace.[1] There will come a time, a new historical aeon, when the eschatological meaning of creative power will finally and definitely be made clear. The problem of creativeness leads on to the problem of the meaning of history.

[1] See *The Destiny of Man.*

PART FOUR

The Problem of History
and Eschatology

CHAPTER VIII

*1. The world as history. Aeons. Messianism and history.
Cosmic time, historical time, and existential time. Prophecy
and time. 2. Society as nature and society as spirit. Spirit
overthrows the apparently everlasting foundations of society.
The break-through of freedom and love. The communist and
anarchist ideal. 3. Spirit, nature and technology. Culture and
civilization. The power of base and evil ideas*

I

There are two points of view from which the world may be regarded. From one of them the world is above all a cosmos. From the other the world is before all else history. To the ancient Greeks the world was a cosmos, to the ancient Hebrews it was history. The Greeks and the Hebrews lived in different times, not *at* a different time, but in a different kind of time. The view which sees the world as a cosmos is cosmocentric. That which regards the world as history is anthropocentric. The point at issue is this: must man be interpreted in terms of the cosmos or the cosmos in terms of man? Is human history a subordinate part of the cosmic process or is the cosmic process a subordinate part of human history? Is the meaning of human existence revealed in the cyclic movement of cosmic life, or in the fulfilment of history? This is also the issue between a static and a dynamic view of the world, between interpreting the world as primarily in space, and interpreting it as primarily in time. Reality is always historical—it can be nothing else. And what we call 'nature' has its history in time, the stars in the heavens have it, so has the crust of the terrestrial globe. But it can be understood as cosmic infinity into which human history breaks, in which case there are in it no events which are important in virtue of their own meaning; or it can be understood as entering into human history as a preparatory part of it, and in that case it is given a significant meaning.

No philosophy of history could arise among the Greeks, on account of their cosmocentric way of looking at the world. Their golden age was in the past, and their gift for the creation of myths was due to this. They had no great expectation to turn their minds towards the future. It was only in connection with messianic eschatological thought that a philosophy of history could arise, and that was to be found only in the people of Israel and among the Persians who had influenced them.[1] These people have an intense sense of expectation. They looked for a great manifestation in the future, for the appearance of the Messiah and the messianic kingdom, in other words, for the incarnation of Meaning, of the Logos, in history. It might be said that it is messianism which makes the historical. The philosophy of history is derived from Iranian, Hebrew and Christian sources. The nineteenth century doctrine of progress, which was so non-Christian externally, springs nevertheless from the same source of messianic expectation.

Doubts and objections have been raised about the possibility of a philosophy of history.[2] It is indeed beyond dispute that it is impossible to construct a purely scientific philosophy of history. We live within historical time. History has not yet come to an end, and we do not know what sort of history is yet to come in the future. What element of newness is still possible in the history of mankind and the world? In such circumstances how are we to grasp the meaning of history? Can history reveal itself before it reaches its conclusion?

A philosophy of history has been possible, and it has existed,

[1] See a curious book by Charles Autran: *Mithra, Zoroastre, et la préhistoire aryenne du Christianisme.*
[2] See W. Dilthey: *Einleitung in die Geisteswissenschaften.*

precisely because it has always included a prophetic element which has passed beyond the bounds of scientific knowledge. There cannot be any other sort of philosophy of history than prophetic. It is not only the philosophy of history contained in the books of the Bible and in St Augustine which is prophetic and messianic, so also is the philosophy of history of Hegel, Saint Simon, Auguste Comte and Karl Marx.[1]

The philosophy of history is not merely knowledge of the past, it is also knowledge of the future. It always endeavours to bring meaning to light and that can become clear only in the future. When people divide history into three epochs, and from the third synthetic epoch of the future look for consummated fulfilment, for a perfected consciousness of freedom of spirit, and for an embodiment of spirit in a perfect and just state of society, that is prophecy; it is a secularized form of messianism or chiliasm. When Hegel asserts that in the Prussian State there will be a manifestation of that freedom which is the meaning and goal of world history; and when Marx maintains that the proletariat will be the liberator of mankind and will create the perfect social order; or again when Nietzsche affirms that the appearance of the superman as the result of human evolution will make plain the meaning of this earthly life—all alike are sanctioning messianic and prophetic thought, they are all announcing the coming of the thousand years' reign. There is nothing of that sort that can be asserted by science.

In Hegel, history is sacred history.[2] The messianic and prophetic character of the philosophy of history is settled by the fact that the meaning of history depends upon the unknown future. And the difficulty of the philosophy of history is due to the fact that it is knowledge not only of that which has not yet been, but also of that which still is not. It might, therefore, be said that it is pro-

[1] See Georges Dumas: *Psychologie de deux Messies positivistes, Saint Simon et Auguste Comte*.
[2] See Hegel: *Vorlesungen über die Philosophie der Geschichte*.

phecy not only about the future but also about the past. Historical reality becomes a thing which cannot be captured, for the present which is with us cannot be retained until the following moment.[1] Everything flows, everything is in a state of movement and change. In actual fact no knowledge contains that concrete reality of the present which we desire to grasp. But the case of the phenomena which the natural sciences study is different from that of the knowledge of history in view of their repeatability and the possibility of experiment. The philosophy of history can be nothing but a religious metaphysic of history. The problem of messianism is of fundamental significance for it.

If we took a deeper view of history we should be able to see that messianism, true or false, open or disguised, is the basic theme of history. The whole tragedy of history is due to the working of the messianic idea, to its constant effect of causing division in the human mind. Messianism is of ancient Hebrew origin, and it is the contribution of the Hebrew people to world history. The intensity of the messianic expectation of the Hebrew people even led to the appearance of Christ, the Messiah, among that people. The messianic idea was foreign to the Greeks, they had a different vocation. The messianic hope is born in suffering and unhappiness and awaits the day of righteous judgment, and, in the end, of messianic triumph and the messianic reign of a thousand years. From the psychological point of view this is compensation. The consciousness of messianic election compensates for the experience of suffering. The sufferings of the Hebrew people, the sufferings of the Polish people, of the Russian people, the sufferings of the German people (and I say of the people, not of the State), and of the labouring classes of society operate favourably to the rise of a messianic frame of mind.

There is also a messianic expectation of mankind as a whole which arises from the enormous suffering of man on this earth. If suffering does not utterly crush a man or a people, it becomes a

[1] See J. Guitton: *Le temps et l'éternité chez Plotin et St. Augustin.*

source of terrible power. Happiness and tranquillity weaken and demoralize and there is nothing more disintegrating than a serene and cheerful scepticism. The appearance of the Messiah is accompanied by constant doubt and questioning whether this is the true Messiah or not. In the Gospels we see this constant questioning about Jesus: is he the Christ? There have indeed been many false Messiahs and many false forms of messianic belief. Anti-Christ will be a false Messiah. Messianic belief may be national or it may be universal, there is an individual messianism and a collective messianism, it is sometimes triumphant and sometimes it suffers, there is a form of messianic hope which belongs to this world and a form which belongs to the other world.[1]

Every type of messianic thought and expectation is represented in the history of Israel. In the prophets universal messianism triumphs over national messianism. On the overthrow of the conception of a conquering messiah, the form of the suffering messiah comes to the forefront. The figure of the suffering servant in Deutero-Isaiah may be applied both to the sufferings of the messianic people—to Israel itself and to a prophetic premonition of the sufferings of Christ the Messiah. And, at the same time, it was extraordinarily difficult for the Hebrew people to reconcile themselves to the idea that the Messiah would be manifested on earth not in the conquering figure of a king, but in the person of one who suffers and is crucified. The attitude of the Hebrew people to suffering was highly complex and it was two-sided. This can be seen in the Book of Job, and in the Psalms. Yahweh was the God of the poor and the protector of the oppressed. The prophets demand that those who are first, the rich, the strong, those who are in power, shall be brought low and punished, and that those who are last, the poor, the weak, and the lowly, shall become the first.

And this indeed will come to pass when the messianic hour in history strikes. The religious sources of the social-revolutionary

[1] See A. Causse: *Les pauvres d'Israel* (Prophètes, Psalmistes, Messianistes).

doctrines of history and of all socialist movements are there, in the prophets and the messianic thought of Israel.[1] The fundamental theme of theodicy was already propounded in the Bible, that same theme which torments us also: how are the power and the goodness of Yahweh to be reconciled with the misfortunes of the Hebrew people and the injustices of earthly life? Messianism was indeed the answer to the problem of theodicy. Israel suffers for the sins of the world. That is the form which universal messianism takes. But for a long while the messianic outlook continued to be the expectation of a conquering Messiah within the life of the world.

The messianic hope is not concerned with belief in personal immortality; that belief is of late growth. Other-worldly messianism is associated with the apocalyptic writings, which are different from the prophetical books. A heavenly world arises, and Messiah is a heavenly being. The new Jerusalem comes down from heaven with the Messiah. The future begins to be represented as supernatural. The messianic beliefs of the apocalyptic writers are bound up not only with national triumph but also with personal salvation.[2] Persian influences upon the Hebrew apocalyptic writers are undoubted. A *rapprochement* between the Judaic and Hellenistic worlds also takes place and thus the way was prepared for Christian universalism.

Messianic consciousness passes into the Christian world, and there it is transformed. Despite much theological opinion to the contrary, it must be stated that Christianity is essentially messianic. The first appearance of the Messiah, the first realization of the messianic hope does not bring to an end the messianic orientation to the future, the looking for the Kingdom of God, for the transformation of the world, and for a new heaven and a new earth. The eschatological interpretation of Christianity is alone its deep

[1] See G. Walter: *Les origines du communisme.*
[2] See S. Trubetskoy: *The Doctrine of Logos,* which contains much of interest.

and true interpretation.[1] The preaching of Jesus about the coming of the Kingdom of God, which after all forms the principal part of the contents of the synoptic Gospels, is eschatological preaching. The idea of the Kingdom of God has an eschatological meaning; it indicates the end of this objective world and the coming of another, a transformed world. There is no Kingdom of God as yet, it has not yet come. 'Thy Kingdom come'! The Church is not the Kingdom of God as St Augustine asserted and as the majority of Roman Catholic theologians after him have likewise thought. The Church is only a pathway within earthly history.

Primitive Christianity was eschatological in its frame of mind. The first Christians awaited the second coming of Christ, the Messiah, and the end of the world. The eschatological character of Christianity was weakened, messianic thought was well-nigh extinguished, when the path of history between the first appearance of the Messiah and the second came into view, and the adjustment of Christianity to historical conditions began. The objectification of Christianity took place, historical Christianity arose. The phenomenon crushed the noumenon. Seductive temptations began to make themselves felt, and degradation was the result. The very principles of Christianity were tainted by it. The seduction did not lie in the human sins of Christian bishops and of the Christian rank and file, but in the perversion of the very teaching itself under the influence of social ideas; in other words it was the triumph of historical objectification over spirit.

In the wilderness Christ, the Messiah, had rejected the temptation of the kingdoms of this world. But Christian people in history have yielded to that temptation. This has left its impress upon the actual dogmatic teaching which historical Christianity has elaborated. The ancient Hebrew idea of the Messiah-King

[1] Among those who defend the eschatological interpretation of Christianity upon scientifically historical principles Weiss and Loisy should be specially mentioned. The most remarkable religious and philosophical exposition of Christianity as a religion of the Spirit and of belief in an era of the Paraclete is provided by Cieszkovsky. See his book, *Notre Père*.

passes into Christian thought. The historical Christian theocracies came into being as the result of this, and that is the very greatest perversion of Christian messianic belief. Theocracy in all its forms, both Eastern and Western, has been a betrayal of Christianity, it is a betrayal and a lie. And theocracies were doomed to perish. The thing to which they gave effective realization was opposed to the Kingdom of God, to the Kingdom of freedom and love. The spirit of imperialism, and the will to power have been the breath of life to theocracies, and their controlling force. They have imparted a sacrosanct character to earthly power and this has resulted in the perpetration of monstrous violence upon men. They attached Christian symbols to realities which have nothing in common with Christianity.

Once more messianism became national and added a character of universality to national pretensions, in spite of the fact that after the appearance of Christ, the Messiah, national messianism was once for all done away with and rendered inadmissible. National messianism and theocracy were brought to an end not only by the Gospels, but also by the prophets. The theocracies of history, and sham messianism, crumbled into dust, but in the nineteenth and twentieth centuries messianism appeared in a new garb, in secularized forms. A messianism of the chosen race and of the chosen class takes shape. The old chiliasm is brought into theories of social life and one is bound to say that there has been more of Christian truth and right in the liberation movements than in the theocracies of history.[1] The double-edged nature of messianic belief in the teaching of Dostoyevsky about the Russian God-bearing people, for instance, is very striking. This double-edged nature was already to be seen in the old doctrine of Moscow and the Third Rome.

The one and only true messianic belief is the messianism which looks for a new era of the Spirit, for the transformation of the world and for the Kingdom of God. This messianic

[1] V. Soloviëv always insisted upon this.

belief is eschatological and it stands in direct opposition to all the theocracies of history and to all efforts to turn the State into something sacred. It is only the quest for truth and right in the ordering of society which enters into the true messianic belief.

But those who seek after such an ordering of society may also be seduced by the kingdom of this world and repudiate the Cross. Hebrew messianic belief is still with us in its false form. The deceptions of the messianic consciousness will continue to exist until the end of time, and it is this that makes history a drama. This accounts for the fact that the principal content of history continues to be war. It is the fate of Christianity to find itself, as it were, in an *entr'acte* in history. The spiritual forces of historical Christianity are becoming exhausted, the messianic consciousness in it has been extinguished, and it has ceased to play a guiding rôle in what are known as the great events of history. The creative process goes on, as it were, outside Christianity, and in any case outside the visible Church. Nothing but a transition to eschatological Christianity, and a turning to the light which streams from the future can make Christianity again a creative force. But the transition to eschatological Christianity does not involve the repudiation of the experience of history and culture; on the contrary, recognition of the religious significance of that experience is precisely what it does involve. The messianic theme continues to be the theme of history, and it is a theme which is connected with the problem of time. The philosophy of history is above all a philosophy of time.

History presents itself to us as events in a stream of time—eras, decades, centuries, millenia. But do the events of history take place in that same time in which the phenomena of nature occur? A certain body expanded through the generation of heat, a combination of chemical elements took place, bile was secreted; or, again, the Peloponnesian War broke out, Luther nailed up his theses, the Bastille was stormed. Here is a series of events in which 'time' varies in significance and has differing relations to the meaning of the events in question.

I have already written in other books of mine about the fact that there are different sorts of time. At the moment I repeat only the most important points. There is cosmic time, there is historical time and there is existential time. Cosmic time is calculated by mathematics on the basis of movement around the sun, calendars and clocks are dependent on it, and it is symbolized by the circle. Historical time is, so to speak, placed within cosmic time and it also can be reckoned mathematically in decades, centuries and millenia, but every event in it is unrepeatable. Historical time is symbolized by a line which stretches out forward into the future, towards what is new. Existential time is not susceptible of mathematical calculation, its flow depends upon intensity of experience, upon suffering and joy. It is within this time that the uplifting creative impulse takes place and in it ecstasy is known. It is symbolized above all by the point, which tells of movement in depth.

History moves forward in its own historical time, but it cannot either remain in it, or come to an end in it. It moves on either into cosmic time, in which case it makes an affirmation of naturalism and is in tune with the final objectification of human existence, when man takes his place as merely a subordinate part of the whole world of nature. Or it issues into existential time, and this means moving out from the realm of objectification into the spiritual pattern of things.

Existential time, which is known to everyone by experience ('those who are happy do not watch the clock'), is evidence of the fact that time is in man, and not man in time, and that time depends upon changes in man. At a greater depth we know that temporal life is consummated in eternity. The development of the spirit in history is supra-temporal. Hegel is of opinion that in historicity the spirit overcomes history and realizes eternity, but he does not understand the tragedy of history. In existential time, which is akin to eternity, there is no distinction between the future and the past, between the end and the beginning. In it the eternal accomplishment of the mystery of spirit takes place. In consequence of events which occur in existential time there is development and enrichment in history, and a return to the purity of its sources. From time to time limpid springs are brought into view which well up from existential depths and then an illusion is created by which the revelation of the eternal is transferred to the far distant past. Time is not the image of eternity (as in Plato, Plotinus), time is eternity which has collapsed in ruin. Cosmic time and historical time do not resemble eternity. But, nevertheless, Christianity attaches a meaning to time and to history within time.

History in time is the pathway of man towards eternity, within it the enrichment of human experience is accumulated. But it is absolutely impossible to conceive either of the creation of the world within time or of the end of the world within time. In objectified time there is no beginning, nor is there any end, there is only an endless middle. The beginning and the end are in existential time. The nightmare doctrine of predestination became a possibility thanks only to a false and illusory interpretation of objectified time. Upon the same soil springs up the doctrine of the eternal pains of hell. All this is a projection upon the external, upon the realm of objects, of events which take place in existential time. The eternal destiny of man is not a destiny within endless time, the decision upon it is reached through the coming of an end to time. The doctrine of pre-existence is a profound one, for it is based upon the memory of existential time.

The idea of progress has a messianic basis and without that it turns into the idea of natural evolution. Judgments of value are connected with this messianic basis and not with natural evolution, which may lead to what is bad and undesired. Progress must have a final goal and in that respect it is eschatological. But historical progress contains an insurmountable antithesis within it, one which cannot be resolved within history. This antithesis is due to the fact that man is a historical being; it is only in history that he realizes the fullness of his existence, but, at the same time, there is a clash between human personality and history, and it is a clash which cannot be subdued within the confines of history.

Man puts his creative strength into history and does so with enthusiasm. But history, on the other hand, takes no account of man. It uses him as material for the creation of an inhuman structure and it has its own inhuman and anti-human code of morals. History consists moreover in the bitter strife of men, classes, nations and States, of religious faiths and of ideas. Hatred is its controlling power and its most dynamic moments are associated with hatred at its keenest. Men carry on this senseless strife in the name of historical aims, but it inflicts grievous wounds upon human personality and is the cause of measureless suffering among men. In fact, history has become something like a crime.

Yet at the same time we cannot simply cast aside the history of thousands of years nor can we cease to be historical beings. That would be too easy a way out. But it is impossible to see in history a progressive triumph of reason. In Dostoyevsky's *Letters from the Underworld* the hero says: 'It's monotonous: they fight and fight, they are fighting now and they fought before; you agree that there is really too much monotony about it all. To put it in a nutshell, you can say anything about world history, things which only the most disordered imagination could put into your head. There is only one thing you cannot say—and that is you cannot call it reasonable.' This links up with Dostoyevsky's fundamental theme —the self-will of man and world harmony. Man ranks his self-will higher than his happiness. The will to power and the will to impose unity upon the world by force, goad and torment man. Men torment both themselves and others with the illusory aims of historical might and majesty. The foundation and the destruction of kingdoms is one of the chief purposes of history. The first philosophy of history—the Book of Daniel, speaks of this, and there the fate of kingdoms is foreseen. Almighty and majestic kingdoms for the sake of establishing which the sacrifice of numberless men has been made are doomed to perish, and have perished.

All the ancient empires of the East crumbled into ruin; the Empire of Alexander of Macedonia perished and at the time of his death he was aware of the fact that it would do so. The Roman Empire likewise perished, so did the Byzantine Empire. All the theocracies collapsed and we ourselves have witnessed the fall of the Russian Empire. And in the same way all empires which are yet to be founded will perish. The kingdom of Caesar and the glory of it pass swiftly away.

History postulates the freedom of man. The determinism of nature cannot be transferred to history. Dostoyevsky had a profound understanding of this, a deeper sense of it than anyone else. History presupposes human freedom, yet it denies man's freedom and sets it at naught; it scarcely allows him liberty to breathe freely. The tragedy and torment of history are above all else the tragedy and torment of time. History has a meaning solely because it will come to an end. The meaning of history cannot be immanent in history, it lies beyond the confines of history. Progress, which has a habit of offering up every living human generation and every living human person as a sacrifice to a future state of perfection, which thus becomes a sort of vampire, is only to be accepted on the condition that history will come to an end, and that in that end all previous generations and every human person who has lived on earth will be able to enjoy the results of history. Historical pessimism is justified to a remarkable degree, and there are no empirical grounds for historical optimism. But the ultimate truth lies beyond pessimism and optimism. It all goes back to the mystery of the relation between time and eternity. There are such things as moments of communion with eternity. These moments pass, and again I lapse into time. Yet it is not that moment which passes, but I in my fallen temporality: the moment indeed remains in eternity. The task that faces me is that personality as a whole should enter into eternity, not the disintegrated parts of it.

There are three forces which operate in the history of the world—God, fate and human freedom. That accounts for the complexity of history. If it were only God who was active, or only human freedom, that complexity would not exist. It is a mistake to think that Christianity ought to deny fate. What Christianity recognizes about fate is that it can be overcome. Christ was victorious over inevitable fate. But it is only in Christ that fate can be conquered. And those who are outside Christ, or opposed to him, put themselves in subjection to fate.

The terrible power of fate is active in the history of peoples, societies and States. Fate is at work in the formation of great empires, and in the destruction of them, in revolution and counter-revolution, in the insane pursuit of riches and in the ruinous collapse of them, in the seductive lure of the pleasures of life and in its enormous suffering. Fate turns human personality into a plaything of the irrational forces of history. Hegel's 'cunning of the reason' is fate. Both irrational forces and rationalizing forces alike are expressions of fate. The power of technical skill, which has been built up by the human reason for the increase of human might, is the work of fate.

At certain times in their history, nations are especially apt to fall into the power of fate, the activity of human freedom is weakened, and a period of Godforsakenness is experienced. This can be felt very strongly in the destiny of the Russian people, and of the Germans as well. Such decrees of destiny are particularly significant in the present era of history. Godforsakenness, accompanied also by enfeeblement of freedom, is an experience both of individual men and women and also of whole peoples. The meaning of history cannot be grasped nor can it be examined in its objectification, for in the view of things taken in objectification, the end of history is concealed from sight.

Given the naturalistic outlook upon history, one can speak only of the youth and old age of a people, one cannot talk about progress. The highest aim that can be acknowledged is only to experience the uplifting impulse which springs from the strength of youth. Decadence, which is both refined and complex, is succeeded by the comparative crudity and primitiveness of the vital forces of peoples. In comparison with the animal world there are endless possibilities of development in the world of human beings, although this does not apply to organic, biological development, in which respect there is rather regress. There is an eternal principle in man which shapes his destiny. But man is not an unchanging quantity in history. In history man does change, he undergoes new experiences, he becomes more complex, he unfolds and develops. There is human development, but it does not take place along a straight ascending line. In the historical destiny of man the part played by freedom varies, and it is impossible to follow Hegel and say that there is in history a progressive development towards freedom.

Freedom such as man has not known may indeed evolve, but so also may human servitude of a kind unknown before. Noumenal realities operate behind the phenomena of history and for that reason only are freedom and development possible. Beyond history meta-history is concealed, and the sphere of the historical is not absolutely isolated from that of the meta-historical. What is happening in existential time lies hidden behind what is taking place in historical time. The appearance of Christ the Liberator is a meta-historical fact and it occurred in existential time. But in that central messianic manifestation meta-history breaks through into history, albeit history receives it in a troubled setting.

It is not that event alone, central and full of meaning as it was, which is meta-historical. A meta-historical element, which is not open to explanation by the determinism of history, is to be found also in every manifestation of creative genius, always a mysterious thing, and in every true liberation from the determining power of the phenomenal world. The meta-historical arrives out of the world of the noumenal into this objective world and revolutionizes it. A real profound revolution in the history of the world is a noumenal revolution, but it gets into a state of tangled confusion owing to the terrible determinism of the phenomenal world. The history of Christianity provides cases in point.

The revolution of the spirit has not been successful in history and, therefore, a transition to eschatological Christianity is inevitable. But in eschatological Christianity there is a retrospective action upon the historical past, an action which resuscitates. The secret of the fascination of the historical past is due to the transfiguring action of memory. Memory does not restore the past as it was, it transforms that past, transforms it into something which is eternal. Beauty is always revealed in creative transformation and is a break-through into the objective world. There was too much that was criminal and ugly in the objective phenomenal reality of the past. That is suppressed by transforming memory. The beauty of the past is the beauty of creative acts in the present. The contradictions of history are amazing: the beauty of the past is seen in association with injustice and cruelty, and, on the other hand, an age which has striven after justice, equality and freedom appears ugly.[1] This is due to the impossibility of attaining completeness within the confines of history and to the illusions of objectifying thought. The end of history means passing through death, yet in order to attain resurrection. Eschatological Christianity is a resuscitating Christianity. The godlessness of Heidegger's philosophy, which is very characteristic of the present day, lies in the fact that from its point of view the present condition of being and the anxiety that belongs to it are unconquerable.[2] Being which inclines towards death is anxiety, and anxiety is being which inclines towards death.

And this is his final word. It is a word which is the very opposite

[1] This forms the basis of K. Leontiev's whole philosophy of history and sociology.
[2] See his *Sein und Zeit*.

of a religion of resurrection, of an eschatological religion. Hegel's philosophy is godless in another way. There is in it no consciousness of the conflict between the personal and the universal, nor is there any divine pity for suffering man, nor divine compassion for the created thing in its pain. One can become reconciled to the horrors of history and to progress as on its way it deals out death, only if one cherishes the great hope of a resurrection of all who have lived and are living, of every creature who has suffered and rejoiced.

2

Man is not only an historical being, he is a social being also, and that by no means in the sense that he is a determined part of society and a member of society in the way the sociologists assert. On the contrary, society is in man and sociality is one of the aspects of human nature. Man realizes himself in community with other human beings. Sociality is indeed already embedded in the foundations of cosmic life. It is there among the animals, too, and human beings even copy social life as seen in the animal world, the ant heap and the bee hive, for example. The world of nature sought to live in union and it lives in discord. Human life does actually realize unity in that it has created society which potentially is included in it. Without society and outside it man could not carry on the struggle for life against the menacing elements of the world.

Society has two aims, co-operation, the common effort of men in the struggle, and community, the union of men. The former of these aims has indeed been realized more effectively than the latter; yet even so it has been brought about by way of enslavement and injustice. It is precisely within the destinies of societies that man is exposed to the greatest seductions. In society reciprocal action takes place and also conflict between spirit and nature, the struggle of freedom, justice and humanity against violence, pitiless strife, the favoured selection of the strong, and dominating power. The organization of society is the objectification of human existence, a process which crushes human personality. The fall is in the very rise of society. But the Biblical legend of the Fall is expressed in the fallen human mind. An event which belongs to the noumenal spiritual world presents itself to man as one which belongs to the phenomenal natural world, to man, that is, who is already in a state of servitude to objectification and ejection into what is outside his existence.

But originally, in the depth of existence, the Fall was also a loss of freedom, as it were, and enslavement to the external objective world; it was a process of exteriorization. It was not indeed disobedience to God, which is a form of words appropriate to the fallen, social world and to the servile relations which have grown up in it. It was a rather separation from God into the external sphere in which everything is determined from without, one imposing his will upon another in a realm of enmity and compulsion. God is freedom, and he desires freedom, just as he is love and desires love, and as he is a Mystery which is unlike all the properties and relations of the natural, historical and social world. This decides the fact that the Fall is slavery, determinism, in which everything is decided from without, and enmity, hatred and violence. That is the impress which the Fall has stamped upon human life.

Sociality, which has been effectively realized in society both enriches the life of man and is also a source of slavery to him. The sociomorphism of a fallen state decides and distorts even the form of the knowledge of God. Christianity in history has been highly social in the bad sense, disfigured by the objectification of spirit, and it has not been social enough in the good sense, as that which actually realizes a sense of community. The Kingdom of God, the seeking of which is the essence of Christianity, is not only the saving of separate souls, but also a spiritual society, a communion of men. It is social in the metaphysical sense of the word.

Christian society has very easily become feudal or bourgeois, but it finds great difficulty in becoming social, using the word 'social' not in the sense which implies community which comes into being from without, but rather of that which is revealed within and issues from spirit. A Christian group, society, family, and so on, can only be thought of in terms of community, not of hierarchy; it must be conceived as a free union in the spirit of brotherhood.

The problem of the shared life, of overcoming the state of being shut up in oneself, and living in isolation is a fundamental problem of human life. Solitude is a late product of advanced culture. Primitive man knew no solitude, he lived too much within his social group for that.[1] Collectivism is earlier than individualism. The experience of solitude raises the question of the shared life in a new way. And for man of the present day, who has fallen away from his organic life, there is no more painful problem. Man lives in a disintegrated world and the final truth is in the fact that the true sharing of life, a true sense of community is a possibility only through God: it comes from above not from below.

The objectification of human existence establishes communication among men. This communication in the last resort comes compulsorily from outside: it is a necessary thing, and it is not through it that the truly shared life is attained.[2] In history man is exposed to two processes, one of individualization and the other of socialization. And he who is most highly individualized comes tumbling down into the conditions of socialization at its maximum. This is a sphere in which an exacerbated conflict goes on. It is a mistake to suppose that socialization builds up a great sense of community among men, it may even lessen it. Socialization, which corresponds to coercive objectiveness, happens in every sphere of existence. Even the process of getting to know things is socialized, and about that I have already spoken. The growth of

[1] See Lévy-Bruhl's books: and Bachofen's *Das Mutterrecht*—a book of genius.
[2] See my *Solitude and Society*.

sociology in theory and of socialism in practice reflect the process of socialization.

In the nineteenth century the ideals which mark out the boundaries of the social life of men were brought more and more to light. But they grew up in an atmosphere of the extreme objectification of human existence; they were an active revolt against the degradation of man, against injustice and slavery. The communist ideal and the ideal of anarchism mark the limits. They take their stand beneath the great symbol of bread and freedom. The break-up of the objectified social life of men leads to this, that they offer people either freedom without bread or bread without freedom. But the combination of bread and freedom is at once the most difficult of tasks and the greatest of rights. It seems to be beyond the power of our era to achieve, this era in which the human masses are offered bread in return for their refusal of freedom of spirit. This is the theme of Dostoyevsky's *Legend of the Grand Inquisitor* in which his genius foresees the paths of history.[1]

Human societies, and especially those of them which have incorporated Christianity into their experience, undergo in various forms the three temptations which Christ rejected in the wilderness. There is in man a profound need not merely for 'bread' which is a symbol of the very possibility of human existence, but also for world-wide unity. And so man follows those who promise to turn stones into bread, and establish the kingdom of this world. People love slavery and authority. The mass of mankind has no love for freedom, and is afraid of it. What is more, freedom has at times been terribly perverted, and even turned into a means of enslavement. Freedom has been wholly interpreted as a right, as a thing which people are entitled to claim, whereas what it really is above all is an obligation and a duty. Freedom is not something which man demands of God, but that which God requires of man.

Freedom, therefore, is not a trifle to be lightly assumed; it is a

[1] See my *Dostoyevsky*.

difficulty and a burden which man ought to take upon himself. And there are but a few who assent to this. Freedom, in the spiritual sense, is aristocratic, not democratic. There is a bourgeois freedom also, but that is a perversion and an insult to spirit. Freedom is a spiritual thing, it is spirit. It issues out of the noumenal world and overthrows the settled order of the world of phenomena.

The ideal of anarchism, if accepted in its ultimate depth, is an ideal which marks the limit of human liberation. It ought not by any means to be taken to denote the rejection of the functional importance of the State in this objectified world. What anarchism ought to oppose is not order and harmony, but the principle of power, that is to say, of force exercised from without. The optimism of most of the theories of anarchism is false. In the conditions of this objectified world we cannot conceive of the ideal society, without evil, strife and war. Absolute pacifism in this world is a false ideal, because it is anti-eschatological. There is a great deal of truth on this subject in Proudhon.[1]

All political forms, democracy and monarchy alike, are relative. What must be supported throughout to the end are those forms, relative as they are, which provide the greatest possibility of real freedom, of the recognition of the value of personality, and which acknowledge the supremacy of truth and right over the State. But the ideal can be nothing but the supersession of all power, on the grounds that it rests upon alienation and exteriorization, and means enslavement. The Kingdom of God can only be thought of apophatically, as achieved absence of power and a kingdom of freedom. Hegel says that 'law is the objectivity of spirit', and thus admits that he assigns a realm to objectification. And it is he too who says that the State is a spiritual idea in the *Äusserlichkeit* of the human will to freedom. *Äusserlichkeit* is indeed the fundamental mark of the State and of power.

There are two ways of understanding society, and two paths

[1] See Proudhon: *La Guerre et la paix*.

that it follows. Either society is understood as nature or it is interpreted as spirit. Society is either accepted as nature and, therefore, ordered in accordance with the laws of nature, or it is built up as a spiritual reality. In this way the ideals of society, and the character of its conflict are decided. As nature, society is under the power of necessity; its motive power is the struggle for predominance and mastery; natural selection of the strong holds good in it; it is built up on the principles of authority and compulsion, and relations which occur within it are settled as object relations. As spirit, on the other hand, society finds its motive power in the quest for freedom; it rests upon the principle of personality and upon relations which are subject relations. Its controlling motive is the desire that love and mercy should be the basis upon which the fabric of society rests. Society as nature is submissive to the law of the world; as spirit, it desires to be submissive to the law of God. All this has been given a different interpretation by such defenders of the organic idea of society as Schelling, Franz Baader, Möhler, Khomyakov and Soloviev; but that is just romantic illusion from which one must set oneself free.

As a matter of actual experience society is both nature and spirit, and both principles are at work in it. But the natural predominates; that which is of the world predominates over the spiritual which is of God, necessity predominates over freedom, coercive objectivity over personality, the will to power and mastery over mercy and love.[1] But the great lie has been that the 'natural' basis of society, the struggle for existence and predominance, emulation, war, the exploitation of man and scorn of his dignity and worth, coercion of the weak by the strong— that all these have been regarded as eternal and even spiritual foundations of society. And among the ideologists of authority and hierarchical order there has even been an idealization of these

[1] It will be clear that I am using the words 'nature' and 'natural' in a different sense from that in which Rousseau and Tolstoy, or the champions of 'natural' right, employ them.

vile things, these things that ought not to be. In the eyes of the world society as nature is strength. Society as spirit is truth and right, to which the world may all too often be blind.

Society, as nature, is objectification, self-estrangement of spirit, alienation of human nature into the external, in a word enslavement, which sums it all up. Corresponding to it is naturalism in sociology, which endeavours to provide scientific sanction for the selection of a race of the powerful and dominant, and for the crushing of personality by society understood as an organism.[1] Given the organic conception of society some mitigation might have been introduced in the past by the fact of patriarchal relationships. Society as an organism which is constructed upon traditional patriarchal relations, is not rent by the furious and unrestrained strife of men, social groups, classes, tribes and races. It establishes a relative social harmony which is based upon hierarchical inequalities, to which popular religious beliefs give sanction.

In capitalist societies and in those which are known as individualist, which were originally inspired by a set of ideas about the natural state and natural harmony, a conflict of all against all has come to light. And in them the greatest social inequalities have been created, which have the sanction of no popular beliefs at all and of no traditions, and are absolutely shameless. This is a soil which is favourable to the growth of riot and revolt, and they have some right and justice in them, but they assume the character of movements which belong to society as nature, not to society as spirit. Marxism wants to liberate man from the enslaving power of economics, but it looks for the liberating act within economics, to which it assigns a metaphysical significance.[2]

Contrary to the ideas of sociological and economic naturalism,

[1] N. Mikhailovsky displayed great perspicacity when as far back as the seventies of the last century he already exposed the character of the organic theory of society, Darwinism in sociology, and so on, as reactionary and injurious to human personality. See his *The Struggle for Individuality*.

[2] In this connection the early works of Marx are important, and especially his *Philosophie und Nazionaleconomie*.

non-objectified spirit does break into the natural life of society with its evil passions and its false ideological sanctions, which are worse than the passions themselves, and with its power of determinism. And in so breaking in, spirit seeks to order society after a different pattern, to introduce freedom, the dignity and value of personality, compassion and the brotherhood of men. This is reflected in distorted form in the philosophically naïve idea of the social contract. In clarifying the conventional and confused state of the terminology it is interesting to note that what ought to be called spiritual right is in fact known as natural right. The 'natural' rights of man are precisely those which are opposed to society as nature, to natural determinism in society, and such rights are, therefore, spiritual and not natural.[1]

The doctrine of what is 'natural', in the history of European thought, of natural reason, natural morals, and natural right, has very close links with the fight for the liberation of human nature and of nature in general from the stifling suppression they suffered during the middle ages. But the time is at hand when it must be decisively shown that it is precisely the 'natural' which is an enslaving power proceeding as it does from the objectified and determinate world. Whereas liberation is spiritual; it proceeds from spirit, which is freedom and lies outside the sway of objective determinism. Some of the greatest misunderstandings are due to this. There is, for instance, no more horrifying misunderstanding than to regard materialism as a philosophy of emancipation and the spiritual view of life as a philosophy which enslaves. Such misunderstanding arises from the fact that men have made use of the spiritual view of life as a means for the enslavement of others, in the interests of sanctions in the realm of ideas, which belong to society precisely as nature, and not to society as spirit. The greatest evil has been not in the primary elements of nature, but in these sanctions in the realm of ideas. And it is all due to a false understanding of spirit.

[1] See Ellinck: *A Declaration of the rights of man and citizen.*

In actual fact, natural matter is a conservative and reactionary principle, while spirit is a creative and revolutionary principle. Spirit overthrows the naturally servile foundations of society and tries to create society after its own image. It is the non-eternal, transitory character of these servile hierarchical foundations of society which are exposed to condemnation. But the revolution brought about by the spirit, in its own expression in social life, easily falls under the power of objectification, and new and yet newer forms of slavery are continually coming to light. The process of invasion by liberating spirit is interrupted, there is no direct development in a straight line. The real revolution of the spirit is the end of objectification as belonging to this world; it is the revolution of noumena against the wrong line which the world of phenomena has taken. When that time comes the spiritual society, the realm of Spirit, the Kingdom of God will be made plain, decisively and finally.

But the action of fate in history, which dislodges the operation of God and human freedom, gives rise to its own physical embodiments and leads to its own extreme objectifications. The State, that kingdom of this world and pre-eminently of its prince, has had functions to perform which are necessary for this evil world. But there have also been built into it the evil demoniacal will to power and paramountcy, the will to fortify the strength of the iniquitous kingdom of this servile world; there has been a glut of enmity and hatred. And the image of the State will be shown in the final end to be the image of the beast which issues out of the abyss. It is said with much zeal and love that perfection is impossible on earth and so there cannot be a perfect society. And people say this chiefly because they do not want such perfection and because their interest lies in upholding the wrong. But it is true that there can be no perfect society within this 'earthly' scheme of things, and the expectation of such perfection is merely a utopian illusion.

But that is not by any means the question. The question is: is the conquest of this objective world a possibility, not the annihilation of what is 'earthly', but its liberation and transformation, its transition to a different scheme of things? And that is an eschatological question. It becomes Christians at any rate to believe that the only kingdom which can achieve success is the Kingdom of God. The Kingdom of God is not merely a matter of expectation: it is being founded, its creation is beginning already here and now upon earth. This requires that we should interpret eschatology in an active and creative way.

3

The most revolutionary and cataclysmic event in the history of the world is the emergence of technological knowledge, that triumphant advance of the machine which is determining the whole structure of civilization.[1] The machine and technical skill have in very truth a cosmological significance. In the machine something new makes its appearance, something which has not hitherto been in the life of the world. The machine is a combination of physical and chemical forces but it is not a natural phenomenon. In addition to inorganic bodies, and organic bodies, organized bodies are making their appearance. This is nature which has been handled by human activity, and subordinated to the purposes of men. By technical skill forces are extracted from the heart of nature which had been asleep and had not come to light in the cycle of natural life. To have achieved the splitting of the atom is paramount to a cosmic revolution which issues from the heart of civilization itself.

At the same time the growing power of technological knowledge in the social life of men means the ever greater and greater objectification of human existence; it inflicts injury upon the souls, and it weighs heavily upon the lives of men. Man is all the while more and more thrown out into the external, always becoming

[1] See my essay: 'Man and the Machine', and F. Dessauer: *Philosophie der Technik*.

more and more exteriorized, more and more losing his spiritual centre and integral nature. The life of man is ceasing to be organic and is becoming organized; it is being rationalized and mechanized.

Man falls out of the rhythm which corresponds to the life of nature; he gets out of step with nature, he gets further and further away from it (I am not using the word 'nature' here to mean the object of mechanical natural science), and his emotional life, and the life of the soul suffer from deficiency.

The dialectic of technical progress consists in this: that the machine is a creation of man and at the same time it takes a line against man: it is born of the spirit, yet nevertheless it enslaves the spirit. The progress of civilization is a self-contradictory process, one which creates a division in the mind of man. In the life of society, spirit, primitive nature and technology act and react upon each other and are in conflict with one another. Technical knowledge of an elementary kind already exists from the very outset, from the very beginning of civilization. The struggle for life in the teeth of the elemental forces of nature requires it. But at the height of civilization the part played by technical knowledge becomes predominant and takes the whole of life into its scope. This provokes a romantic reaction of the 'natural' against technology. Man, suffering from the wounds inflicted by technical civilization would like to return to the organic life of nature which begins to seem to him to be paradise. But this is one of the illusions of the mind. There is no such return to that paradise. A return from the life which is technically organized to the life which is naturally organic is an impossibility.

Both an organic element and a technical element enter into society considered as spirit. Hence arises the problem of the relation between civilization and culture, a question which has arisen with peculiar trenchancy in Russian and German thought.[1] The

---

[1] The Slavophils, Hertzen, K. Leontiev and others raised this question long before Spengler.

relation between the two must not be supposed to be a matter of time. The tendency for civilization as a type to predominate over culture always showed itself, already in the ancient world. It is a theme which was known as long ago as the time of the prophets who took up arms against the growth of capitalism.

Culture is still linked with the naturally organic, but civilization breaks that link, for it is possessed by a will for the organization and rationalization of life, by a will for increasing power.

With it goes a dizzying increase of speed, a frenzied acceleration of every kind of process. Man has no time for recollection or for looking inwards into his own depth. An acute process of dehumanization takes place and it is precisely from the growth of human might that it takes its rise. There is paradox in this.

In a bourgeois age of technical civilization an unbounded increase of wealth takes place and these riches are periodically destroyed by fearful wars. There is a sense in which these destructive wars which are brought about by the will to power are the fate of societies which are based upon the dominating influence of technical civilization and steeped in bourgeois contentment. The instruments of destruction are immeasurably more powerful than those of construction. Civilization at its height is extraordinarily inventive in devising means of killing, but it has no resuscitating forces in it. And that is its condemnation.

The part played by technology raises the problem of spirit and the spiritual mastery of life in an acute form. Technology puts into men's hands fearful means of destruction and violence. A group of men who have seized power with the help of technology can hold the whole world under the tyranny of their rule. This means that the question of the spiritual state of men is a matter of life and death. The world may be blown up because of the debased spiritual state of the men who have got possession of the means of destruction. The simpler weapons of time gone by brought no such possiblity within the reach of men. The power of technology reaches the limits of the objectification of human existence, it turns man into a thing, an object, a nameless thing. The victory of society considered as spirit would mean that the objectification of human existence would be overcome, it would be the triumph of personalism. The machine raises the eschatological question, and leads up to the breaking of the seals of history.

The major evils and the principal sufferings of life are due not so much to the baseness and wickedness of individual people, but rather to the base and wicked ideas which take possession of their minds, to social prejudices, beliefs which have become vague and cloudy, which have degenerated into a mere inheritance from the environment in which they arose. The evil and suffering which were caused by such people as Torquemada, Philip II, Robespierre and many others and the cruelty they inflicted were not due to the fact that they were themselves vile and evil men, as individual people they were not base and cruel. It was due to the fact that their minds were possessed by evil ideas and beliefs which appeared to them to be good and indeed lofty.

The head of a family, a member of some particular estate, the head of a government department, the director of some enterprise, a prelate of the Church, a general, a minister or a king are liable to be cruel and to spread suffering around them. And the main reason for it is a result of their consciousness of their own position in a hierarchy. By nature and as individual persons it may well be that they are not at all cruel. But the constitution of their minds is by tradition such that it imposes upon them a tendency to be merciless and cruel and to achieve their ends by force. Such people insist with a distorted conscience, upon the honour and might of the family, the estate, the army, the ecclesiastical establishment, the State to which they belong, and in general lay stress upon the principle of authority and the power of rank. What a number of human lives have been crippled and ruined as a result of wrong ideas about the authority of parents and superiors!

The idea of objective rank in a hierarchy based upon the generic and the common is a rejection of the dignity and value of personality; the impress of a fallen state of existence is stamped upon it. It is only the idea of hierarchy in a subjective, spiritual and charismatic sense which maintains the dignity and worth of the man himself, of personality together with all its qualities. Objective hierarchical principles, which are worse than plague and cholera, always sacrifice personality, the living human being who is capable of suffering and joy, for the sake of the family, the race, the class, the State, and all the rest.

The subjective principle of hierarchy on the other hand is a human form of it. It is a hierarchy which depends upon gifts, upon the *charismata* of prophets, apostles, saints; it is the hierarchy of men of genius in human power to create, the hierarchy of personal nobility of character and beauty of soul. There is a metaphysical inequality among human beings in accordance with their individual gifts, and it goes with the preservation and support of personality and the worth of every living creature, of all the children of God. It recognizes an equality of the unequal.

The objective social idea of hierarchy almost never corresponds to the subjective and spiritual idea of it. All too often it includes the selection of the worst, the most debased in personal qualities. The objective principle of hierarchy is a most cunning invention of the objectified fallen world. In that world men who stand at the highest level, judged by their gifts and qualities, are liable to be made victims, they are persecuted and crucified. How tragic is the fate of the prophet and the genius in this world! What a triumph it accords just to the talents of mediocrity, day to day routine and the readiness to adapt oneself! It is only the captains and the men of power who share in that sacrosanct character which is ascribed to tribes and towns, nations and States. But this has been and always is sheer paganism. If only the protagonists of the objective idea of hierarchy would stop talking about the impossibility of equality among men, about the inequality which by nature exists among them and the mastery of some over the others!

The idea of equality as such is in reality hollow and derivative. The primary matter is the idea of freedom, of the value of every man as a person, even if he be a person in only a potential State. And all that equality means is that freedom and worth are secured for every human person, for all men, and that no single man shall be treated as a thing or a mere means to an end. It is precisely in society considered as spirit that a metaphysical charismatic inequality and a qualitative diversity among men should really come to light. In society regarded as objective nature on the other hand a monstrous inequality, the lordship of some and the slavery of others is combined with a process of reducing personalities to the same level, with the subjection of personality to the generic mind and the dominance of society over man.

What is needed is to set humanity, pure divine humanity, a human idea of hierarchy and a charismatic sense of it against the fearful slavery of man in objectified society, against the vampire-like tyranny of inhuman and inhumane hierarchical principles and generic ideas. In the last resort this means the substitution of society on a charismatic basis for society established by law, of a society, or to speak more truly, a community of emancipated men in the Spirit. The only thing to set against the servitude of man, which takes the most varied forms, including forms which are liberal and socialist, is personalism which has noumenal foundations. Such personalism, which is social, not individualist, is a personalism of the community.

But a personalist spiritual revolution can only be conceived in terms of eschatology. It means the end of the objectified everyday world, the world of determinism and a transition to the realm of freedom, which is the new era of the Spirit. But this personalism which embraces every living thing is already being established here and now. It is not merely in the future, it is in the present also. It points out the way, although it does not look in an optimistic spirit for victory within the conditions of this world. To the dull and humdrum social world this personalism is miraculous, it meets objectified nature with resistance, it is a different order of existence.

In order to avoid misunderstanding it must be said that compulsion is inevitable in those parts of the objectified world which are most material in character. It is impossible to endow crude materiality with complete freedom. But the higher we rise towards spirituality so much the more out of place and intolerable does objectified compulsion become and so much the more ought the freedom of subjectivity, freedom of spirit, to be established. And another thing that must be said is that a true sacred tradition does exist. It is a resuscitating memory through which the link with what is eternal in the past is preserved. But the base tradition, tradition which is generic without expressing the 'togetherness' of *sobornost*, the tradition of inertia, of objectification instead of spirituality, such evil traditions must needs be overcome

CHAPTER IX

1. The end of the objective world. The discovery of freedom and personal existence in concrete universality. The removal of the opposition between subject and object. Epistemological and metaphysical account of eschatology. 2. Personal eschatology and universal-historical eschatology. The pre-existence of souls and re-incarnation on different levels. Liberation from hell. 3. Freedom and Grace. Chiliasm, true and false

I

I have already said that the history of the world and the history of mankind possess meaning solely upon the condition that they will come to an end. Unending history would be meaningless. And if within unending history uninterrupted progress were revealed, that is not an idea which our minds could accept, because it would mean that every living thing, living now or called upon to live in the future, every generation that lives, would be made into a means to serve future generations, and so on for ever, endlessly. Everything in the present is a means to the future. Endless progress, an endless process, means the triumph of death. It is only the resurrection of all that have lived which can impart meaning to the historical process of the world, a meaning, that is, which is commensurable with the destiny of personality. A 'meaning' which is not commensurable with the destiny of personality, with my personal fate, and has no significant bearing upon it, has in fact no meaning. Unless the universal meaning is at the same time a personal meaning also, it is no meaning at all. I cannot live within a 'great whole', the 'great whole' ought to live in me. I ought to reveal it in myself. If there were a God and that fact meant nothing to me and had nothing to do with my eternal fate, it would be equivalent to there not being any God.

An end points also to the infinity of human existence. The absence of an end, that is, an evil infinity, would, on the other hand, indicate the finiteness of human existence, final and definite finiteness. God is infinite not in the bad sense but in the good sense of the word, and it is from him that an end comes to everything which appeared to be infinite in the bad sense. The rationalization of religion has sought to ascribe a bad finiteness to God. My life is devoid of meaning if death means the final end of it; and even the values with which that life might be filled, would not save it from absurdity. But my life would be just as absurd if it went on endlessly in this objectified world; that would not be eternal life. Historical life is senseless if death is all the while triumphant in it; and if there is no end of death, no victory over it, if death is endless. Unending history under the conditions of the objective world means the triumph of finiteness, that is, of death. The endlessness of history, if that history has no existential significance in relation to human beings and their existence, is a most horrible absurdity. It is only an end which can give meaning to personal and historical existence, an end which takes the form of resurrection into which the creative attainments of all human beings enter.

The meaning lies beyond the confines of history, beyond the boundaries of individual and world history. It is not immanent in it, in relation to history it is transcendent. But the very words 'immanent' and 'transcendent' are here relative and conditional. The transcendent, lying beyond the confines, acts immanently. The immanent in history is a power which is transcendent in relation to it. Time does not contain eternity, yet at the same time, eternity moves out into time, and time moves out into eternity. The paradox of the relation between the finite and the infinite, between time and eternity, is fundamental. Everything moves through the antithesis of the finite and the infinite, the temporal and the eternal. Our whole life rests, or rather is restless, upon this.

Man is a finite, limited creature but he holds infinity within him, and he demands infinity as an end. Metaphysics inevitably become an eschatology. And the weakness of all the old systems of metaphysics lay precisely in the fact that they were not eschatological. The weakness of eschatology in systems of theology, on the other hand, was that they were epistemologically and metaphysically speaking naïve. An epistemological and metaphysical account of eschatology is an imperative task. That is to a great extent precisely the purpose of this book of mine. It connects the problem of the end with the idea of objectification, which to me is fundamental. That being granted the relation between this world and the other is interpreted in an absolutely different way.

The metaphysical and epistemological meaning of the end of the world and of history denotes the end of objective being and the overcoming of objectification. At the same time it is the removal of the antithesis between subject and object. Indian religious philosophy has sought to take up a position on the other side of the antithesis of subject and object, and it is that which has constituted the truth in it. But it has signally failed to relate itself to history and the experience of human creative power, and this was evidence of the limitation of that philosophy. The end means also the victory of existential time over historical and cosmic time. It is only in existential time, which is to be measured by the degree of vigour and tension in the condition of the subject, that the way out towards eternity can be made clear. It is impossible to think of the end as taking place within historical and cosmic time: there it is under the sway of an evil infinity. This is bound up with the fundamental antinomy of the End.

From the philosophical point of view, the paradox of time makes the interpretation of the Apocalypse, considered as a testimony about the end, very difficult. The end of the world is not to be conceived as occurring in historical time, on this side of history, that is to say, the end must not be objectified. Yet at the same time we cannot think of the end of the world as entirely outside history, as an event which is altogether on the other side.

This presents an antinomy of the Kantian type. There will be time no longer, there will not be the objectified time of this world. But the end of time cannot be within time. It is not in the future that everything happens, since the future is a fragmented part of our time. This means that the end takes place in existential time. It is a transition from the 'objectness' to the 'subjectness' of existence, a transition to spirituality. Man as a noumenon is at the beginning and as a noumenon he is at the end, but he lives out his destiny in the phenomenal world. That which we project into the sphere of the external, and call the end, is the existential experience of contact with the noumenal, and with the noumenal in its conflict with the phenomenal. The experience is not one of development from one stage to another, it is an experience of shock and catastrophe in personal and historical existence.

In view of the objective state of the world, and given the fallen condition of human existence, the end assumes the form of a fatality which weighs heavily upon the conscience of a sinful world and sinful mankind. It is before all else the last judgment. There is in the end an unavoidable moment of judgment by conscience, which is, as it were, the voice of God within man. But the end includes also the coming of the Kingdom of God. And this involves an antinomy which arises from the fact of freedom.

The end is not only the operation of a divine fatality (the very association of those two words is bad), it is also a matter of human freedom. This is no less an antinomy than the one which is linked with time. Out of it arose that keen insight of N. Fedorov's genius in realizing the conditional nature of apocalyptic prophecy.[1] If there is to be no Christian 'common task', if freedom is to have no concern with the realization of the Kingdom of God, then indeed there will be but one thing, and that will be a dark and terrible end. If, on the other hand, there is a 'common task' of men, then something different will happen, there will be a trans-

[1] See his *The Philosophy of the Common Task*.

232

formation of the world and the resurrection of every creature that has lived. Fedorov, however, did not arrive at a philosophical expression of this problem. His philosophy was naïvely realistic and simple-minded.

The true, deep-down existence of man, his noumenal self does not belong to the world of objects. The end of the world will be an end of that world of objects, but it will come as the effect of processes which have taken place elsewhere than in the objective world. The transcendent light in the world does not issue out of the world, if by 'world' objective phenomena are understood, it can issue only out of noumenal subjects. The paradox of time leads to this, that the end of the world is always near. The touch of it is always in an act which gives a shock. And at the same time the end of the world is projected upon the future and tells of the coming of an apocalyptic era. The end is perceived and accepted not as a fated doom, but as freedom; and it is the discovery of personality and freedom in the concrete universality of spiritual existence, in eternity. It is the transformation of the world, and man creatively and actively takes his part in it. It is the new heaven and the new earth.

The real existential relations which hold among existent beings may be expressed in laws, but they are not subject to laws, in the sense of dominating forces which hold the mastery over them. Change, therefore, is possible in those relations which hold in the world, and the objective nature of such relations may be brought to an end. Such a change in the relations is a victory over the power of necessity, and that, from the point of view of the determinist way of looking at things, is miraculous. It is a reasonable way of interpreting the miraculous.

In the history of European thought two beliefs have collided with each other and found themselves in opposition—belief in God, and belief in man. But that was merely the swing in the dialectic of thought. At a higher level of consciousness man grasps the truth that belief in God presupposes belief in man, and belief in man postulates belief in God. Christianity, therefore, must be understood as the religion of God-manhood. The one and only reason for belief in God is the existence of the divine element in man. And no degree of human degradation, truly terrible as it is, can give grounds for the denial of this grandeur in man. Belief in God without belief in man is one of the forms that idolatry assumes. The very idea of revelation is made meaningless if he to whom God reveals himself is a creature of worthless insignificance who in no respect corresponds to the One who reveals himself.

The rejection and depreciation of man in Barth makes Barthian theology non-dialectic. As against Schleiermacher it might be said that religion is not the consciousness of human dependence but a sense of the independence of man in relation to the world, in virtue of that which constitutes the divine principle in man, the hypostasis of his interior sonship to God. In the existential dialectic, however, man passes through a state of abasement and depression, and some have wished to suggest to him that that abject state is the one and only nature he has. But man is not merely one of the phenomena in a world of objects. His noumenal essence remains in him. And in acts which take their rise from that noumenal essence he can change this world.

It is a mistake to separate this world and the other altogether. It is in fact precisely the concrete life in this fallen objective world, the concrete life of men and women, animals, plants, of the earth with its mountains and fields, its rivers and seas, of the stars and expanses of sky, which contains the noumenal core in it; a noumenal core which is not to be found in the abstractly common, in the hypostatized hierarchy of universals. But the fallen world creates images of fictitious things too, which have no noumenal core—straw which must be separated from the weeds, repulsive reptiles and insects, fantastic monsters. The eschatological outlook, the transformation of the world, is a possibility precisely because there is a noumenal basis within the concrete life of the world, even in the most ordinary of its manifestations. And in any case there is more of this noumenal basis in it than in the life of States, or in the technical skill of civilization, in both of which all individual life is crushed by the abstractly common.

2

There are two forms of the eschatological outlook, the individual and personal and the universal and historical, and, owing to the paradox of time, it is extraordinarily difficult to bring the two into harmony with each other. In traditional Christian theology the view which eschatology opens out has never been clearly explained in a satisfactory fashion. On the one hand, the individual decision upon personal destiny after the death of a man is maintained. On the other hand, the decision upon the destiny of the whole world and mankind is expected at the end of time, when history comes to a conclusion. Between these two prospects there is a period of time which is empty.

My eternal destiny cannot be isolated; it is linked with the destiny of history, with the destiny of the world and of mankind. The fate of the world and of all humanity is my fate also, and, *vice versa*, their fate cannot be decided without me. My failure, or the failure of any creature whatever will be world failure too, it will be the failure of humanity as a whole. To say that my own individual fate is of no less significance to me, is indeed of greater significance, than the fate of the whole solar system, is not an expression of extraordinary human egoism, it is an affirmation of the truth that man is a microcosm.

Meanwhile, the vengeful and cruel instincts of people have built up a vengeful and cruel eschatology. However sad it may be, it has to be recognized that religions which proclaim salvation shew a disposition to welcome the idea of hell. Even the Christian Apocalypse is not free from the eschatology of vengeance. It was a source of inspiration even to the great Christian poet Dante. It has even been taught that the justified in paradise find delight in

235

contemplating the pains of sinners in hell. (The Book of Enoch, Pope Gregory the Great, Thomas Aquinas, Jonathan Edwards).

It is untrue to suppose that the doctrine of eternal torment serves merely to frighten people, it provides them also with a source of satisfaction and content. And that happens not only among cruel, malicious, revengeful people. Thomas Aquinas was a holy man, not in the least malicious, rather he was a gentle and kindly person. But he derived exultant pleasure from the triumph of righteousness indicated by the torments of sinners in hell. The idea of justice can assume the form of retaliation. The conception of hell has been of immense importance. In an altered form it operates even in a mind which has lost its old faith. Hatred, revenge, a merciless attitude towards an enemy always lead to the desire for a hell.

The doctrine of an eternal hell establishes a dualism from which there is no escape; it is absolute, not relative, dualism, and it means the fated failure not only of man, but above all, of God, the failure of the creation of the world, failure not in time, but in eternity. The final horror in the sphere of religion, comes not from God, but from the conviction that there is no God, that God has gone away and is cut off from me. The experience of hell is the experience of godlessness. It is a striking fact that the Persians who are regarded as the source of the dualist idea, did not think of hell as eternal and in that respect revealed a superiority over the Christians who profess the doctrine of an eternal hell.

The problem of hell is of fundamental importance in eschatology. The eschatological outlook which envisages hell is slavery to fallen objectified time. It goes to show that the eschatological problem by which man is faced is insoluble within the sphere of objectification. Yet at the same time the traditional doctrines of theology in the realm of eschatology are entirely under the sway of objectification. They apply to the noumenal world what can be applicable only to the phenomenal world. They attribute to eternity what can be attributed only to time and *vice versa*. Here,

236

upon this earth, man knows what it is to experience the torments of hell and these torments appear to him to be infinite and to have no end in time.[1] But in such an experience man is left in the power of fallen time. He is not issuing out towards eternity. And as a result of the illusions of consciousness which arise from objectification he projects his experience of the pains of hell upon the life of eternity. He objectifies the evil of this present life into a diabolical kingdom of hell parallel to the Kingdom of God.

But if we free ourselves from the nightmares which are born of our own objectified minds, behind which lies the depth of the sub-conscious, then the light can shine through upon us in our experience of the paradox of time. There is a hell; only a frivolous optimism can entirely deny it. But hell belongs to this side, not the other, it is phenomenal, not noumenal; it belongs to time not to eternity. It is related more closely to the field of magic than to the sphere of mysticism. And at the same time, for me light is thrown upon the truth that hell, though it were for me alone (and there are moments when I regard myself as fit for it), would be the failure of all creation and a schism within the Kingdom of God.

And, *vice versa*, paradise is a possibility for me, if there is not to be any everlasting hell for any single creature who lives or has lived. One cannot be saved in loneliness and isolation. Salvation can only be a corporate experience, a universal release from suffering. The very word salvation is but an exoteric expression for illumination and transfiguration. Unless it is understood in this way it is impossible to reconcile oneself to the idea of creation at all.

Among the ancient Hebrews the hope of immortality was linked not with the doctrine of the soul, but with the doctrine of God—with God's fulfilment of the promises which he had made to his people. This is the messianic faith and hope. In Christianity that messianic faith and hope assume a universal character. It is a

---

[1] See my *The Destiny of Man.*

hope which looks for a general resurrection and transfiguration, for the coming of the Kingdom of God. The doctrine of an ever-lasting hell in Christian eschatology, indicates that a universal consciousness has not yet been completely attained and that the spirit of love has not yet won the victory over the ancient spirit of vengeance. The Christian mind has not yet been emancipated from the residuum of a retaliatory and penal eschatology. There is still needed a purgation of Christian thought from the ancient fear, the *terror antiquus*.

In that ancient terror, the fear of this world with its threat of suffering for man was mingled with the fear of God. The idea of God was stifled by the categories of sociomorphism, anthropo-morphism and cosmomorphism with all their limitations. But this revealed a very imperfect sense of reverence before the Divine Mystery. Reckonings to settle accounts, which were human, all too human indeed, were transferred to God and to his relations with the world and with man. God was thought of in terms of the life of here and now; in terms of power, might, government and legal processes. But God is not like anything at all in the world of objectification. God is not even being, much less is he power in this world's sense, nor is he authoritative might: He is spirit, freedom, love and eternal creativeness.

The weakness of eschatology lies in its tendency to return into time, when the matter in question concerns eternity. In escha-tological thinking which is not set free from the power of objectification (projecting as it does the End in a form belonging to this world) not only is the picture of hell intolerable, but the picture of heaven also. The sublimated earthly kingdom of the senses, and our narrow social categories are transferred to heaven. Judgment upon the infinite is passed in terms of the finite. There are times when the desire rises within one to prefer our sinful earth with its unsatisfied infinite aspirations and its various forms of contradiction and suffering, to that narrow, finite and contented paradise. Dostoyevsky's insight was shown in his idea of paradise and in the dialectic which he showed to be connected with that idea.[1]

We must not form our conception of the end by transferring to it the marks of the finiteness of our world. And that means that we must not objectify the end, we must not form an estimate of eternity in terms of time. A passionate dream of paradise lives on in man, a dream of joy and freedom, of beauty, of soaring creative power, a dream of love. Sometimes it takes the form of evoking the memory of a golden age in the past. At other times it finds its expression in messianic expectation which is directed towards the future. But it is one and the same dream, the dream of a being who has been wounded by time and who longs eagerly to make his way out of time.

In art and poetry there is a memory of paradise. But in his attitude towards the future man is painfully divided. He expects

[1] In that work of genius *The Dream of a Ridiculous Man*, Dostoyevsky wrote these amazing words: 'They looked sorrow in the face and they fell in love with it; they thirsted for suffering and said that it is only through suffering that truth is reached. There their punishment was made manifest. When they became evil they began to talk about brotherhood and humanity, and they understood these ideas. When they became criminal they invented justice and wrote themselves whole volumes to conserve it, and as a symbol of these treatises on law they set up the guillotine. They scarcely ever remembered what they had lost; they were even unwilling to believe that at one time they had been innocent and happy. They even laughed at the possibility of this former happiness of theirs, and called it a dream. . . .

'Having lost all belief in past happiness, having called it a fairy tale, they had such a desire once more to be innocent and happy again, that they prostrated themselves before the wishes of their own hearts, like children. They made a god of this desire of their heart, they built churches and began to offer prayers to this same idea of theirs, to this their own desire, while at the same time they were wholly convinced of its impracticability and of its non-existence. All the same, if it were a thing within the range of possibility that they should go back to that state of innocence and happiness which they had lost, and if someone suddenly pointed it out to them and asked them whether they would like to return to it, they would in all probability refuse. The guilty one who has forfeited paradise says: ' "They sang the praises of suffering in their songs. I went about among them wringing my hands and wept over them. But I loved them, even more perhaps than before, when there was still suffering in their faces and when they were innocent and so beautiful. I came to love their earth which they had defiled even more than when it was paradise, simply because sorrow had appeared in it".'

not only joy and liberation from captivity, he expects also the possibility of pain and suffering. The very term 'future' is a category of the fallen world in the sense that it implies objectiveness, a falling away from existential time, from the depth of existence. There are people who possess occult faculties which overcome the limitations of space and time. What are known as telepathic phenomena are associated with this, and it is impossible to deny that they exist. It may not in itself indicate any special spiritual attainment. A truly spiritual victory over the limits of space and time will, however, belong to the new spiritual era, the era of paracletism. In the Spirit everything will appear in a new and different light.

The ancient doctrine of the transmigration of souls, which has been made very popular by the theosophists, raises questions which merit serious consideration. An endless uniform transmigration going on upon earth among different people, and even animals, is a different sort of eschatological nightmare from the nightmare of the eternal pains of hell. But the idea of the transmigration of souls may nevertheless afford some relief in comparison with the idea of everlasting hell. Reincarnation does at least mean that there is no final decision upon a man's destiny on the basis of the short moment of his existence between birth and death, with all the limitations of human experience which are due to the fact of his living in the conditions of space and time. It means that there is a just demand for a wider experience and it does not include that terrorist idea that after death no enrichment of experience is possible and no change for the better.

If we refuse to accept the terrorist and servile doctrine of everlasting hell we ought to admit the pre-existence of souls in another sphere before their birth on earth, and a path for the soul in another sphere after death. This means that a reincarnation on one level cannot be admitted, since it contradicts the integral nature of personality, and the unchangeableness of the very idea of man. But we can accept of idea of reincarnation on different levels which makes a man's destiny dependent also upon his existence in a sphere other than that of the objective phenomenal world. Leibniz rightly speaks not of metempsychosis but of metamorphosis. In any case the teaching of Origen is more acceptable than the traditional theological doctrine of the creation of the soul at the moment of conception, or of its coming into being in the process of birth by way of hereditary transmission. It is impossible, in any case, to tie up the eschatological fate of a man exclusively with the phenomenal world, which I call the world of objectification.

Man's existence in the setting of this world is but a moment of his spiritual journey. But his destiny is sunk deep in eternity and cannot depend solely upon this fallen time. The Fall of Man did not occur in this phenomenal world nor in this time. On the contrary the reverse is the case, for this phenomenal world and its time are a product of the Fall. Therefore, the way man takes, the path which decides his destiny cannot be simply the one which he follows in this world and in this world aeon. Popular teaching about reincarnation remains essentially in this time which is thought of as unending and carries with it no recognition of an issue into eternity. The doctrine of hell also recognizes no egress from time into eternity. This directs attention to the fundamental significance of the problem of time in the subject of eschatology.

The whole difficulty of eschatological thought lies in the fact that it is conceived in terms of past and future. But the outlook of eschatology lies outside these categories. It is for this reason, therefore, that the doctrine of endless reincarnation and the doctrine of the everlasting pains of hell are alike to be rejected. They are two forms of the rationalization of a mystery.

The popular doctrine of reincarnation in a single sphere disintegrates human personality, for it denies the importance to personality of the form of the body, of the unbreakable link which unites personality with that form, with the unique countenance of a man. Reincarnation on more than one level, on the other hand, does not necessarily involve this transition into another body. The material of the body is changed, but not its form, which is spiritual. It is a mistake to think that 'this world' means a world of the body, and 'the other world' means a bodiless world. Materiality and corporeality are not one and the same thing. 'The other world' is also corporeal in the sense that there exists an eternal form, eternal countenances, and the eternal impression upon them. The quality of the body depends upon the state of the spirit and soul. Spirit-soul creates its own body. It is from this that the doctrine of the resurrection derives its outstanding truth and depth; it is a resurrection, that is, of the complete human being, not the conservation of disrupted parts of him. What occurs is a new clothing in bodily form, a new incarnation, not only of an individual creature, of man, but also of the whole world. The eschatological sense is a feeling for this process which is going on, of reclothing in bodily form, and reincarnating the whole world. The process may be experienced as death, but this death is not final and complete. It is a false direction of spirit which strives eagerly to condense the world and reduce its bulk. What one must strive for is victory over the burdensome weight of the world, that is to say, for its transfiguration.

The religious philosophy of India includes a doctrine of *Karma*, the effect of men's actions even after death; of *Samsara*, the eternal cycle of rebirth through *Karma*; of *Sahnhara*, the painful character of the new births; and of *Maksa*, which is deliverance from the suffering of the new births by overcoming *Karma*. There is truth in all this, but it is partial and it is all within a setting of cosmo-centric thought which recognizes no escape from the power of the world. Man lives out his fate, submerged in the cosmos. Christianity teaches a doctrine of the deliverance of man from the power of the world, from the cosmic cycle and the hierarchy of cosmic spirits and demons. It is in this that the unique character of the light of Christianity is to be found, and the distinctiveness of Christian eschatology. In respect of its eschatology, theosophy is in the power of cosmic hierarchies, nor is it free from demon-olatry. But the environment in which man lives out his destiny is a world of many spheres. Man can attain to spiritual freedom from the power of the world but he cannot separate himself from the world, he cannot steal away from it.

Man's relation to the world can follow two paths. Either man is subordinated to the world as a part of it, or he absorbs the world into himself and the world becomes, as it were, part of him. It is the second alone which is the path of spiritual emancipation. Christianity is a historical religion, not a naturalistic, a spiritual, not a cosmic religion. Christian eschatology, therefore, is a messianic eschatology. But two dangers lie in wait for eschatological thought. There is the risk of its falling into the monistic naturalism of the doctrine of reincarnation. And there is the risk of its falling into the dualistic satanism of the doctrine of everlasting hell. Each of these dangers remains in the power of objectification and objectified time. In reality eschatology can only be revealed in the epoch of paracletism, it will be a revelation of the Spirit.

The objectified, phenomenal world is under the power of the generative process, and within it generative thought is predominant. The personal, the unrepeatable and individual is cramped and crushed in it. Hence arises the metaphysical problem of sex and love. Sex is not only biological, it is a metaphysical phenomenon also. Through reproductive sex the generative elements in the world have their triumph, the individual disintegrates and a multitude of new individuals arises in the uninterrupted life of the race. Both birth and death are linked with sex. Reproductive sex sows the seed of death, and re-establishes life afresh. The new life shoulders out the old. The seed of this life is scattered everywhere in the world of men and animals. Generative sex is entirely under the sway of fallen time in which the future devours what has gone before.

But generative sex poses its tragic problem only for the mind which is keenly aware of personality only in connection with the personal destiny of a man. The man who is wholly submerged in the generative element, on the other hand, is not in the least aware of any tragic problem. I am inclined to go so far as to place the dominance of universals, the supremacy of the genus in the logical sense, on a level with the dominance of the genus in the biological, sexual sense. The actual emergence of the objective phenomenal world may be connected with sex, which is antagonistic to personalism, and here is the point at which the fate of the world and of man is decided. The transformation of the world is above all else the mastering of fallen sex. This fact is but little recognized.

A sense of sin and a feeling of shame are associated with sex, an awareness of unhappiness at the very source of life, and at the same time a consciousness of the very greatest intensity of life. This is a most mysterious side of human existence and an extreme form of its objectification, its loss of personality. Sex, which marks a cleavage within the complete androgynous form of man, is a living contradiction within his essential being. The attraction to each other and the repulsion from each other of the sundered male and female principles are due to it. With it are associated phantom pleasure and real suffering.

The dividedness, the ambiguity of sex is indeed in touch with *eros,* which is a power issuing from another source and bearing a different character. The meaning of love is personal, not generative. Love is bestowed upon the unique, individual person. But *eros* can be impersonal also, when it is either subjected to the lower elements in sex or when it rises to the ideal world, as in Platonism. *Eros*-love becomes distorted, debased and profaned more than anything else in the world. Sexual life is intertwined with it and so is economic life, which belongs to the lower world.

But love has the vocation of redeeming the sin of sex and of recalling thoughts of the eternal personal destiny which lies outside the generative impulse. In the world of objects man submits himself to the generative life, and bestows upon the impersonally

244

common predominance over the personally individual. With this degrading sins are associated, but with it are bound up also great generic virtues. And at times it happens that one is doubtful which are the worse, these sins or these virtues. Many ethical philosophers have connected altruistic virtues with the generative instincts, almost identifying the personal with the egoistic. This is a typical confusion, and it arises from the objectifying of human existence.

In actual fact, the personal, far from being connected with the egoistic, is even opposed to it. It is the noumenal in man, whereas the generative impulse belongs to the phenomenal world in which man is turned into an object among other objects. It is this, moreover, which gives such importance to the problem of sex and love from the metaphysical point of view. Sex is a fall, it is a disruption which seeks to reestablish wholeness but does not succeed in doing so within personal existence, within the primary reality. Love is an energy which issues from the noumenal world, it is an energy which transforms. The objective world thrusts love out of the way, and rejects it because it is linked with personality and refers to personality rather than to race.

The results of love, as indeed of all creative actions, are objectified. And, therefore, the servitude of man within the generative natural process is continually prolonged. I am speaking of all types of love. All love is an energy of the noumenal world, Christian *agape* and *philia,* as well as *eros*-love. And in this world all love is subject to the process of objectification, the love which is compassion and mercy, and *eros*-love; falling in love; the love which moves downward and the love which ascends. Everything which is noumenal, aflame and creative, leads to the making of objective structures in which that which originally took fire is extinguished. Real love, illumined and serene, includes a coinherence of compassion and the experience of being enamoured. But in the disrupted state of human existence in the world a dissociation of these two principles takes place. Falling in love may be pitiless and cruel; compassion and mercy may be dried up and lose all personal attractiveness and sympathy.

In love, in all love in this world, there is a tragic breakdown.[1] In its essential nature love is radiation, radio-activity, both falling in love and compassionate love, and its course is always from one person to another person, it is the vision of a person through the crust of objectivity. In other words, it is the overcoming of objectification. *Eros*-love in its proper meaning is the overcoming of the objectiveness of sex, it is the triumph of the person over the genus, that is to say, it prepares the way for the transformation of the world. Sex gives rise to fallen time and to death. Love ought to triumph over time and death and turn towards eternal life. Woman's nature is the more closely linked with sex as a cosmic element; hence the cults of the Great Mother, of the elemental Mother Earth. But there is also something base and sinister in the female element, a principle which both enslaves and is itself enslaved. The cult of the Mother of God, of the Most Holy Virgin, is essentially distinct from the pagan worship of the female principle; it is worship of the womanhood which is entirely illumined and serene, which has achieved victory over the base element in femaleness.

3

History has a messianic theme. Deep down in the whole historical process, there is a tangled dialectic of the messianic idea. Messianic thought is historical and eschatological, it is concerned with history and with the end, with the historical future and with eternity. And Christianity itself is historical and eschatological. It runs its course within existential time; it is objectified in

[1] In the middle ages there were two schools of thought on the subject of love —physical love (in Thomas Aquinas) and ecstatic love (among the mystics). It was love towards God which was the question at issue. Physical love means that man always loves himself and expects happiness for himself through his love for God. It would be truer to say that love towards God is a return which God needs. See P. Rousselot: *Pour l'histoire du problème de l'amour au moyen âge.*

historical time and it is deeply embedded in this world. It is the end of this world. It announces victory over the world, and, in its objectified condition, it has been vanquished by the world.

The dialectic of history, which is a dialectic of existence and not merely of thought, is different from Hegel's teaching about it. It is capable of solution only in the end of the world, and it exerts an attraction towards that end. All solutions within the course of history are attended by failure. Until the end of the world and of history, dualism remains in power. It is only after the end that monism, unity, wholeness can be asserted, that is to say, only outside objectification, outside the determinate world of phenomena. History, in which to all appearances determinism, and even fate, reign supreme, is full of an inward dialectic of freedom.

Freedom involves the freedom of evil as well. Without the freedom of evil, good would not be free, it would be determined and imposed by force. At the same time, however, the freedom of evil gives rise to the necessity of servitude. Slavery itself can be the child of freedom, and there would be no freedom if it did not carry with it this possibility of giving rise to slavery; there would be but the servitude of good. But the servitude of the good is an evil thing, and the freedom of evil can be a greater good than the good which is a result of compulsion. It is a paradox to which no solution can be found within the confines of the history of the objective world, and it exerts a pull towards the end.

Another side of this existential dialectic is provided by the dialectic of freedom and grace. Grace must be the power which is called upon to resolve the contradiction between freedom and necessity. Grace is a more exalted thing than the freedom and necessity which are in this world: it emanates from the higher world. But just here is the most tragic of facts. Grace likewise is objectified in this world and for that reason is, in a sense, made subject to the laws of this world. Grace stands at a higher level than law, it is a different sort of thing from law. But the possibility exists of a sort of forensic grace, circumscribed by legal formalities, grace which is tied to something else, grace which is allowed to exist only within a system of formal regularities. The history of Christianity is full of this. People, so to speak, tie God up in history. Within the confines of history, therefore, grace does not resolve the paradox of freedom, the conflict between freedom and necessity. The solution can be conceived only in forms of eschatology.

The subject of evil is a fundamental theme in the life of the world. But one's relation to evil and to evil persons and things is also dialectical. This is one of the fundamental inconsistencies of the objectified world. A pitiless and evil attitude towards evil and towards people and things that are evil may turn into a new evil. And how frequently it has so turned! Just as freedom can give rise to slavery, so the merciless destruction of evil can do the same. Vengeance wreaked upon evil men has ever new forms of evil as its outcome. Man falls into a magic circle from which there is no way out. The teaching of the Gospels about a man's attitude to his enemies belongs to this subject; it is one expression of his attitude towards evil. The world has been unable to find a place for the truth of the Gospel. They have expressed the mystery of redemption in the narrow categories of this world. But the mystery of Christianity lies deeper than that. Man is powerless to conquer evil: but God the Creator also is powerless to conquer evil by an act of power. It is only the God of sacrifice and love who can triumph over evil, the God who took upon himself the sins of the world, God the Son, who became man.

The opposition between the two theories about man, that man is by nature sinful and evil, and that man is by nature good and sinless (Rousseau and the humanists) is superficial and does not go very deep. The first, the harsh traditional doctrine of man has served to oppose optimistic teaching about the goodness of human nature, together with the so-called progressive and revolutionary deductions that have been drawn from it. It was demanded that a tight hold should be kept upon man. Only no explanation was offered of the fact that the very people who made this demand excluded themselves from the necessity of submitting to the tight hold.

In actual fact, what is revolutionary in a really profound sense, is not optimism, which in the last resort is conservative, but rather the pessimism which cannot come to terms with the world. But this pessimism is not absolute, it is relative, and the messianic hope remains in it. We no longer live in a cosmos in the ancient Greek and mediaeval sense of the word. We are no longer aware of a world harmony, and have fallen out of the world order. This destruction of the cosmos began long ago, it dates from the beginning of modern times with their great scientific discoveries about the world. The ancient cosmos with the earth at its centre, is linked with the Ptolomaic system. Present day physics are obliged to reject the cosmos, they are breaking it up. The world, this planet of ours, has been set reeling. Already man no longer feels the ground firm under his feet, ground which is linked with a world order. There is going on in the world not only a process of evolution, but a process of dissolution also.[1] The world is arriving at a fluid condition. The homogeneity towards which the phenomenal world is moving is what is called in the second law of thermodynamics, entropy.

All this should make the eschatological sense more intense. A double process is going on; the world is becoming more and more dehumanized, man is ceasing to be aware of his central position in the world structure, and at the same time he is expending collosal creative energies to humanize the earth and the world, and to subject it to himself. The contradiction between these two processes is not capable of resolution within the confines of this world. It is man as noumenon who alone is the centre of the world, man as phenomenon is an insignificant speck of dust in it. Man is

[1] See an interesting book by A. Lalande: *La dissolution opposée à l'évolution dans les sciences physiques et morales.*

249

surrounded by cosmic infinity, by a supra-world and an infra-world. His means of subsistence are very limited, to secure them involves intense labour, and he is compelled to wage senseless and devastating wars. The cross purposes in man's life in the world can be overcome only eschatologically. And man, unhappy in the world, lives by a chiliastic dream which takes various forms and, not rarely, forms which are deceptive.

Chiliasm is esoteric and expresses symbolically the resolution of the messianic theme. The historical process is accompanied by a whole succession of failures and the theme of history is insoluble within the limits of history, for that theme is the Kingdom of God. Thus we are faced by the question: Will there be any sort of positive result of history, or will the result be merely negative? Another way of putting the same question is to ask: Will the creative acts of man have an honourable place in eternal life? Will they enter into the Kingdom of God? To deny to supra-history a positive outcome of history means to deprive history of all meaning, it is to deny that human creative power has any importance in the realization of the fullness of the Kingdom of God. It means to deny the worth of the divine likeness in man.

The failure of human creative power is due to the objectification of all the products of that power. But the actual creative power itself moves out beyond the limits of objectification and is directed towards a new life, towards the Kingdom of God. The products of great creative minds prepare the way for the Kingdom of God, and enter into it. Greek tragedy, the pictures of Leonardo, Rembrandt, Botticelli; Michaelangelo's sculpture and Shakespeare's dramas; the symphonies of Beethoven and the novels of Tolstoy; the philosophical thought of Plato, Kant and Hegel; the creative suffering of Pascal, Dostoyevsky and Nietzsche; the quest for freedom and for what is true and right in the life of society— all enter into the Kingdom of God. Chiliasm expresses, in a relatively distorted and limited form, the truth that history will have a positive end also.

There is a false chiliasm and there is a true. In its false form chiliasm objectifies and materializes the thousand years' reign, it pictures it in terms of this fallen world. Such chiliastic thought does not attain the deepest understanding of the antinomy between 'what belongs to this world' and 'what belongs to the other', between history and meta-history, between the world and the spirit. It must be remembered that the subject in question is the new aeon, the epoch of the Spirit, the epoch of the Paraclete, and that our categories are not applicable to that. The Kingdom of God, which is not to be thought of as either order or the absence of it, nor as necessity, nor as an arbitrary decision, must exist upon earth too, in spite of the fact that it is at the same time a heavenly kingdom. It is only eschatologically, only in the Kingdom of God and not in the earthly realm, that God can be all in all.

Only in the second coming of Christ, in the form of Christ, the Coming One, will the perfection of man appear in its fullness. And into that perfection and fullness all the creative activity of man will enter. This was not brought to light at the first advent of Christ; it remained concealed. The passive interpretation of the Apocalypse, as the mere endurance of the end and of judgment, as a denial of any importance to man and his creative activity in the actual coming of the end, is an expression of the slavery of man and of his subjection. An active interpretation of the Apocalypse stands in opposition to all this.[1]

The end of the world is a divine-human enterprise, the activity and the creative work of man also enters into it. Man not only endures the end, he also prepares the way for it. The end is not merely the destruction of the world, and judgment, it is also the illumination and transformation of the world, the continuation, as it were, of creation, the entry upon a new aeon. The creative act of man is needed for the coming of the Kingdom of God,

[1] There are some admirable thoughts on this subject in Cieszkovski, the chief Polish philosopher of messianism, and so there are in our own N. Fedorov also.

God is in need of and awaits it. The future coming of Christ presupposes that the way has been prepared for it by man. And, therefore, we can think of the end only in terms of a dual tension and antinomy. The end is a spiritual event which takes place in existential time. When we project the end upon the time of this world and objectify it in history, the end divides into two and may present itself alike as pessimistic and optimistic, as destruction and construction.

For this reason the chiliastic hope is inescapable. For this reason the eschatological idea both can and should be active and creative. Through the contradictions and the conflicts there comes about a return to what is primary, but in its fullness, enriched by the experience of creative activity. Such are the ways of the Spirit. In a deeper sense the whole world process, the historical process, can be absorbed into eternity. And then it is an interior movement in the accomplishment of the mysteries of the spirit. Eternity embraces time.

Kant said that philosophy has its own chiliasm. To affirm that life has a meaning is inevitably an affirmation of chiliasm, but it is only the deeper spiritual interpretation of it which is important. And here we come upon an astonishing thing. Official traditional theology is fond of talking about the almightiness of God, and about the omnipresence of God in the world. But very little has been done to present him to us. Its exponents believe in the divine power in the world and do not expect the coming of the Kingdom of God. If their belief were stronger, they would not be constantly giving religious sanction to violence and necessity in the world. They believe in something else; they believe that the power, authority and violence of this world are sacrosanct, they believe in a symbolic expression of the power of God in the phenomenal world, which bears no resemblance to God in any respect and is in every way opposed to him. But true, purified, spiritual belief in God is emphatically eschatological belief, it is a belief in the coming of the Kingdom of God.

Into the fullness of faith, faith which is ecumenical, the partial truths of the heresies also will enter—the truth contained in Sabellianism, in Marcionism, in Pelagianism and in Patripassionism, but with their one-sidedness overcome and superseded. All the humanist creative activity of man in modern times will likewise have its place in the fullness of faith, but that again as a religious experience consecrated in the Spirit.

Necessity and the lure of practical advantage which is bound up with it act upon me from all sides and I cannot overcome it in the conditions of the objective world. But not one whit do I desire to ascribe a sacred character to this necessity and practical advantage. I know that this necessity is illusory and I believe that it can be conquered and that the power through which such a victory is possible, is called God—God the Liberator. But my faith in victory is eschatological and my religion is prophetic. What is needed is not so much to set certain ends before one and to realize them in the practical world, making use of evil means in doing so, as to display, express and radiate a creative energy of one's own, in knowledge, in love, in a sense of community, in freedom and in beauty, and to be self-determined in the strength of one's awareness of the end.

Everything is steeped in the mystery of spirit. But self-alienation, exteriorization and objectification take place in the paths of the Spirit. The creation of the world by God is an objectified interpretation of the mystery of the Spirit. The drama of the relation between God and Man is an inwardly trinitarian drama. In its centre is the Son, the eternal man, and the drama is resolved by the Spirit who proceeds eternally from the Father. This is reflected in inverted fashion in the world which is called created. God is that victory of light over darkness which is being achieved in eternity, the triumph of meaning over senselessness, of beauty over ugliness, of freedom over necessity.

But within the mystery of the Spirit are God and his Other.

This is not covered by the doctrine of the Absolute, which has no knowledge of an Other or of any relation to it. The primary mystery is the mystery of the birth of God in man (who includes the world in himself) and the birth of man in God. In our imperfect language this means that there is in God a need for a responsive creative act on the part of man. Man is not merely a sinner; the consciousness of sin is but an experience which moves him as he treads his path; man is also a creator. The human tragedy from which there is no escape, the dialectic of freedom, necessity and grace finds its solution within the orbit of the divine Mystery, within the Deity, which lies deeper than the drama between Creator and creature, deeper than representations of heaven and hell.

Here the human tongue keeps silence. The eschatological outlook is not limited to the prospect of an indefinable end of the world, it embraces in its view every moment of life. At each moment of one's living, what is needed is to put an end to the old world and to begin the new. In that is the breath of the Spirit. The aeon of the end is the revealing of the Spirit.

A BRIEF OVERVIEW OF
NIKOLAI BERDYAEV'S LIFE AND WORKS

Nikolai Berdyaev (1874–1948) was one of the greatest religious thinkers of the 20th century. His adult life, led in Russia and in western European exile, spanned such cataclysmic events as the Great War, the rise of Bolshevism and the Russian Revolution, the upsurge of Nazism, and the Second World War. He produced profound commentaries on many of these events, and had many acute things to say about the role of Russia in the evolution of world history. There was sometimes almost no separation between him and these events: for example, he wrote the book on Dostoevsky while revolutionary gunfire was rattling outside his window.

Berdyaev's thought is primarily a religious metaphysics, influenced not only by philosophers like Kant, Hegel, Schopenhauer, Solovyov, and Nietzsche, but also by religious thinkers and mystics such as Meister Eckhart, Angelus Silesius, Franz van Baader, Jakob Boehme, and Dostoevsky. The most fundamental concept of this metaphysics is that of the *Ungrund* (a term taken from Boehme), which is the pure potentiality of being, the negative ground essential for the realization of the novel, creative aspects of existence. A crucial element of Berdyaev's thought is his philosophical anthropology: A human being is originally an "ego" out which a "person" must develop. Only when an ego freely acts to realize its own concrete essence, rather than abstract or arbitrary goals, does it become a person. A society that furthers the goal of the development of egos into persons is a true community, and the relation then existing among its members is a sobornost.

He showed an interest in philosophy early on, at the age of fourteen reading the works of Kant, Hegel, and Schopenhauer.

While a student at St. Vladimir's University in Kiev, he began to participate in the revolutionary Social-Democratic movement and to study Marxism. In 1898, he was sentenced to one month in a Kiev prison for his participation in an anti-government student demonstration, and was later exiled for two years (1901–02) to Vologda, in the north of Russia.

His first book, *Subjectivism and Individualism in Social Philosophy* (1901), represented the climax of his infatuation with Marxism as a methodology of social analysis, which he attempted to combine with a neo-Kantian ethics. However, as early as 1903, he took the path from "Marxism to idealism," which had already been followed by such former Marxists as Peter Struve, Sergey Bulgakov, and S.L. Frank. In 1904 Berdyaev became a contributor to the philosophical magazine *New Path*. The same year he married Lydia Trushcheva, a daughter of a Petersburg lawyer. In 1905–06, together with Sergey Bulgakov, he edited the magazine *Questions of Life*, attempting to make it the central organ of new tendencies in the domains of socio-political philosophy, religious philosophy, and art. The influence exerted upon him by the writers and philosophers Dmitry Merezhkovsy and Zinaida Gippius, during meetings with them in Paris in the winter of 1907–08, led him to embrace the Russian Orthodox faith. After his return to Russia, he joined the circle of Moscow Orthodox philosophers united around the Path publishing house (notably Bulgakov and Pavel Florensky) and took an active part in organizing the religious-philosophical Association in Memory of V. Solovyov. An important event in his life at this time was the publication of his article "Philosophical Truth and the Truth of the Intelligentsia" in the famous and controversial collection *Landmarks* (1909), which subjected to a critical examination the foundations of the world-outlook of the left-wing Russian intelligentsia. Around this time, Berdyaev published a work which inaugurated his life-long exploration of the concept of freedom in its many varieties and ramifications. In *The Philosophy of Freedom* (1911), a critique of the "pan-gnoseologism" of recent German and Russian philosophy led Berdyaev to a search for an authentically Christian ontology. The end result of this search was a philosophy of freedom, according to which human beings are rooted in a sobornost of being and thus possess true knowledge.

In 1916, Berdyaev published the most important work of his early period: *The Meaning of the Creative Act*. The originality of this work is rooted in the rejection of theodicy as a traditional problem of the Christian consciousness, as well as in a refusal to accept the view that creation and revelation have come to an end and are complete. The central element of the "meaning of the creative act" is the idea that man reveals his true essence in the course of a continuing creation realized jointly with God (a theurgy). Berdyaev's notion of "theurgy" (in contrast to those of Solovyov and Nikolai Fyodorov) is distinguished by the inclusion of the element of freedom: the creative act is a means for the positive self-definition of freedom not as the choice and self-definition of persons in the world but as a "foundationless foundation of being" over which God the creator has no power.

Berdyaev's work from 1914 to 1924 can be viewed as being largely influenced by his inner experience of the Great War and the Russian Revolution. His main themes during this period are the "cosmic collapse of humanity" and the effort to preserve the hierarchical order of being (what he called "hierarchical personalism"). Revolutionary violence and nihilism were seen to be directly opposed to the creatively spiritual transformation of "this world" into a divine "cosmos." In opposing the chaotic nihilism of the first year of the Revolution, Berdyaev looked for support in the holy ontology of the world, i.e., in the divine cosmic order. The principle of hierarchical inequality, which is rooted in this ontology, allowed him to nullify the main argument of the leveling ideology and praxis of Communism—the demand for "social justice." Berdyaev expressed this view in his *Philosophy of Inequality* (1923).

During this period, Berdyaev posed the theme of Russian

messianism in all its acuteness. Torn apart by the extremes of apocalyptic yearning and nihilism, Russia is placed into the world as the "node of universal history" (the "East-West"), in which are focused all the world's problems and the possibility of their resolution, in the eschatological sense. In the fall of the monarchy in February 1917, Berdyaev saw an opportunity to throw off the provincial Russian empire which had nothing in common with Russia's messianic mission. But the Russian people betrayed the "Russian idea" by embracing the falsehood of Bolshevism in the October Revolution. The Russian messianic idea nevertheless remains true in its ontological core despite this betrayal.

In the fall of 1919, Berdyaev organized in Moscow the Free Academy of Spiritual Culture, where he led a seminar on Dostoevsky and conducted courses on the Philosophy of Religion and the Philosophy of History. This latter course became the basis of one of his most important works: *The Meaning of History: An Essay on the Philosophy of Human Destiny* (1923). His attacks against the Bolshevik regime became increasingly intense: he called the Bolsheviks nihilists and annihilators of all spiritual values and culture in Russia. His activities and statements, which made him a notable figure in post-revolutionary Moscow, began to attract the attention of the Soviet authorities. In 1920, he was arrested in connection with the so-called "tactical center" affair, but was freed without any consequences. In 1922, he was arrested again, but this time he was expelled from Russia on the so-called "philosopher's ship" with other ideological opponents of the regime such as Bulgakov, Frank, and Struve.

Having ended up in Berlin, Berdyaev gradually entered the sphere of post-War European philosophy; he met Spengler, von Keyserling, and Scheler. His book *The New Middle Ages: Reflections on the Destiny of Russia and Europe* (1924) (English title: *The End of Our Time*) brought him European celebrity. Asserting that modern history has come to an end, and that it has been a failure, Berdyaev again claimed that Russia (now the post-revolutionary one) had a messianic mission. He wrote that "culture is now not just European; it is becoming universal. Russia, which had stood at the center of East and West, is now—even if by a terrible and catastrophic path—acquiring an increasingly palpable world significance, coming to occupy the center of the world's attention" (*The New Middle Ages*, p. 36). In 1924, Berdyaev moved to Paris, where he became a founder and professor of the Russian Religious-Philosophical Academy. In 1925, he helped to found and became the editor of the Russian religious-philosophical journal *Put'* (*The Path*), arguably the most important Russian religious journal ever published. He organized interconfessional meetings of representatives of Catholic, Protestant, and Orthodox religious-philosophical thought, with the participation of such figures as Maritain, Mounier, Marcel, and Barth.

In the émigré period, his thought was primarily directed toward what can be called a liberation from ontologism. Emigration became for him an existential experience of "rootless" extra-hierarchical existence, which can find a foundation solely in "the kingdom of the Spirit," i.e., in the person or personality. The primacy of "freedom" over "being" became the determining principle of his philosophy, a principle which found profound expression in his book *On the Destiny of Man: An Essay on Paradoxical Ethics* (1931), which he considered his "most perfect" book. This is how he expressed this principle: "creativeness is possible only if one admits freedom that is not determined by being, that is not derivable from being. Freedom is rooted not in being but in 'nothingness'; freedom is foundationless, is not determined by anything, is found outside of causal relations, to which being is subject and without which being cannot be understood" (from his autobiography, the Russian version, *Self-knowledge*, p. 231).

At around the same time, Berdyaev re-evaluated Kant's philosophy, arriving at the conclusion that only this philosophy "contains the foundations of a true metaphysics." In particular, Kant's "recognition that there is a deeper reality hidden behind the world of phenomena" helped Berdyaev formulate a key principle of his personalism: the doctrine of "objectification," which he first systematically developed in *The World of Objects: An Essay on the Philosophy of Solitude and Social Intercourse* (1934) (English title: *Solitude and Society*). This is how Berdyaev explained this doctrine: "Objectification is an epistemological interpretation of the fallenness of the world, of the state of enslavement, necessity, and disunitedness in which the world finds itself. The objectified world is subject to rational knowledge in concepts, but the objectification itself has an irrational source" (*Self-knowledge*, p. 292). Using man's creative powers, it is possible to pierce this layer of objectification, and to see the deeper reality. Man's "ego" (which knows only the objectified world) then regains its status of "person," which lives in the non-objectified, or real, world. Berdyaev had a strong sense of the unreality of the world around him, of his belonging to another—real—world.

After the Second World War, Berdyaev's reflections turned again to the role of Russia in the world. His first post-war book was *The Russian Idea: The Fundamental Problems of Russian Thought of the 19th Century and the Beginning of the 20th Century* (1946), in which he tried to discover the profound meaning of Russian thought and culture. Himself being one of the greatest representatives of this thought and culture, he saw that the meaning of his own activity was to reveal to the western world the distinctive elements of Russian philosophy, such as its existential nature, its eschatalogism, its religious anarchism, and its obsession with the idea of "Divine humanity."

Berdyaev is one of the greatest religious existentialists. His philosophy goes beyond mere thinking, mere rational conceptualization, and tries to attain authentic life itself: the profound layers of existence that touch upon God's world. He directed all of his efforts, philosophical as well as in his personal and public

260

life, at replacing the kingdom of this world with the kingdom of God. According to him, we can all attempt to do this by tapping the divine creative powers which constitute our true nature. Our mission is to be collaborators with God in His continuing creation of the world.

Summing up his thought in one sentence, this is what Berdyaev said about himself: "Man, personality, freedom, creativeness, the eschatological-messianic resolution of the dualism of two worlds—these are my basic themes."

BORIS JAKIM

2009

BIBLIOGRAPHY OF NIKOLAI BERDYAEV'S BOOKS IN ENGLISH TRANSLATION

(IN ALPHABETICAL ORDER)

The Beginning and the End. Russian edition 1947. First English edition 1952.

The Bourgeois Mind and Other Essays. English edition 1934.

Christian Existentialism. A Berdyaev Anthology. 1965.

Christianity and Anti-Semitism. Russian edition 1938. First English edition 1952.

Christianity and Class War. Russian edition 1931. First English edition 1933.

The Destiny of Man. Russian edition 1931. First English edition 1937.

The Divine and the Human. Russian edition 1952. First English edition 1947.

Dostoevsky: An Interpretation. Russian edition 1923. First English edition 1934.

Dream and Reality: An Essay in Autobiography. Russian edition 1949. First English edition 1950.

The End of Our Time. Russian edition 1924. First English edition 1933.

The Fate of Man in the Modern World. First Russian edition 1934. English edition 1935.

Freedom and the Spirit. Russian edition 1927. First English edition 1935.

Leontiev. Russian edition 1926. First English edition 1940.

The Meaning of History. Russian edition 1923. First English edition 1936.

The Meaning of the Creative Act. Russian edition 1916. First English edition 1955.

The Origin of Russian Communism. Russian edition 1937. First English edition 1937.

The Realm of Spirit and the Realm of Caesar. Russian edition 1949. First English edition 1952.

The Russian Idea. Russian edition 1946. First English edition 1947.

Slavery and Freedom. Russian edition 1939. First English edition 1939.

Solitude and Society. Russian edition 1934. First English edition 1938.

Spirit and Reality. Russian edition 1946. First English edition 1937.

Towards a New Epoch. Transl. from the original French edition 1949.

Truth and Revelation. English edition 1954.

262

Printed in the USA
CPSIA information can be obtained
at www.ICGtesting.com
LVHW041048201123
764427LV00006B/111